SETTING THE NEW ...

SETTING THE NEW AGENDA

A Unique Development of Innovation in Cultural Engagement at Academic and Communities Levels Seven Years of Excellence: 2000 – 2007

PROFESSOR ABD AL-FATTAH MUHAMMAD EL-AWAISI

FOUNDING PRINCIPAL AND VICE-CHANCELLOR

Al-Maktoum Institute Academic Press

Published in 2007 (22 February 2007) by Al-Maktoum Institute Academic Press
124 Blackness Road, Dundee DD1 5PE
United Kingdom
Tel: 0044 (0) 1382 908070
Fax: 0044 (0) 1382 908077
www.almipress.com

Copyright © Abd al-Fattah El-Awaisi, 2007
Layout: Khalid El-Awaisi
Cover Design: Alya Rashid Burhaima, alya.burhaima@gmail.com

A catalogue record of this book is available from the British Library.
ISBN 978-1-904436-09-6

DEDICATION

To HH Shaikh Hamdan Bin Rashid Al-Maktoum who gave our contemporary world a practical model for the missing relationship between 'Knowledge and Power' through his continuous support to establish and develop Al-Maktoum Institute in Scotland.

HH Shaikh Hamdan Bin Rashid Al-Maktoum and
Professor Abd al-Fattah El-Awaisi (6 May 2002)

(Photograph: David Martin - Fotopress)

CONTENTS

CHAPTER FIVE: DEVELOPMENT AND ENHANCEMENT OF RESEARCH CULTURE

PART THREE: SETTING THE AGENDA FOR CULTURAL
ENGAGEMENT AT THE COMMUNITIES LEVEL

CHAPTER EIGHT: SERVING THE LOCAL AND NATIONAL
COMMUNITIES... 113

FORWARD

Lord Elder of Kirkcaldy
Chancellor of Al-Maktoum Institute, Dundee - Scotland

The fifth anniversary of the official opening of Al-Maktoum Institute in Dundee, Scotland is an important time to reflect on the history and achievement of the Institute and its Founding Principal and Vice-Chancellor, Professor Abd al-Fattah El-Awaisi, the author of this book. The Institute has come a long way in such a short time, and has already left its mark in a number of areas, both at the academic and community level. It has rapidly built up the foundations for it to continue to make a very significant contribution to debates about the Study of Islam and Muslims, Islamicjerusalem, and multiculturalism, which are of such crucial relevance to the world in which we live today.

The idea for the Institute originated in the vision of our patron, HH Shaikh Hamdan Bin Rashid Al-Maktoum, and his passion for multiculturalism, and education. The creation from scratch of Al-Maktoum Institute, now a leading national and international academic centre in this field has taken only five years. Its standing has been clearly recognised in a number of ways, by other universities and government bodies through memoranda of understanding, official visits, and other such marks of recognition, as meticulously detailed in this book.

At the academic level, the establishment and creation of Al-Maktoum Institute marks a very significant development in the academic discipline of the Study of Islam and Muslims. That is, within the hothouse atmosphere of the twenty-first century, what is often called 'Islamic Studies' needs to be developed into a new agenda, which is in line with the challenges and opportunities of today, and so therefore needs leading scholars to take this initiative to establish the field as the Study of Islam and Muslims.

There have been a number of important steps taken by the Institute, and set out in this book, to further that vision. One has been the pioneering development of Islamicjerusalem Studies. Research and studies in this field began back in 1994 with the establishment at of the

Islamic Research Academy (ISRA), and following several years of development this new field of inquiry – raising so many interesting and provocative questions and issues – was successfully institutionalised with the creation and development of Al-Maktoum Institute.

Through the Institute, Islamicjerusalem Studies has been significantly developed since 2001, in particular through the areas of teaching, research supervision, the establishment of the international *Journal of Islamicjerusalem Studies*, and the publication by Al-Maktoum Institute Academic Press of Abd al-Fattah's book *Introducing Islamicjerusalem*. With the opening of the Institute, there was established the first and (to date) only university level taught programme on Islamicjerusalem Studies (a postgraduate MLitt masters), awarded by the University of Aberdeen. The Institute also established in 2001 the first and to date only Chair in Islamicjerusalem Studies, and is the home of the Centre for Islamicjerusalem Studies.

The publication of the recent report *Time for Change: Report on the Future of the Study of Islam and Muslims in Universities and Colleges in Multicultural Britain* which Abd-al Fattah and Malory Nye co-edited is a significant contribution that is likely to set the terms of this debate for future years.

At the heart of Al-Maktoum Institute is a multicultural ethos in which both staff and students work together in an environment that recognises differences between peoples, cultures and religions as a positive and necessary part of education. Indeed the Mission Statement of the Al-Maktoum Institute is 'to build bridges between communities and people at all levels across the world', and it summarises the purpose of the Institute as follows:

> As a unique academic post-orientalist institute that is working to serve the communities and to promote a greater understanding of different religions and cultures, multiculturalism is at the heart of Al-Maktoum Institute's vision and structure, and is to be practically implemented in all aspects of its work. (Al-Maktoum Institute Mission Statement)

As an implementation of this vision on the academic level, Al-Maktoum Institute established at the first and only UK chair (professorship) in Multiculturalism, a Centre for Research on Multiculturalism and Islam and Muslims in Scotland, a think-tank titled the Multiculturalism Research Unit, and has recently overseen the introduction of a new taught postgraduate masters programme, MLitt in Multiculturalism, to be taught for the first time in September 2007.

Two examples of the academic promotion of these multicultural values are the organisation by the Institute of two major international conferences on the topic. The first of these was organised by the Institute in April 2006, on the theme 'The Challenges of Multiculturalism', and the second is being jointly organised by the Institute and Zayed House for Islamic Culture, UAE, to be held in Abu Dhabi in April 2007 on the theme 'Multiculturalism and Cultural Engagement: Mapping an Agenda for the 21st Century'.

The multicultural work of Al-Maktoum Institute extends beyond the academic promotion of this vision, and Abd al-Fattah has continually striven to develop the mission of the Institute to work with communities at all levels, at the local, national, and international levels.

The achievements of the last five years are clearly the product of the huge commitment and untiring effort by all of the staff of the Institute. In this, the leadership of Abd al-Fattah as Founding Principal of the Institute has been key. In just five years, the establishment from scratch of the Institute as a leading centre of excellence, as a practical implementation of this vision for multiculturalism and education has been hugely impressive. It is no understatement to say he has put a very significant part of himself into the Institute and that the Institute's great achievements so far reflect directly back on its Founding Principal.

As we now look ahead to the next five years, it is clear that the next challenge is to continue to see the Institute's growth and the further development of the New Agenda as a necessary and essential contribution to multiculturalism and cultural engagement for today's world.

PART ONE
SETTING THE SCENE

INTRODUCTION

On 6 May 2007, the Institute celebrates the fifth anniversary of its official opening. Although the Institute was officially opened by His Highness Shaikh Hamdan Bin Rashid Al-Maktoum, Deputy Ruler of Dubai, and the United Arab Emirates Minister of Finance and Industry, and Patron of the Institute, on 6 May 2002, the first academic year started in October 2001 (nearly one month after we moved into the current campus in late August 2001). Al-Maktoum Institute for Arabic and Islamic Studies is a new and exciting development in teaching and research in the Study of Islam and Muslims in Scotland. Indeed the Institute is a distinctive and unique development in British higher education and Scotland's first academic institute of its kind.

To celebrate the last five years of excellence, a series of events and celebrations have been planned. As part of this, I was encouraged by my colleagues, friends and students to write the story of setting the new agenda for this unique development of innovation in cultural engagement at academic and communities levels. As a historian as well as the Founding Principal and Vice-Chancellor of Al-Maktoum Institute, it is my honour to write and document this distinguished history of achievements and contributions for our time and for the coming generations to prove that there is nothing impossible in this life.

When the Institute was founded on 24 October 2000 and I was appointed as the Founding Principal and Vice-Chancellor on 1 January 2001, I was happily aware of the big challenges ahead of me in establishing the Institute. In simple terms, I knew my task was not only to set up a new institute of higher education from scratch but to build, lead and develop the newborn Institute from the start right through to its successful establishment and day-to-day running. That meant finding the basic elements for the running of an academic institution, which other Principals and Vice-Chancellors do not need to worry about when they start their new jobs. This includes, for example, finding a 'home' for the Institute at both physical and academic levels: buying the building, appointing an appropriate academic and non-academic team, and finding a Scottish partner university to validate our programmes.

As I was the only individual employed at that time at the Institute, I had to do almost everything and didn't even have a proper desk. In addition, I was working day and night from the first day we moved into the current campus in late August 2001, preparing to start offering our postgraduate programmes. Major works were undertaken to renovate the campus, not to mention the time and energy spent to ensure academic preparations for the commencement of teaching were well organised. I much appreciate the encouragement, support and help I have received from the whole of my family: my wife Aisha, sons and daughters.

I would like to take this opportunity to thank everyone who has contributed to our successes and achievements. Special thanks to HH Shaikh Hamdan Bin Rashid Al-Maktoum for his continuous support for Al-Maktoum Institute. I would like to thank my family, and all my friends and colleagues for their support in the last five years. Huge thanks to all the members of Al-Maktoum Institute family, both staff and students. Thanks also to everyone in Dundee and Scotland who continuously supported the work of the Institute. They are the ones who have made all the achievements possible.

The aims of this book are to provide:

i.   a historical document, providing a detailed record on our important achievements
ii.   an open and accessible introduction to the work I have undertaken through the Institute
iii. a possible model for future developments, offered for those who wish to take forward this agenda and possibly implement some of its ideas, aims and ambitions.

Within an introduction and a conclusion, this book has been divided into three Parts with eleven chapters. Part One, Setting the Scene, includes the introduction and chapter one. Chapter One, Outstanding Start, introduces the historical background for establishing the Institute, and also discusses the reasons for choosing Dundee as its home (a question I am often asked). Important issues such as campus development, the official opening, the appointment of the new chancellor, the establishment of the first senior academic posts, the creation of the first department, and the validation of the Institute postgraduate programmes are also highlighted.

Part Two, Setting the New Agenda for Cultural Engagements at the Academic Level, has six chapters. Chapter Two, The success and niche of the Institute, presents the Institute's academic strategic development with a focus on the Dundee Declaration, and the New Agenda for the Study of Islam and Muslims globally. Particular attention will be paid to specific subjects, such as the major research and report on the future of the Study of Islam and Muslims in Universities and Colleges of multicultural Britain. Chapter Three, Unique Programmes in the Study of Islam and Muslims in Scotland, presents the first unique programmes and courses. Particular attention will be paid to programmes review and developments, the proposal for distance learning and an overview of the relationship with the University of Aberdeen. Chapter Four, Creating and Enhancing the Learning Environment and Community, focuses on the students training and development. It also highlights how we successfully established a learning community. Particular attention will be paid to the issues of communications, library and IT facilities, students' involvements, remembering and recognising senior figures, and marketing and recruitment. Chapter Five, Development and Enhancement of Research Culture, presents how the Institute has build up a vibrant research culture. It also focuses on the Research Centres and their activities, the research seminars, the Research Development Funds, and the Al-Maktoum Institute Academic Press. Chapter Six, International Academic Links and collaborations focuses on the establishment of the Institute's international academic network. Chapter Seven, Achievements: Achieving Academic Excellence presents reports from external examiners, student enrolment statistics, graduates statistics, Alumnus Network, and Honorary Fellowships.

Part Three, Setting the New Agenda for Cultural Engagement at the Communities Level, includes four chapters. Chapter Eight, Serving Local and National Communities, presents how the Institute became an integral part of Dundee and Scotland society fabric through serving the communities and its contribution to the regeneration of Dundee. It also highlights the links and activities with three of Dundee City Council departments, other organisations, clubs, and leaders of the communities. Particular attention is paid to the creation of Al-Maktoum Foundation in Scotland, the project to establish Al-Maktoum Multicultural Centre in Dundee, and the sponsorship and support of local organisations in Dundee. Chapter Nine, Serving the International Communities, presents an understanding of how the Institute has been working with international organisations. It also highlights specific events where the Institute hosted senior international delegations in Dundee. Chapter Ten,

The United Arab Emirates and Scotland as an Example, presents how the Institute developed its agenda for cultural engagements at the communities level by providing a working model as an example. It focuses on the key role played in building strong links and bridging the two countries. Chapter Eleven, Annual Summer Schools, presents a more focued working model for cultural engagements. It highlights the training programme in multiculturalism and leadership for female students from the UAE (including students from Qatar University); the training programme on English language, multiculturalism and leadership for local UAE from Dubai Media Incorporated and the establishment of the summer school alumnus network.

I am very grateful indeed to my colleagues, Professor Malory Nye, Depute Principal for Academic Affairs, Dr Alhagi Manta Drammeh, Head of the Department of the Study of Islam and Muslims, Mrs Annemarie Smith, Administration and Communications Officer (Principal and Vice-Chancellor's Office), Mr Abubaker G. Abubaker, Administrator, and Mr David Whitton, Public Relations Consultant of the Institute for their valuable comments and feedback on reading the first draft of this book. I am especially indebted to Miss Alya Rashid Burhaima, one of the 2006 Summer School students, for the cover design and to Dr. Khalid El-Awaisi, lecturer in Islamicjerusalem Studies, for the layout of the book.

1

OUTSTANDING START

The Institute was born after I had undertaken years of hard work through the Islamic Research Academy (ISRA)[1]. In April 1999, a delegation from ISRA chaired by Lord Watson of Invergowrie visited Dubai at the invitation of HH Shaikh Hamdan Bin Rashid Al-Maktoum, Deputy Ruler of Dubai and the United Arab Emirates Minister of Industry and Finance. At the meeting on 3 April 1999, His Highness Shaikh Hamdan generously offered to fund several postgraduate scholarships in Islamicjerusalem Studies each year, to be administered by ISRA.

The Historical Background for Establishing the Institute

In 1999, the Management Committee of ISRA began the process of establishing a Centre for Islamicjerusalem Studies. On 27 August 2000, ISRA decided that it was better to widen the scope of the project and to establish an Institute for Arabic and Islamic Studies. HH Shaikh Hamdan once again demonstrated his extraordinary generosity in recognising the work and achievements of ISRA by offering to fully sponsor the establishment of the Institute in Scotland. This understanding was made official by the signing of a Joint Agreement between ISRA and Al-Maktoum Foundation in Dubai, with regard to the establishment of Al-Maktoum Institute for Arabic and Islamic Studies during the Fourth ISRA International Academic Conference on **24 October 2000** at the School of Oriental and African Studies, London. In recognition of the support and generosity of His Highness Shaikh Hamdan Bin Rashid Al-Maktoum who has been, and remains, a strong

---

[1]   See Aisha al-Ahlas (2004), *Islamic Research Academy: 1994-2004, background, activities and achievements, with special reference to the new field of inquiry of Islamicjerusalem Studies* (ISRA, Scotland).

and devoted champion of this new and exciting academic endeavour, it was decided to name the Institute 'Al-Maktoum Institute for Arabic and Islamic Studies'. On 29 December 2000, I was authorised to approach Mr Mirza Al-Sayegh with the intention of appointing the first Board of Directors for the Institute, and on **30 December 2000** this was done. The appointments also meant that the Institute became a separate and independent entity from ISRA.

At the same time, the Management Committee of ISRA also began searching for a '' 'home' for the project. The Committee approached all the Scottish Universities to introduce this project, and several showed interest. After lengthy discussions with Principals and Deputy Principals of these Universities, and after detailed consultation with Al-Maktoum Foundation in Dubai, it was decided that our first academic link would be with the University of Abertay Dundee.

Dundee Home for the Institute

The extensive search in Scotland for a home for the Institute finally landed on the lovely sunny City of Dundee, the 'City of Discovery'. There were several reasons for this choice. Dundee has had a very strong link with the Arab and Muslim countries for over a century, in particular through the jute industry. The Study of Islam and Muslims was not a field of study offered by any academic institution in Dundee. In the twenty first century, Dundee is re-innovating and regenerating itself as an academic city, and it was felt that it was also high time there was an institution like ours within its boundaries. As the first institution in Dundee to offer the Study of Islam and Muslims at the academic level, the Institute has surely helped to strengthen this link, further boosting Dundee as an academic city, and raising its profile at both national and international levels. Indeed, the establishment of the Institute outside the traditional Edinburgh home for Islamic Studies showed that there was strength in Islamic Studies right across Scotland. It also demonstrated that Dundee is just as capable as other Scottish cities of housing major institutes.

The establishment of the Institute in Dundee should, hopefully, also be seen as one way of expressing thanks for the hard work and commitment shown by my close friend, Mr Ernie Ross (former MP), who has been working very hard for many years on issues related to the Arab and Muslim countries, especially the Arab-Israeli conflict.

Several options were available to the Institute Board to establish its first campus in Dundee, but as a historian, I was keen to find a historical building. After several visits to Dundee, the current campus of the

Institute at 124 Blackness Road, in the City's West End was purchased for the use of the Institute by Meadowbrook Limited from Dundee College. It is a beautiful grade B-listed building which was built in 1908 as a Catholic primary school. The campus of the Institute is very conveniently located. All amenities are nearby and both the libraries of the University of Dundee and the University of Abertay Dundee are within walking distance. The city centre, main train and coach stations and Dundee Airport are also close by.

Campus Development

When we first moved into the building in August 2001, we realised that there had to be a serious investment to renovate and refurbish the premises, to make it a comfortable academic place for both students and staff. In very simple terms, nearly everything had to be started from scratch and I was the only individual employed at that time at the Institute. Accordingly, I had to work day and night and put all my energy into ensuring the suitability and safety of the building to start our academic activities.

Major works were undertaken to renovate the campus. Two of the main external works undertaken were to completely replace the roof and to restore the stonework to ensure durability. These took several months to complete and the final touches to the stonework were only finished in February 2002.

In the first few months of occupancy, we were faced with a considerable vandalism which resulted in nearly all our windows being broken. The problem continued even after we had contacted the police and the local councillor. We were aware that the act of vandalism was committed by teenagers who probably have felt that they were vandalising an unoccupied building. We reached this assumption because after the boards covering the windows were taken down, no more such incidents were reported. Additionally, following advice from Tayside Police, it was decided to replace the glass windows with polycarbonate, a material guaranteed to be shatter-proof. Since that time, we have not experienced any vandalism or problems of that kind.

Internally, the building was required a major clean-up after being unused for many years. At the time we moved into the premises, old furniture was scattered around the building and nearly all the furniture that we required was not available. Indeed, there were not even any suitable desks. There were also many children's furniture and toys left by Dundee College. In an effort to create links with the local communities, we decided to donate these toys and furniture to the nursery at Dundee

University. The old furniture we did not require, was donated to local charities.

Another major project undertaken within the building was the installation of networked IT and telecommunication facilities. This work was done from scratch as the necessary infrastructure was not available on-site. The Institute is particularly proud of the videoconferencing facility installed in Shaikh Rashid Conference Hall. From an empty space we transformed it into a state-of-the-art hall with equipment bearing the latest technology, one of the very few such available in Dundee. This enabled students, staff and researchers to benefit by being able to linkup with scholars lecturing from anywhere in world. The equipment and technology we provide may be used by both academics and the general public.

Almost all the renovation and refurbishment works were contracted out to local companies, in line with the Institute's commitment to serve the local communities, especially in Dundee. The roofing, furnishing, painting, decorating, cleaning and many other works were all undertaken by companies based locally.

Structure of the Current Campus

The ground floor of the campus comprises the reception and lobby area, the Institute Office, Shaikh Rashid Conference Hall, Shaikh Hamdan Library, Al-Maktoum Foundation Office, Shaikh Maktoum Garden, the Postgraduate Research Students' room, one multi-purpose room, and a Dining area which also includes common and quiet rooms. The second floor holds the Depute Principal for Academic Affairs Office and ISRA Office.

The third floor is the main teaching floor and has three seminar rooms, including the Michael Adams Seminar Room, each of which can accommodate up to 20 students at any one time. There also are the offices of the Head of the Department of the Study of Islam and Muslims, the academic staff, the Visiting Scholars Room, Shaikh Muhammad IT Centre, Al-Maqdisi Boardroom, the Majlis (Meeting) room, and the Al-Maktoum Institute Academic Press Centre. The fourth floor is the Principal's Suite.

Announcement of the Establishment of the Institute in the House of Commons

Even though the Institute was still at the foundational stage, we had already been given very positive exposure within the context of the House of Commons. The establishment of the Institute was announced there during the Eid Reception on 18 December 2001. The reception was attended by the British Prime Minister, The Rt Hon Tony Blair MP, the Foreign Secretary, The Rt Hon Jack Straw MP and the Home Secretary, The Rt Hon David Blunkett MP. The reception is an annual event organised by Labour Middle East Council (LMEC) at the House of Commons, and every year of approximately 300 representatives of the British Muslim communities attend the reception. Other dignitaries such as Muslim Ambassadors in Britain, MPs, members of the House of Lords and senior members of the British government are also present.

Official Opening

The Official Opening Ceremony on 6 May 2002 brought the Institute to the attention of the whole academic world, when it was privileged to have His Highness Shaikh Hamdan Bin Rashid Al-Maktoum himself to perform the ceremony[2]. The senior delegation consisted of 17 senior officials from the United Arab Emirates and well-known corporate figures, including representatives of universities in the UAE, and leading figures in industry, health services and local economic development. Among the delegates were:

1. Mr Mirza Al-Sayegh (Director of the Office of HH Shaikh Hamdan Bin Rashid Al-Maktoum and Chairman of the Institute Board)
2. Mr Mohamad Obeid Bin Ghannam (Secretary-General of Al-Maktoum Foundation and member of the Institute Board)
3. HE Mr Juma Al-Majid
4. HE Mr Qasim Sultan (then Director-General, Dubai Municipality and Chairman of Dubai Health Board)
5. Dr Hanif Al-Qassimi (then Vice-President, Zayed University)
6. Dr Hadef Bin Jouan Al-Dhahiri (Vice-Chancellor, UAE University)
7. Dr Said Al-Hassani (Under-Secretary, UAE ministry of Higher Education)

---

[2]   Together with Mr George Foulkes (MP), Minister of State at the Scottish Office representing Her Majesty's Government, HH Shaikh Hamdan cut the tartan ribbon at the main entrance of the Institute, signifying the Institute's entry into a new era. Following the welcoming speech, I invited HH Shaikh Hamdan to officially open the Institute by unveiling a commemorative plaque, accompanied by Mr George Foulkes.

8. Dr Sulaiman Musa Al-Jasim (then Director, Higher Colleges of Technology, UAE Ministry of Higher Education)
9. Mr Abd al-Rahim Al-Mirri (Cultural Attaché, UAE Embassy in London)
10. Mr Abd al-Rahman Al-Ghurair (Vice-Chairman, Dubai Chamber of Commerce and Industry)
11. HE Mr Muhammad Ali Al-Abbar (Director-General, Dubai Economic Development Department)
12. HE Mr Qadi Mawarshid (Director-General, Dubai Health Board)
13. Mr Ahmad Al-Shaikh (Dubai TV)
14. Mr Ali Khalifah (Dubai TV)

The event was attended by senior government officials, business leaders, and the academic communities of Dundee. It was indeed a historic and excellent day for the City of Dundee and Scotland offering an opportunity to establish links with Dubai and the United Arab Emirates.

HH Shaikh Hamdan declared the Institute officially opened in his address, after the unveiling of a commemorative plaque to mark the auspicious occasion. The Institute also published a commemorative booklet to mark the historic day.

First Chair in Islamicjerusalem Studies

The academic activities of the Institute started with the appointment of the First Chair in Islamicjerusalem Studies. The vacancy for this first post was advertised widely in the academic world and we received some very good applications before the closing date of 16 April 2001. Three short-listed candidates - one each from the United Kingdom, Germany and Switzerland - were interviewed on 5 May 2001 by an independent Appointing Committee consisting of four academics from the University of Stirling, University of Manchester Institute of Science and Technology, University of Wales and University of Leiden in The Netherlands. The Appointing Committee decided to offer the post to Professor Abd al-Fattah El-Awaisi.

First Chair in Multiculturalism, Islam and Muslims in Britain

The Institute took another bold step forward on 11 October 2002 by appointing Professor Malory Nye as the First Chair in Multiculturalism, Islam and Muslims in Britain. The position was created in response to the dire need to engage in a more serious and structured way in research and teaching of multiculturalism, with a focus on Islam and Muslims in

Britain. This appointment further enhanced the Institute's reputation as a centre of research excellence.

Appointment of New Chancellor

A special dinner was held on 15 January 2003 at Dundee Hilton to announce the appointment of The Lord Elder of Kirkcaldy as the new Chancellor of Al-Maktoum Institute for Arabic and Islamic Studies. During the dinner, Lord Elder was welcomed by the Chairman and members of the Institute Board, senior academics, politicians, business representatives and leaders of the communities in Dundee, including the Lord Provost of Dundee Mr John Letford.

Lord Elder is the second Chancellor of the Institute. The first Chancellor was Lord Watson of Invergowrie who was appointed as the Chancellor on 1 January 2001. However, he stepped down on 27 November 2001 upon being appointed as the Scottish Executive Minister for Tourism, Culture and Sport.

Lord Elder has served, and is still serving, the British public in various distinguished posts. His presence as the Institute's Chancellor further boosts our ability to serve the communities of Dundee and Scotland, as well as Britain as a whole. Indeed, with Lord Elder being a member of the Institute's family, we are in an even stronger position to act as a bridge between the Western and Muslim countries, especially between Scotland and the United Arab Emirates.

Lord Elder's first official engagement as Chancellor of the Institute was to visit Dubai on 28 – 31 March 2003. Accompanied by Professor Abd al-Fattah El-Awaisi, the Principal and Vice-Chancellor, Lord Elder attended several high-powered meetings with senior officials within the education sector in Dubai. Visits were arranged to Zayed University, UAE University in Al-Ain, Dubai University College, Dubai College of Arabic and Islamic Studies, Juma Al-Majid Centre for Culture and Heritage, Dubai TV, Dubai Internet City, Shaikh Saeed House, Dubai Museum and Higher Colleges of Technology (Dubai Women's College). An audience with HH Shaikh Nahayan Bin Mubarak Al-Nahayan, Chancellor of Zayed University and the UAE Minister of Higher Education, was also held during the visit.

Scottish Parliament

I was invited to lead the weekly Time for Reflection at the Scottish Parliament on 20 November 2002. In my address, I talked about Scottish Muslims and Muslims in Scotland and how Islam encourages integration and cooperation. I also mentioned the good work the Institute is doing for the benefit of Scotland as a whole. The speech received a positive response and was covered by the local media.

Prior to the Time for Reflection session, I met the (now former) Scottish Parliament's Presiding Officer, Sir David Steel. Sir David was briefed about the first Al-Maktoum Institute Delegation to the UAE, and he was especially pleased to hear about the proposal for Emirates Airline to direct flight to Scotland. I also met Sir David Steel when he visited the Institute on 29 November 2002.

First Qur'anic Recitation in the history of Kirking Ceremony

On Tuesday, 6 May 2003, Al-Maktoum Institute for Arabic and Islamic Studies once again became part of an historic occasion in Scotland. During the Kirking of the Second Scottish Parliament at St Giles Cathedral, Edinburgh, a student from the Institute recited the Holy Qur'an in front of HRH The Prince of Wales, MSPs, academics and political and community leaders from all over Scotland.

This was the first time in history that the Holy Qur'an had been read in a Kirking Ceremony. The recitation was done by Mr Khalid El-Awaisi, former President of the Al-Maktoum Institute Student Society. Khalid received a letter of thanks from the Scottish Parliament which stated: '... thank you most sincerely for the wonderful rendition you gave of Surat al-Hujurat from the Holy Qur'an[3] at the Kirking of the Parliament ceremony in May. Everyone I have spoken to about it was as impressed as I was and to many it opened their eyes to a new dimension.'

---

[3]   'Oh you who believe! Men should not ridicule others; maybe they are better than themselves. Nor should any women ridicule other women; maybe they are better than themselves. And do not find fault with one another or insult each other with derogatory nicknames. How evil is it to have a name for evil conduct after coming to faith! Those people who do not turn from it are wrongdoers.

Oh you who believe! Avoid most suspicion. Indeed some suspicion is a crime. And do not spy and do not backbite one another. Would any of you like to eat his brother's dead flesh? No, you would hate it. And have piety of God. God is Ever-Returning, Most Merciful.

Oh Humankind, we created you all from a single pair of a male and a female, and made you into nations and tribes so that you should get to know one another. The noblest among you in the sight of God is the one with the most piety. God is All-Knowing, All-Aware.' (Qur'an, 49: 11-13)

400th Anniversary of the Union of the Crowns

The Rt Hon Jack McConnell (MSP), Scottish First Minister, hosted a dinner to mark the 400th anniversary of the Union of the Crown. The dinner was held at the Royal Museum in Edinburgh on Tuesday 1 July 2003 and was attended by Her Majesty the Queen and HRH the Duke of Edinburgh. I was invited by Mr McConnell to join other senior officials from around Scotland at the dinner.

Appointment of PR Company

The Institute Board appointed Mr David Whitton of Whitton PR Ltd as the public relations representative of the Institute in May 2003. Mr Whitton has been involved in the public relations industry since 1970 and his experience in dealing with the media is vast. Among other responsibilities, Mr Whitton was Special Adviser and Official Spokesman for the former Scottish Secretary, the late Donald Dewar; and Special Adviser and Official Spokesman to the first First Minister and the Scottish Executive (1999-2000).

Creation of the Post of Depute Principal for Academic Affairs

Professor Malory Nye, who holds the chair of Multiculturalism, Islam and Muslims at the Institute, was appointed in March 2004 to this new post of Depute Principal for Academic Affairs. In his new role, he became responsible for continuing the expansion and growth of the Institute's academic activities and for leading the further development of our aims to pursue excellence in our key areas of teaching and research.

As a leading expert in the field of multiculturalism and the study of religious diversity in the UK, Professor Nye has been great assistance in building the reputation of the Institute, both nationally and internationally, as a leading institution for the academic study of Islam and Muslims.

The First Validation of the Masters Taught Programme

The Institute started its first two postgraduate taught programmes by offering two courses, one leading to the award of MLitt in Islamic Studies and the other to MLitt in Islamicjerusalem Studies. The proposal for the these courses had undergone detailed examination by the University of Abertay Dundee's Committee for Academic Standard and Quality (CASQ). The document outlining the content of both courses was first examined by the School of Social and Health Sciences Board on 14 November 2001. After its approval, it was then examined by a Scrutiny Group on 23 November 2001 followed by a Course Validation

Advisory Group (CVAG) on 14 December 2001, both of which were set up by CASQ.

The document received a very positive response from CVAG and the committee even complimented the Institute on the robustness of the validation that had been undertaken and the quality of the programme documentation. Following the very good review by CVAG, CASQ decided on 11 January 2002 to recommend to University's Senate that the course leading to the award of MLitt in Islamic Studies/Islamicjerusalem Studies, to be delivered by the Al-Maktoum Institute, be validated without limit of time. The Principal of the University took a Chairman's Action to approve the document on behalf of the Senate on 18 January 2002 and this was subsequently approved by the Senate on 20 February 2002.

University of Abertay Dundee

The first academic link to validate our postgraduate programmes was established with the University of Abertay Dundee. On 17 October 2001, the Senate of the University of Abertay Dundee decided to approve the academic partnership between the Institute and the University. This was followed by approval from the University Court on 26 October 2001. On the same day, a Memorandum of Agreement was then signed by me as Principal and Vice-Chancellor of the Institute, and Professor Bernard King, Principal and Vice-Chancellor of Abertay.

Although the Institute was at that time constituted by the University of Abertay as a Division of its School of Social and Health Sciences, it is important to note that the Institute has always been an autonomous and independent body. Additionally, the Institute Board discussed at length on 24 June 2002 the relationship between the Institute and Abertay, and decided that the Institute should continue to remain an autonomous and independent establishment.

After a meeting between Lord Elder, the Institute Chancellor, and Professor Bernard King, Principal of the University of Abertay, in February 2004 it was resolved that the previous validation agreement between the Institute and Abertay would cease. In May 2004, Lord Elder wrote to Professor King confirming these changes and reaffirming the Institute's appreciation of the University of Abertay's validation our programmes in the first two and half years of the Institute's history. Of course, this change in the validation arrangements has not diminished the Institute's strong commitment to the development of its relationship with the city of Dundee.

University of Aberdeen

I initially visited the University of Aberdeen on 24 October 2003 to meet Lord Professor Sewel, Senior Vice-Principal. This was followed on 13 January 2004 by another visit to the University of Aberdeen to meet Professor Duncan Rice, the Principal and Vice-Chancellor of the University of Aberdeen, Aberdeen Business School, and the Dugald Baird Centre for Research on Women's Health and the Health Economics Research Unit. The Institute delegation also included Mirza Al-Sayegh, and Mohamed Obeid Bin Ghannam.

University of Aberdeen Validation Agreement

On 16 March a panel of senior members of the University of Aberdeen visited the Al-Maktoum Institute as part of the process of their consideration of the validation agreement. This visit was carried according to the standard procedures for universities in the UK, as set out by the Quality Assurance Agency. The panel appointed by the Academic Standards Committee (Postgraduate) of the University (ASC PG) was made up as follows:

- Professor Gordon Burgess, Convener of the ASC (PG) and of the validation panel
- Professor Seth Kunin, the Head of the School of Divinity, History, and Philosophy and Director of Research, College of Arts and Social Sciences
- Professor Trevor Salmon, Director of Teaching and Learning, College of Arts and Social Sciences
- Yvonne Gordon, Assistant Registrar
- Dr Gabriele Marranci, Observer, Lecturer in Anthropology of Islam

During their visit, which lasted for the whole day, the panel met me as the Principal and Vice-Chancellor, teaching and administrative staff, toured the Institute campus, and met with students taking both MLitt and PhD programmes. The main items of discussion for the panel were issues of quality assurance at the Institute, student support facilities, and the practical issues that would arise from the change to University of Aberdeen.

At the end of the visit the panel met me and Depute Principal for Academic Affairs again. They confirmed that they were happy with their findings, and they would be submitting a report to University of Aberdeen ASC (PG) recommending the proposal for the validation agreement. The panel commended the Institute on a number of aspects of its provision for students, including the New Student Induction and Summer Postgraduate training research workshops, and it was agreed that under the new agreement the Institute would be fully implementing the University's Quality Assurance procedures. The panel's report was subsequently considered by the ASC (PG), who recommended that the validation agreement be approved for five years from the start of the academic year 2004/5. At the subsequent meeting of the University of Aberdeen Senate on 5 May, this approval was given and the Senate decision was then ratified by the University of Aberdeen Court on 25 May 2004.

On 26th May 2004 the Principals of Al-Maktoum Institute and the University of Aberdeen signed a validation agreement for the MLitt, MPhil, and PhD programmes of the Institute. The result of this agreement was that all new students registering with the Institute from September 2004 would be students of the University of Aberdeen, and receive their degrees from that prestigious institution. Furthermore, existing research students at the Institute was given the opportunity to transfer their registration to the University of Aberdeen if they so chose. A considerable number of our continuing students have transferred to the University of Aberdeen at that time.

This new validation agreement was a very significant step for the Institute and it was very much in line with the Institute's aim to foster excellence in teaching and research in the Study of Islam and Muslims. The University of Aberdeen is one of the oldest Scottish universities, having recently marked its 500th anniversary, and has an international reputation for its teaching and research.

According to the agreement, the Institute is now considered for administration of its academic programmes as a Centre within the University of Aberdeen School of Divinity, History, and Philosophy, which also contains the subject areas of Divinity and Religious Studies, Cultural History, History, History of Art, and Philosophy. In the 2001 Research Assessment Exercise (RAE) Divinity and Religious Studies were awarded the high rating of 5.

Students at the Al-Maktoum Institute have full use of the University of Aberdeen's facilities, as well as the Institute's own facilities in Dundee. All teaching and supervision takes place on the Institute's campus in Dundee.

The Institute works closely with the University of Aberdeen in a number of areas of collaboration in the fields of research and teaching.

Creation of the Post of Head of Department for the First Department at the Institute: Department of the Study of Islam and Muslims

From 1 February 2003 to 1 October 2006, the role of Head of Department was held by Professor Malory Nye. Initially this was Professor Nye's main administrative role, and then from 1 March 2004 he also became Depute Principal for Academic Affairs. A number of the duties and responsibilities of the role of Head of Department were combined with his duties as Depute Principal for Academic Affairs, mainly for the efficient day-to-day running of the Institute.

With the growth and development of Al-Maktoum Institute, and particularly because of the development of an academic staff group who now have some experience, the Institute took the decision to re-establish the position as a role for a member of academic staff, to enable the efficient mid-level management and administration of academic affairs.

The primary role of the post is defined in terms of academic leadership, particularly in the areas of teaching and research of the appointed academic staff of the Institute. This is being implemented through the following duties: management of academic staff, taking an active role in promoting and developing the Institute's new agenda for the Study of Islam and Muslims, administrating senior academic-related matters as required, and chairing several committees of the Academic Council. The Institute Board makes the appointment of the Head of Department(s) for a fixed period of no more than two years, with the expectation that it will normally be rotated amongst suitably able/qualified academic staff.

Dr Alhagi Manta Drammeh, who holds the lectureship in the Study of Islam and Muslims at Al-Maktoum Institute, was appointed on 1 October 2006 as Acting Head of the first department to be established here: The Department of the Study of Islam and Muslims.

PART TWO
SETTING THE NEW AGENDA FOR
CULTURAL ENGAGEMENT AT THE
ACADEMIC LEVELS

2

THE SUCCESS AND NICHE OF THE INSTITUTE

At the heart of the work of the Institute, both in our academic activities and in serving the communities, is my vision and passion for the twin pillars of education and multiculturalism. On 23 June 2004, all our work came together in a single document titled 'Shaikh Hamdan Bin Rashid Al-Maktoum's Vision for Multiculturalism'. In this document, Shaikh Hamdan sets out the importance of the vision of Islamicjerusalem as a model of a common space in which people from different backgrounds can live together – a place which radiates goodness and blessings, and is not closed and insular, but is instead a centre in which diversity and pluralism thrive in a spirit of mutual respect and co-existence.

Through the creation of the Al-Maktoum Institute in Scotland, through our teaching programmes in Islamicjerusalem Studies and the Study of Islam and Muslims, through the new agenda for the Study of Islam and Muslims, through our implementation and investigation of the central concept of multiculturalism, and through our continuing efforts to serve the communities, we are setting a new agenda for cultural engagement in both academic and communities levels; and encouraging dialogues across cultures and peoples, which will enhance greater understanding and appreciation between the Arab and Muslim worlds and the west.

The passion for Islamicjerusalem and the vision for the implementation of this model into practical steps have created the foundations for co-operation and the encouragement of a multicultural ethos of mutual respect and common understanding for the whole world. In the last five years, we have been very keen to continue providing many examples in cultural engagement for people to learn from.

Strategic Academic Developments

The central aim of the Institute is to pursue excellence in teaching, research and consultancy in the academic study of Islam and Muslims, in particular to promote intelligent debate and understanding of Islam and the role of Muslims in the contemporary world, and to be a place of knowledge and reflection on the issues facing a diverse and multicultural world in the 21st century.

The success of the Institute comes from the fact that it is one of the key Post Orientalist and Post-Traditionalist institutions in the world. We recognise the need to develop the study of Islam and Muslims as a discipline with long established roots but which must now face the challenges and opportunities of a diverse and multicultural word in twenty-first century. To this end, we are actively working to educate the next generation of scholars both nationally and internationally in the study of Islam and Muslims. Our programmes are based on current and progressive research and take into consideration the needs and preferences of our local, national and international students.

At the Institute, we look at Islam and Muslims in many different ways and in many global contexts. We are distinct from traditional approaches, where the focus has been to study Islam and Muslims from just one limited perspective. The Institute does not seek to offer Islamic Studies within a single methodology. We offer training in the study of Islam and Muslims within a number of *different* methodologies, eg history, political science, anthropology, geography, and area studies as well as traditional approaches in Islamic Studies. We provide our students with an interdisciplinary and multidisciplinary approach so that they can appreciate and understand the various schools of thought within a specific line of study. Indeed, our approach reflects a diversity of teaching and research interests spanning a variety of subject areas and methodological approaches. We are committed to the interdisciplinary and cross cultural study of a variety of fields in the study of Islam and Muslims.

To reflect this vision of Post-Orientalist, Post-Traditionalist and multicultural approaches, the Institute established its strategic objectives through setting the new agenda as announced initially in 18 March 2004, 'Dundee Declaration for the future development of the study of Islam and Muslims'.

The First International Symposium on Islamic Studies

On 17-18 March 2004 the Institute hosted, in collaboration with the Islamic Universities League, a major international symposium on the development of Islamic Studies in Higher Education. Professor Jafaar Abdelsalam, Secretary General of the Islamic Universities League, led a delegation of academics from the League, including scholars from Al-Azhar University, the oldest university in the world. The symposium looked at case studies in the teaching of Islamic Studies in Egypt and the UK, as well as the development of the new field of inquiry of Islamicjerusalem Studies, and also looked at past and future issues in the teaching of particular areas of the study of Islam and Muslims.

Dundee Declaration

One strong theme of the symposium was the sense of the emergence of a new agenda for the development of the field of the Study of Islam and Muslims. After long discussions, the delegates at the event agreed to issue a statement called 'The Dundee Declaration for the future development of the study of Islam and Muslims'. This innovative and very important document sets out in detail key issues for the field, stressing the importance for scholars engaged in this area to face the challenges of the twenty-first century. The Declaration made it clear that the Study of Islam and Muslims must seek to develop and define itself as Post-Orientalist and multicultural, in which it is recognised that there is no single methodology or approach, but is both interdisciplinary and multidisciplinary. (The full text of the Dundee Declaration is in Appendix 6).

The New Agenda for the Study of Islam and Muslims Globally

We recognise the need to set the agenda for the future development of Islamic Studies (and other related subject areas) into the Study of Islam and Muslims. Since the drafting of the Dundee Declaration the Institute has begun the process of strategic planning for developing, disseminating and implementing this new agenda. We played a key role, not only by innovating an agenda for research and teaching that links directly with the needs of our contemporary era – the challenges of globalisation and multiculturalism which all engaged in the field must face – but also pioneering a new approach which includes scholars under a broad umbrella of ideas and issues in the study of Islam and Muslims, coming from different backgrounds and faiths who are united by a common intellectual goal and an ethic of mutual respect for differences.

Indeed, we have taken a leading role in the establishment and implementation of this new agenda, for example by working in partnership with other academic institutions. We were very keen to work in co-operation with our partner universities across the world to find ways in which the new agenda may be developed and implemented worldwide. In the last three years, the Institute have discussed, with our partner universities, the practical ways to take this further.

The following points summarise this new agenda:

Post-Orientalist

- The Study of Islam and Muslims is a field with long established roots, but which must now face the challenges and opportunities of the twenty-first century.
- The Study of Islam and Muslims is based on a principle of mutual respect by all involved in this field of academic study, in which both Muslims and non-Muslims can share together a common sense of purpose and belonging, and a common intellectual goal.
- Scholars working in this focused field share a common aim to build bridges and to provide a meeting point between the Muslim and Western worlds of learning and to encourage scholarship and academic co-operation at this crucial time.
- The current crisis in the contemporary Muslim world is caused in part by the absence of co-operation between knowledge and power.

Post-Traditionalist

- The Study of Islam and Muslims is about the study of Muslim people, societies and cultures as well as the religion of Islam.
- The Study of Islam and Muslims is not only a faith-based field. It extends far wider than traditionalist approaches based on a theological pursuit of 'faith seeking understanding'.
- Universities in Muslim and Western countries should ensure that the teaching of Arabic and English languages go hand-in-hand for the development of the study of Islam and Muslims in the twenty-first century.
- A better understanding in the West of Islam and Muslims can only be achieved by critical engagement and constructive dialogue based on analytical academic discourse through multicultural education.

Interdisciplinary and multidisciplinary

- As a field, the Study of Islam and Muslims must seek to develop and redefine itself as post-orientalist, post-traditionalist, and multicultural, in which it is recognised that there is no single methodology or approach, but is both inter-disciplinary and multi-disciplinary.

- Such interdisciplinary and multidisciplinary training in the study of Islam and Muslims should be based in a number of different methodologies, including history, political science, anthropology, sociology, geography, gender, and area studies as well as traditional areas in Islamic Studies.

Highest standards

- We are in pressing need to encourage, support and develop research and teaching which achieves the highest quality, and which is based on critical, analytical and scientific standards.
- Scholars, researchers, and teachers within the Study of Islam and Muslims are expected to be trained to the highest possible standards in the field of their research, and as active researchers should strive to maintain the international standards of publication, peer review, dissemination, and continual engagement with contemporary scholarship.
- At the root of this field is a shared ethic of research, which is based on principles of multimethodology, multiculturalism, academic freedom, human rights and tolerance.

New field of inquiry

- The new field of inquiry of Islamicjerusalem Studies is a central and vital element of the Study of Islam and Muslims, and must be developed as an example of the field based on the above principles.
- Islamicjerusalem Studies is a new branch of human knowledge based on interdisciplinary and multidisciplinary approaches. It aims to investigate all matters related to the Islamicjerusalem region, explore and examine its various aspects, and provide a critical analytic understanding of the new frame of reference, in order to identify the nature of Islamicjerusalem and to understand the uniqueness of this region and its effects on the rest of the world in both historical and contemporary contexts.

Multiculturalism

- The Study of Islam and Muslims should be based on the principle of 'One Discipline, Many Approaches', which is pursued by a cross-cultural academic body which may include people of any background.

- The differences between our cultural and religious backgrounds are what give strength and importance to this field of study, and the different cultural lenses that we each bring add to our pursuit of a common intellectual goal.

New innovative initiative (2004 – 2006): Major Research Project on the Future of the Study of Islam and Muslims in Universities and Colleges in Multicultural Britain

In April 2004 the Institute's Research Committee decided to allocate funds for a significant research project that investigated the teaching and research in the study of Islam and Muslims in the UK. In line with the Institute's strategic objective to develop the new agenda for the study of Islam and Muslims, the Institute resolved that an empirical survey and a theoretical analysis of the issues facing those currently working in the field in the UK would make a very important contribution to this area. The aim of the project was to contribute to our understanding of the study of Islam and Muslims at this critical stage, and of course hopefully provide useful research findings to indicate the key issues that the field must face over the next few decades.

Therefore, the Research Development Funded project involved the appointment of two research fellows – Dr Steven Sutcliffe and Dr Maria Holt – to work from April through to September 2004, to achieve the following objectives:

- To provide a review of the historical development of the study of Islam and Muslims in the UK, particularly with regard to institutional contexts for teaching and research in this area.
- To bring together information on current institutional activities in this field, particularly with reference to HE departments and centres of Islamic Studies, Middle-Eastern Studies, and Arabic Studies.
- To produce an interim report on the data and findings of the research, detailing a comparison of methods, approaches, and experiences of departments and centres in the field, along with an overview of the present standing and development of Islamic Studies in the UK.

In line with this, Dr Sutcliffe and Dr Holt were engaged for six months in 2004 with interviewing, visiting and sending questionnaires to all departments and academic centres in the UK that are working in the areas of Islamic Studies and Middle Eastern Studies.

The information and data collected from this research was collated and the research fellows submitted their summary findings to the project directors, Professor Malory Nye and I, along with the data that had been collected. We worked towards the production of a report and analysis of the findings of the research for dissemination in the wider academic community.

Major Research Report: Time for Change

In 2006, we completed this major research project on teaching and research in the Study of Islam and Muslims in the UK higher education. The research led to a new major Report entitled 'Time for Change' written by Professor Malory Nye and I, which was launched in the House of Lords on 25 October 2006.

The research examined 55 higher education departments and centres where Islam and Muslims is taught, including Islamic Studies, Religious Studies, Middle Eastern and Arabic Studies, and also departments of Politics and International Relations.

The Report not only provides a very important overview of the current situation, it also examines some of the key issues and challenges facing the field. In addition, it makes recommendations for how the field must be reshaped and developed to face the challenges and opportunities of the twenty-first century. It concludes that Islamic studies in Britain's higher education establishments are failing to meet the needs of today: 'There must be better education at university level...which reflects the needs of our contemporary multicultural society.'

The Report says that there is an urgent need for a new agenda to develop Islamic Studies into the Study of Islam and Muslims to question both the more traditional approaches that were often faith-based and excluded non-Muslims and the orientalist approaches that often alienated Muslims. Indeed, the call for a new agenda is timely and necessary to prevent the misguided and narrow interpretations of Islam which are the source of so many problems in our multicultural world. It is only through multicultural education we can work to eliminate extremism and fundamentalism.

Indeed, there is a clear and very obvious need for the Study of Islam and Muslims to be developed as a significant field of study across all levels of education in Britain. This is not only for the education of British youth as global citizens with a good knowledge and understanding of the contemporary world, it is also essential as a means of understanding our own multicultural society.

Teaching on Islam and Muslims has been an important part of university curricula in the UK for well over 250 years. But now is the time for change. We need to develop this field of study for today's world and, in particular, to rethink many of the loosely understood ideas that frame so much of the public debate surrounding this.

As a Scottish research-led higher education institution, Al-Maktoum Institute was very keen to develop the discussion and widen the debate of the issues raised by the Report on a scholarly level. For this purpose, the Institute organised a national symposium on 'Time for Change: the Future of the Study of Islam and Muslims in Universities and Colleges in Multicultural Britain' held at the Institute in Dundee on 19 January 2007. The Institute invited academics, policy-makers and individuals with an interest in the field to attend and participate in the discussion.

3

UNIQUE PROGRAMMES IN SCOTLAND IN THE STUDY OF ISLAM AND MUSLIMS

The academic activities at the Institute are governed by the Academic Council chaired by the Principal and Vice-Chancellor of the Institute. All academic development at the Institute has been strategically planned in order to ensure that we are able to provide our students with a unique learning opportunity, as well as to enrich their learning experience.

The First Unique Programmes and Courses

The course in Islamic Studies is distinctive in that it is not focused narrowly on a specific subject. It is designed in such a way that it is not linked to the study of a specific area (e.g., Middle Eastern Studies) or a particular topic (e.g., Muslim History). The course covers a range of topics related to the Study of Islam and Muslims and it allows students to develop a strong grasp of the field. Students are encouraged to approach the field from a wide angle and this will enable them to acquire the knowledge and skills befitting those who have undergone postgraduate training.

The course in Islamicjerusalem Studies is a course unique to the Institute. Indeed, it is the first and only institution that offers the academic study of Islamicjerusalem. The field was pioneered by Professor Abd al-Fattah El-Awaisi himself. The course structure reflects the Institute's commitment to advance an exciting and multi-disciplinary approach to a relatively new field of inquiry.

All our courses are distinctive and exciting developments in the world of academia in Scotland, and even in Britain as a whole. The main features of the programme are:

i.   Contemporary – It is based on current and progressive research, and takes into consideration the needs and preferences of national and international students.
ii. Flexibility - It allows students to transfer between the Certificate, Diploma and Masters, and part-time students to transfer to full-time and vice versa.
iii. Quality – The quality of teaching inputs and outputs are assured and maintained by regular reviews undertaken by the Institute.
iv. Diversity - The programme does not seek to offer Islamic Studies training within a single methodology. Rather, an inter-disciplinary approach is used so that students will appreciate and understand the various schools of thought within a specific line of study.

The First Group of Taught Masters Students

The Institute celebrated the launch of our taught academic programmes on 4 February 2002, the historic day on which the first group of taught students started their study here. Nonetheless, with my very small team at that time, we were working day and night since the first day we moved into the current campus in preparation for that very day. Major works were undertaken to renovate the campus, not to mention the time and energy spent to ensure academic preparations for the commencement of teaching were well organised.

Programme Review and Development

During the academic year 2003/2004, the Institute saw significant developments through a process of restructuring, intended to enhance our quality assurance systems, both for the delivery of our teaching programmes and for the strengthening of the Institute's research culture. These developments were also to address the exciting growth of the Institute and the wider network of relationships which had been developed in the previous years.

The main focus of these developments was to incorporate the new agenda for the future development of the study of Islam and Muslims into the Institute's teaching and research activities. Indeed, this new agenda laid the foundation for the strategic development of the Institute to develop as a Post-Orientalist, Post-Traditionalist and multicultural institution.

The new validation agreement with the University of Aberdeen in 2004 brought the opportunity to review and develop the two MLitt programmes that we offer in Islamic Studies and Islamicjerusalem

Studies. These two programmes were first constructed in 2001, and taught for the first time in February 2002, and so the new validation gave us a timely opportunity for such a review. A key issue for the Institute has been to ensure that the programmes reflect the development of the field of the study of Islam and Muslims, and in particular issues raised by the new agenda and how this can be reflected in the teaching that takes place at the Institute.

Therefore, a fundamental review of the programmes took place in autumn 2004, and the Academic Council of the Institute on 4 November 2004 gave approval to a new structure for both MLitt programmes which were subsequently approved by the University of Aberdeen, and taught for the first time in 2005.

The key changes that the review brought about were as follows:

- Focusing of the teaching, by reducing the total numbers of courses students take. This brought the programmes into line with the MLitt teaching in the School of Divinity, History and Philosophy at the University of Aberdeen.

- For the MLitt in Islamic Studies there were two new core courses for students, in Islam and Muslims in History and Society, and Islam and the West: globalisation, multiculturalism, and Muslims. These are taught alongside a revision of our existing core courses, Core Sources and Approaches in the Study of Islam and Muslims. These three courses provided a diverse, multidisciplinary backbone to the MLitt in Islamic Studies programme, which equipped students with an excellent knowledge and understanding of the general field of the study of Islam and Muslims.

- For the MLitt in Islamicjerusalem Studies, the core courses have revised to incorporate and develop the recent research that the Al-Maktoum Institute has pioneered and promoted since its opening. The main core courses are: The Theoretical Framework of Islamicjerusalem, History of Islamicjerusalem I: from 'Umar to Salah al-Din, and History of Islamicjerusalem II: from the late Crusades to the contemporary era.

Together both programmes established the Institute as providing taught postgraduate courses that are unique and innovative, indeed unlike any other programmes offered in the UK.

Revision and review of the programmes took into account feedback from many quarters, and the changes addressed in particular some of the issues that students have identified to us in the existing programme – in particular the previous over-emphasis on classroom time at the expense of independent research time for the development of postgraduate reading and critical analytical skills. Our aim is to produce MLitt graduates who are trained to the highest possible standards, but whose academic skills are as much based in their capability for further research as in a broad knowledge of their subject field.

Quality Assurance Systems

These developments in the arrangements for the validation of our programmes were initiated as part of the Institute's overall goal to enhance the quality of our students' learning environment and to build a world-class centre for excellence in teaching in the study of Islam and Muslims. Further restructuring within the Institute to strengthen the systems for the delivery, maintenance, and monitoring of our quality assurance were put in place in the academic year 2003-2004.

Academic Council

At the centre of all aspects of the delivery of academic quality assurance at the Institute is the Academic Council, a committee chaired by the Principal and Vice-Chancellor for overseeing and developing all aspects of teaching, research, and academic-related activities in the Institute. In 2003 and 2006, the Academic Council made fundamental reviews of the structure of committees that it administers and in 2006, it decided to create new structure committees as shown below.

Thus, oversight of the key areas of academic activity in the Institute is now constituted into four dedicated committees of the Academic Council. These committees together ensure that there are clear and effective mechanisms for the quality control and provision of all aspects of academic activities within the Institute. As a major part of this restructuring, in September 2004 the Institute also developed for the first time a calendar schedule of all meetings of these committees and sub-committees.

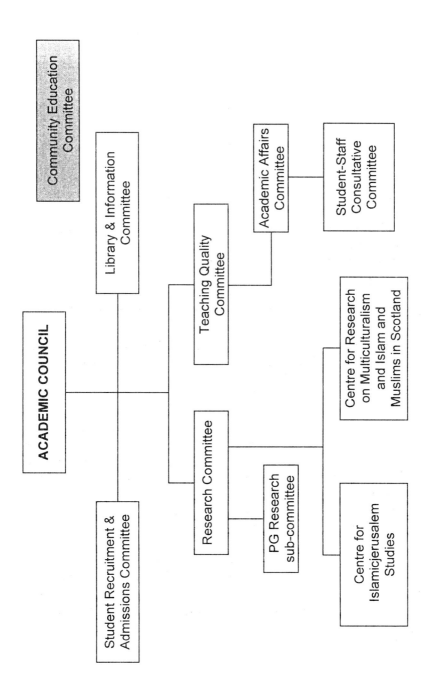

Working Group for Monitoring the Implementation of the Agreement with the University of Aberdeen

Following the signing of the validation agreement with the University of Aberdeen a working group was established at the Institute to consider all the practical issues related to the change from UAD to the University of Aberdeen.

To address the students concerns regarding the facilities available to them in the evenings, such as library facilities, the Institute implemented a late opening policy from 4 October 2004. During the autumn semester the Institute opened until 9.30 pm Monday to Friday to facilitate access to working space and computer facilities. In addition, students still have access to libraries of the other universities in the area.

To address also the other issues raised by our students including Library Access, Borrowing & Inter-Library Loans, Sport/Leisure, Health, and Social Facilities, the Institute set a special budget year under the heading of Students Support.

Development of New Taught Masters Programme and Courses

The two new MLitt Programmes in Islamic Studies and Islamicjerusalem Studies were offered for the first time to our new Master's students in September/October 2005. This new programme was based upon our new agenda for the Study of Islam and Muslims and the unique research developed at the Institute on Islamicjerusalem Studies.

The Institute is actively seeking to develop student recruitment, and as part of this, it has been in extensive discussion with colleagues in the University on the development of new taught programmes, both to develop its existing postgraduate profile, and also to extend into undergraduate teaching.

Following discussion with Professor Duncan Rice on the broad idea of an undergraduate programme on the Study of Islam and Muslims, to be delivered at Al-Maktoum Institute, Professor Rice reiterated his enthusiasm for this development and that the University would be proud to be associated with it. In subsequent discussions with senior staff, the broad idea was developed into a clearly structured programme, but particular difficulties of funding of students have yet to be resolved and require further discussion before the concept can be effectively implemented.

At the postgraduate level, the Institute developed proposals which were submitted to the College of Arts and Social Sciences in November 2006, for three new taught MLitt programmes, in the areas of:

- Multiculturalism
- Muslims, Globalisation, and the West
- Islamic Education

These are proposed to be delivered from Autumn 2007, together with our existing MLitt programmes:

- Islamic Studies
- Islamicjerusalem Studies

The Institute has also proposed some revisions to these programmes to include the provision of new courses, and also to rename the previously titled MLitt in Islamic Jerusalem Studies to bring it into line with the development of research in this new field of inquiry which Al-Maktoum Institute is pioneering.

Together we expect these programmes to greatly expand our student recruitment base, they are very much in line with the overall strategic vision of the Institute for a new agenda for the Study of Islam and Muslims, as well as the recommendations of the report on the development of this field of study which was published in October 2006.

It is hoped that these programmes will raise a lot of interest from potential students looking to engage in the post-orientalist, multicultural, and interdisciplinary agenda in the study of Islam and Muslims that is set out in the new agenda.

Distance Learning on MLitt programmes

Further expansion of our student recruitment base is also being proposed, for the delivery of our programmes through distance learning mode, along with the existing campus based mode. The Institute proposes to extend the delivery of its two current and three new MLitt programmes through distance learning to potential students on a part-time basis, both to students resident in the UK and also within the Gulf region, within easy access of Dubai and the UAE (with a potential market that could also extend to SE Asia).

The Institute recognises that there are two other important recruitment markets, which is seeking to develop. These are:

- Potential students resident elsewhere in the UK with a strong interest in our programmes, but who are unable to move to study at the Institute in Dundee, but who would be able to visit Dundee for two days per course.

- Potential students in the UAE, and the Gulf region, who are increasingly taking the opportunities for distance learning postgraduate study being offered by other Scottish and UK universities – for example by Heriot-Watt and Robert Gordon Universities.

The aim of the Institute is to offer postgraduate taught programmes to students in these two markets through a combination of printed learning materials, student contact support by Institute staff (from Dundee), online discussion (classroom/chat rooms) in a virtual learning environment (VLE), and intensive campus based seminars either in Dundee or Dubai (a two day seminar per course each semester).

The learning materials will be provided to students primarily through printed course documentation (prepared by academic staff at the Institute). The delivery of courses will also make use of a virtual learning environment for student support and virtual discussion (either UoA WebCT or web based discussion groups accessed through the Al-Maktoum Institute website).

The timetable for the introduction of such distance learning is from September 2007 onwards, rolling out the proposed five MLitt programmes on a gradual basis.

University of Aberdeen
(Overview of the First Two Years: 2004 - 2006)

With the Validation Agreement being signed between Al-Maktoum Institute and the University of Aberdeen in May 2004, the academic years 2004-05 and 2005-06 saw the implementation of this agreement in its first two years of operation.

The initial issues for this implementation in the first year focused in particular on the transfer from the University of Abertay of those students at Al-Maktoum Institute who wished to take the opportunity to continue their studies with the University of Aberdeen and the setting up of arrangements for the registration and teaching of new students (PGT and PGR) beginning in the 2004-05 academic session. To a large degree these issues were implemented successfully. The first group of new students registered with the University of Aberdeen entered the MLitt programme in September 2004.

The second year was a period of important growth and development of the relationship between the Institute and the University, marked by a number of significant developments. There is now a successful track-record of implementation of the validation agreement, and the relationship between the Institute and the University is well established and matured.

Through the first two years, there have been a number of discussions between senior staff of the Institute and the University, partly to establish and develop more efficient administrative procedures but more fruitfully to look towards the further successful development of the relationship. These areas have been in particular, the development of new programmes by the Institute, and the development of the validation agreement into accreditation.

One very significant landmark of the past two years was the first and second graduation of University of Aberdeen students, which took place at Al-Maktoum Institute on 1 December 2005 and 1 December 2006, with the degrees awarded by Professor Stephen Logan, the Senior Vice-Principal of the University of Aberdeen.

Al-Maktoum Institute has close relationships with a total of 17 universities and research centres across the world, including Europe, Africa, the Gulf States, and South East Asia. In particular, the Institute considers the University of Aberdeen to be a very important strategic partner and has given strong emphasis since the signing of the validation agreement to fostering and developing academic links and cooperation between the Institute and the University at all levels.

In 2004, November 2005 and December 2006, the Institute organised and funded visits for all our new students (MLitt and PhD) to the University of Aberdeen, where they were able to see the School of Divinity, History and Philosophy, as well as have a tour of the library and receive a talk from library staff on the electronic resources available to Aberdeen University's students.

In addition to this, staff from the University Library and Information Services have visited the Institute on three occasions to meet the Institute students: Gillian Dawson, 'Introduction to library facilities and online resources', at the Summer Postgraduate Research Training Workshop in June 2005, and also 'Practical use of e-research facilities' in January 2007; and Susan McCourt and Elaine Shallcross, 'Introduction to Ref Works', at the Summer Postgraduate Research Training Workshop in May 2006.

We were also very pleased to include Professor Angela Black, Director of the Graduate School, College of Arts and Social Sciences in the programme of the Summer Postgraduate Training Workshop in May 2006, when she gave a talk 'The Research Experience' to our students, and outlined the development of the Graduate School. Prior to this, two members of academic staff from the University of Aberdeen gave papers at the Institute's Winter Postgraduate Training Workshop in January 2006: Dr Claire Heristchi, Politics and International Relations, on 'Project Management', and Dr Johan Rasanayagam, Anthropology, on 'Anthropological Fieldwork'. In addition, Dr Tony Glendinning, School of Social Science, gave paper at the Winter Workshop in January 2007 on 'Strategies of Social Research: a practical introduction'.

The second year was also very fruitful for academic discussion and collaboration between staff of both institutions. Academics from the University visited the Institute on the following occasions to give presentations on their research:

- Dr Nadia Kirwan, French, on 'A 'Truncated' Multiculturalism or a Diversité à la française?' (International Symposium on the Challenges of Multiculturalism, 20 April 2006)
- Dr Johan Rasanayagam, Anthropology, on 'I'm not a Wahhabi': State Power and Muslim Orthodoxy in Uzbekistan'. (Research Seminar, 22 February 2006)
- Dr Claire Heristchi, International Relations, on 'Imperialism and the Academic' (Research Seminar, 29 March 2006)
- Professor Mustapha Pasha, International Relations, on 'Islam and Secularism in a Globalising Age', (Research Seminar, 11 October 2006)
- Professor Robert Segal, Religious Studies, on 'What's wrong with Postmodernism in Religious Studies' (Research Seminar, 8 November 2006)

On 18 May 2006, the Institute organised and hosted a special roundtable meeting for academics working in the study of Islam and Muslims at the University and the Institute. This meeting was attended by, from the University: Dr Clare Heritschi, School of Social Sciences (International Relations), Dr Nadia Kiwan, School of Languages and Literature (French), Dr Martin Mills, School of Divinity, History and Philosophy (Religious Studies), Professor Mustapha Pasha, School of Social Sciences (International Relations), Dr Johan Rasanayagam, School of Social Sciences (Anthropology); and from Al-Maktoum Institute: Professor Abd al-Fattah El-Awaisi, Professor Malory Nye, Dr Maher Abu-Munshar, and Dr Alhagi Manta Drammeh,

The aim of the meeting was to explore not only areas of common research interests but also to explore potential areas of collaboration at the research level. One area of potential collaboration coming out of these discussions could be practical steps towards the development of a network or centre of excellence for the University and the Institute in research in the Study of Islam and Muslims. The meeting included extensive discussion on Al-Maktoum Institute's New Agenda for the Study of Islam and Muslims and a detailed exploration between colleagues on how this new academic agenda can be taken forward through further research collaboration. We look forward to following up these discussions with further meetings in the future.

Developing the relationship between Al-Maktoum Institute and the University

There have been a number of very fruitful meetings between the senior management of both institutions in the past two years, leading to several significant developments of this important relationship. For example, there has been real development with the University of Aberdeen through a succession of productive meetings with Professor Duncan Rice, and Professor Steven Logan. Both institutions are proud of this strategic relationship.

Professor Duncan Rice, Principal of the University of Aberdeen, made his first visit to Al-Maktoum Institute on 6 December 2005 for the first of the regular (bi-annual) meetings of the senior management of the University and the Al-Maktoum Institute. On 16 August 2006 I met with Professor Rice at the University of Aberdeen. It was agreed that this would be an important mechanism for developing the relationship.

On 6 December 2005, Professor Duncan Rice, Principal and Vice-Chancellor of the University of Aberdeen, together with Professor Stephen Logan, Senior Vice-Principal of the University, visited Al-Maktoum Institute to discuss ways in which to further develop this strategic relationship. On this first formal meeting at the Institute, I welcomed Professor Duncan Rice and Professor Stephen Logan and outlined how Al-Maktoum Institute considered the University to be a very important strategic partner. In response, Professor Duncan Rice stated how pleased the University of Aberdeen is to be working with Al-Maktoum Institute, and how it considers the work of the Institute to be making an important contribution to the work of the University.

Validation matters

The first area of discussion focused on the core element of the relationship, which is those matters covered by the validation agreement, in particular the procedures for the administration of the MLitt and research degree programmes. I made it very clear that the Institute considers the first one and a half years of the validation arrangements to have been very successful, and that in particular the Institute was very pleased to have received a very glowing evaluation from the University's validation committee, which had said:

The Institute should be congratulated in providing two solid postgraduate programmes. In particular, it was felt that the combination of the ... Islamic Studies programme with the more intellectually innovative Islamic Jerusalem Studies programme provided a solid combination of established and research-led teaching that would provide the necessary environment for fostering research students (dated 2 November 2005).

Undergraduate degree
I outlined the development of the Institute's initial consideration of the idea to introduce an undergraduate degree in the field of the Study of Islam and Muslims. This had come to fruition in particular in the context of the needs of contemporary society, the social climate following the July 7 bombings in London, major national security issues, and the urgent need to educate all sections of the communities in the Study of Islam and Muslims within the new agenda that the Institute has pioneered, in order to combat extremism and the threat of terrorism and to enhance multicultural Scottish society. The idea of an undergraduate programme, validated by the University of Aberdeen, was very enthusiastically welcomed by the Principal and Senior Vice-Principal, and the discussion focused on establishing a mechanism for this idea to proceed.

Development from validation to accreditation
The Institute considers the initial validation arrangements between the Institute and the University to be a first step in a developing relationship, and that this should lead at some point to an accreditation agreement. Professor Duncan Rice agreed that the move from validation to accreditation was a 'natural progression' in the relationship, and it would be the aim for the University of Aberdeen to achieve this.

With the successful track record of the implementation of the validation agreement, the Institute and the University have agreed that this relationship should be developed from validation to accreditation. Both the Institute and the University also agreed that a timescale would have to be developed in order to achieve this. In November 2006, Al-

Maktoum Institute proposed that the formal process for moving from validation to accreditation be started during the academic year 2006-07.

Other activities
From 16 to 21 December 2006, I travelled with Professor Duncan Rice to visit the UAE, where he had the opportunity to meet prominent figures within the UAE's education and political areas.

Other meetings between the senior management of the Institute and the University over the second year included:

- 6 February:Meeting between Professors Steven Logan, Abd al-Fattah El-Awaisi, and Malory Nye, in Aberdeen
- 21 February: Meeting between Professors Malory Nye, Bryan Macgregor, Head of College of Arts and Social Sciences, Trevor Salmon, Director of Teaching and Learning, College of Arts and Social Sciences, Robert Frost, Head of School of Divinity, History, and Philosophy, Dr Alhagi Manta Drammeh, and Dr Trevor Webb, Academic Registrar, in Aberdeen
- 18 May:Meeting between Steven Cannon, the Secretary of the University of Aberdeen and Professors Abd al-Fattah El-Awaisi and Malory Nye, at Al-Maktoum Institute
- 21 March: Meeting between Professors Abd al-Fattah El-Awaisi, Malory Nye and Angela Black, Director of Aberdeen Graduate School, at Al-Maktoum Institute
- 9 May:Meeting between Cathy Macaslan, Vice-Principal for Learning and Teaching, and Professors Malory Nye and Trevor Salmon, in Aberdeen
- 29 May:Meeting between Cathy Macaslan, Dr Trevor Webb, and Professors Trevor Salmon and Malory Nye, at Al-Maktoum Institute
- 18 October:Meeting between Julie Mcandrews, Centre for Lifelong Learning, and Professors Trevor Salmon, Angela Black, and Malory Nye, in Aberdeen

The main areas of discussion and development over the second year were as follows:

i.   Developing the procedures for the implementation of the validation agreement, particularly to make the process of administration of student applications more efficient
ii. Development of new programmes to be delivered at Al-Maktoum Institute

iii. Delivery of Al-Maktoum Institute programmes through distance learning
iv. Institute and University committee representation
v. Development of the relationship between Al-Maktoum Institute and University of Aberdeen from validation to accreditation

In summary, Al-Maktoum Institute considers that the implementation of the validation agreement is working very effectively, with now very well established mechanisms for quality assurance. During this academic year, the Institute will be working with the University to further develop our course provision and student recruitment base, particularly through the introduction of three new and unique programmes and also with the development of distance learning on our programmes.

4

CREATING AND ENHANCING THE LEARNING ENVIRONMENT AND COMMUNITY

The past five years have seen a number of very significant new events and initiatives at the Institute which are not only creating and enhancing the learning environment and community of the Institute as a centre of excellence, but are also establishing the Institute as a major innovative contributor to international academic debates on the study of Islam and Muslims.

Student Training and Development

Annual Postgraduate Research Training Workshops

The postgraduate training workshops are a significant event within the academic calendar for the Institute's entire research community. They are attended by both staff and students along with visiting scholars. During the first three years the training was limited to a three-day summer training workshop where members of academic staff presented and discussed related and important research issues in the Study of Islam and Muslims. The workshop ensured that both staff and students were up-to-date with recent and important developments in the Study of Islam and Muslims as well as helping in the training of key postgraduate research skills. The aim of the postgraduate training workshop is to assist and train the students in their postgraduate study by allowing them to discuss issues with fellow students and other researchers, and to enhance their experience by presenting a paper to their audience, and receive feedback in an informal environment.

The first programme was held on 15 – 17 July 2002. For 2003, the workshop was held on 18-20 June 2003. Dr Hussein Abdul-Raof of Leeds University and Dr Jabal Buaben from the University of

Birmingham participated in the training workshop in 2003. Dr Michael Owen of Zayed University briefly attended the workshop and all students and academic staff had an opportunity to meet him. A day and a half was allocated for a paper presentations workshop by the Institute's postgraduate students and during this period, all our research students, including Masters students who were preparing their dissertations, presented findings from their own researches.

26-28 May 2004 saw the third such workshop at the Institute, which was very well attended by the majority of our students, along with staff and several visiting scholars – including Dr Martin Mills and Dr Gabriele Marranci from the School of Divinity, History and Philosophy, University of Aberdeen. Following a similar format to the previous years, members of the academic staff presented and discussed important research issues in the study of Islam and Muslims in the workshop. Dr Mills and Dr Marranci gave presentations on issues in postgraduate training, including writing and research planning, and developing critical and analytic skills within the study of Islam and Muslims. Dr Mahdi Zahraa, of Glasgow Caledonian University, also gave a presentation on the stages of development within a research programme. Most of the second and third days of the workshop were taken up with paper presentations by the postgraduate students (both MLitt and research students) on their dissertation and thesis research.

Students found the Postgraduate Research Training Workshop to be an extremely useful element of their training. Emerging from the final evaluation of the workshop was a strong sense that it could be extended further, as three days was not enough to cover in sufficient depth the variety of activities and training issues students need to explore. Arising from this, the Institute Research Committee decided to develop the workshop as a bi-annual event, which from 2005-06 takes place in the winter (January) and summer (May/June). This not only gave more time for extending the programme, but also meant this event happens more regularly as a key part of the Institute's research culture.

The introduction of the bi-annual Postgraduate Research Training Workshops, in winter and summer, demonstrates a strong commitment to the development of a vibrant research community and culture at the Institute, and one which is strongly rooted in the Institute's commitment to the development of the new agenda. It was planned that future workshops in January and June 2005 and beyond would include sessions that looked at particular action points coming from the new agenda in the Study of Islam and Muslims, and work towards developing and mapping the future growth of this field of studies.

In 2005, the Institute held its first Winter Postgraduate Research Training Workshop from 12 to 14 January 2005; and the Summer Postgraduate Research Training Workshops took place from 1 to 3 June 2005 for all students. In 2006, the Institute organised two postgraduate research training workshops: Winter Workshop from 18 to 20 January 2006, and Summer Workshop from 30 May to 1 June 2006. In 2007, the Institute held the Winter Postgraduate Research Training Workshop from 17 to 19 2007 which included the participation in the national symposium on 'Time for Change: the Future of the Study of Islam and Muslims in Universities and Colleges in Multicultural Britain'. The Summer Workshop will be organising from 30 May to 1 June 2007 which includes the participation in the 9th International Academic Conference on Islamicjerusalem Studies.

Postgraduate Taught and Research Student Induction Workshop

The Institute's commitment is also strongly directed at the Induction of our new students. To welcome our new students at the Institute, a three day comprehensive Induction programme was organised on 17-19 September 2003. This included introducing students to the Institute and life as a student in Dundee as well as an introduction and advice on 'Being a student' and 'Being an academic'. It also provided an opportunity for students and staff to interact on a social level and start developing the spirit of the Al-Maktoum Institute Family with our newest additions.

Following the introduction of an intensive induction programme for all new students in September 2003, it has become an important event in the Institute's calendar, and is indeed part of the student support and research structure. The Student Induction meeting took place in 2004 from 22-24 September, when students were given a detailed introduction to the procedures and structures of the programmes of study that they were starting at the Institute and with the University of Aberdeen. The students were also given talks and advice on student life in Dundee, in particular for those students who had only recently arrived in Scotland from overseas. In addition to this, the Student Welfare Officer had also prepared a booklet giving practical advice and information for international students on living and studying in Dundee, which was sent out to all new students before they travelled to Scotland.

A third day of induction took place a couple of weeks into the teaching semester on Wednesday 6 October, when the focus turned to practical study skills. Students were given detailed advice on core skills such as transliteration of words from Arabic to English, bibliography and referencing, as well as the processes of becoming a critical analytic scholar. This session then led into regular weekly meetings on Friday mornings for our whole student community – both taught and research, new and continuing – under the remit of the Extended Induction Seminars. The first two meetings of these seminars were focused on looking at the Dundee Declaration and the new agenda being mapped out, which has produced some very lively and interesting debates amongst our students. Students continued to develop these issues through the semester, in particular examining how the study of Islam and Muslims can develop new ideas within this post-Orientalist context.

On Monday 3 October 2005 the Postgraduate Taught and Research Student Induction week took place running until 11 October 2005. Students were given a detailed introduction to the procedures and structures of the programmes of study that they were starting at the Institute and with the University of Aberdeen. As in 2004, the students were also given talks and advice on student life in Dundee followed by weekly Extended Induction Seminars in 2006.

Student Welfare Officers

To support the students throughout their learning experience at the Institute, especially on their arrival, the Institute appointed an academic member of staff as Student Welfare Officer (male) and another member of the Institute Office as Student Welfare Officer (female).

Staff Appointments

The Institute continues to invest in its human resources, making a number of appointments. All these appointments came about as a result of the growth of the Institute and to ensure that the Institute is in a position to meet its strategic aims. In the first five years, the Institute made several academic staff appointments, particularly to ensure that the teaching and research conducted developed the Institute's agenda for international quality, and would also contribute to the strategic objective of the aims of the new agenda in the Study of Islam and Muslims.

During the staff recruitment process, the Institute places a strong emphasis on attracting the highest quality of scholars, both as teachers and researchers who can contribute to the development of the vision, mission, aims and objectives of the Institute and who can help us to take forward the programmes emerging out of the new agenda in the Study of Islam and Muslims.

Communication

As part of the Institute's policy of communicating its vision, mission and its new agenda, several plaques were mounted within the Institute:

- HH Shaikh Hamdan's Vision for Multiculturalism
- Al-Maktoum Institute's Mission Statement
- Dundee Declaration
- Islamicjerusalem: A New Concept and Definitions

The plaque displaying the Vision was unveiled by the Chancellor and the Vice-Chancellor on 7 February 2005. The Dundee Declaration Plaque was unveiled by the Chairman of the Board and the Vice-Chancellor on 5 March 2005.

A special booklet entitled 'A New Agenda' was published which includes HH Shaikh Hamdan's Vision for Multiculturalism and is now sent, for example, to all applicants prior to interviews for employment. Internal and external understanding of the Institute's Vision, Mission, New agenda in the Study of Islam and Muslims, and the Institute's aims are clear objectives within the Institute.

Several staff induction sessions and discussion meetings were held to ensure that staff are familiar with the Institute's vision, mission, aims and objectives, policies and procedures. The aim was to enhance our internal communications, brief staff on the latest developments and future plans, and promote the importance of working together as a team.

A staff discussion meeting took place on 21 December 2004 where the staff were presented with Shaikh Hamdan's vision. This meeting helped to finalise the drafting of the Institute's Mission Statement which was approved by the Academic Council, the Institute Council and the Institute Board.

Staff Policies and Procedures

On 15 October 2004, the Institute held its first formal staff induction session. This session followed the development and introduction of a full set of personnel policies and procedures by the Human Resource Committee, and aimed to introduce members of staff to the full range of the Institute policies and procedures. It also served as a useful element of staff training, as it brought all Institute staff together to discuss and share matters of mutual concern.

Staff Induction Sessions and Meetings

Further staff induction sessions were held on 15 October 2004, 23 December 2004, 8 March 2005 and 17 October 2005. These sessions included all new members of staff at the Institute. In 2006, staff induction sessions were organised on 22 February 2006, and 1 September 2006. These sessions were tailored according to the needs of new staff members.

The induction sessions are to ensure that all staff are informed of the Institute's Policies and Procedures upon commencing employment with the Institute. Also they aim to ensure that staff are acquainted with the four documents central to the work of the Institute: Shaikh Hamdan's Vision for Multiculturalism, the Institute's Mission Statement, the Institute Aims and Objectives, and the Institute's new agenda for the Study of Islam and Muslims.

In 2005, I met all staff on several occasions. For example, after the summer break I invited all academic and non-academic employees of the Institute to welcome them back. During the meeting on 23 August 2005 I briefed the staff on the plans for the coming academic year. I stated that the theme for 2005-2006 was to be 'focus and quality'. In 2006, I also met with all staff on several occasions. For example, on the 22 June I hosted a working lunch which all staff attended. This was to ensure that staff were prepared for the forthcoming Fourth Summer School and to provide an opportunity to brainstorm ideas for the coming academic year.

The Al-Maktoum Institute Annual Dinner

To instil a family atmosphere within the Institute, a very successful annual lunch for staff and students was established on 19 June 2003. All staff and students were invited to the lunch, which was the first such event organised by the Institute.

During the Summer Postgraduate Research Workshop, in the evening of Friday 28 May 2004, the second Al-Maktoum Institute Annual Dinner took place at a local restaurant. This is now well established as an important occasion when all staff and students, as well as invited guests, have an opportunity to come together in a relaxing and fairly informal context.

At the end of the summer postgraduate workshop the Institute held a Staff and Student Dinner at a local restaurant on 3 June 2005. In addition, at the end of the summer postgraduate training workshop, the Institute also held a staff and student dinner at a local restaurant on 1 June 2006.

Annual Al-Maktoum Institute Staff Festival Dinner
The second annual Al-Maktoum Institute Dinner took place on the 15 December 2004 at the Hilton Hotel. Now a well established event on the academic calendar, the Institute Annual Dinner seeks to bring the staff together in order to promote the importance of working together as a team and as a family. The theme of the Dinner which is a celebration of both Christmas and Eid is significant in reflecting the Institute's multicultural ethos.

The Third Annual Al-Maktoum Staff Festivals Dinner took place on 14 December 2005 at the Hilton Hotel. The evening provided an opportunity for staff to gather socially and relax. With the attendance of all partners our Institute family grew considerably.

Al-Maktoum Tartan Tea Party
On 7 July 2006, the Institute held a Tartan Tea Party to present Al-Maktoum Tartan to the Institute staff in recognition of their hard work over the past year. All members of staff were presented with gifts made from the Al-Maktoum Tartan which was rediscovered earlier in the year. Assisting me in the presentation of these gifts were the Institute Council member, Jill Shimi, The Lord Mayor of Wurzburg, Dr Pia Beckmann, and local singer/songwriter, Laura McGhee. The event was held in the Shaikh Maktoum Garden and attended by the thirty nine female students from the Fourth Summer School, members of Al-Maktoum Institute Council, and many representatives of the local community. The staff and the guests enjoyed the opportunity to socialise after the presentations, when a Scottish themed buffet was offered.

Campus Development
To create a more friendly atmosphere and to address the diverse needs of the Al-Maktoum Institute family, some more changes were made from the second year in the re-allocation of rooms and offices, especially on the ground floor of the Institute. In addition, the Institute has continued to address the diverse needs of Al-Maktoum Institute family and all those who enter its doors.

Lobby and reception area: the Institute felt the need to create a more pleasant and welcoming lobby. The Institute colours were incorporated into the scheme of the reception area to create a warm and inviting atmosphere has been created to make students, staff and guests alike feel welcome and at home as they enter the Institute. The library was expanded and the library security gates were similarly re-located to leave the reception area clutter-free and open-plan for interaction between people in the Institute.

Dining area: to create a closer interaction between staff and students, and instead of two separate common rooms for staff and students, one inclusive area has been created in which staff and students can socialise. Within this area is a sociable common dining room, with hot and cold vending machines, fridge, microwave and other facilities. There are also sports facilities with a table-tennis table and a pool table and a quiet room.

Multipurpose room: to work towards making our facilities fully accessible to all members of the Al-Maktoum Institute family, one room on the ground floor has now been designated as a seminar and multipurpose room.

Postgraduate Research Students Room: to continue enhancing our learning environment, the Institute moved the PG research Student office to the ground floor near all the other support facilities available to students. In addition, this office is now equipped with several fully networked PCs, some of which have specialist research software such as SPSS. In addition, a wireless access technology is also available.

Creation of the Institute Office: the Institute Office was established on 5 January 2004 with the aim of bringing together all the non academic functions of the Institute. This provides a one stop arrangement for all students' enquiries and services. Staff at the Institute Office share the core duties to ensure that services are available to students at all times. This development came about as a direct result of addressing students' concerns, and to improve communication throughout the Institute. Following the establishment of the Institute Office, the students indicated their satisfaction with the new office as it provides easy access and offers a more convenient arrangement of having all functions in the same office.

The Institute Office continues to work towards the achievement of the Institute's aims and objectives, and continues to play its part in supporting the activities of the Institute. Staff at the Institute Office have played their part in the organisation, and ensuring the success of a number of functions at the Institute. In August 2006 a decision was taken to relocate the Institute Office to the room which was known as the Shaikh Maktoum Exhibition Room. This decision was taken in order that the Shaikh Hamdan Library could be extended to meet the growing demands of the students and the continuing expansion of library stock. The new office allows students and visitors clarity regarding the location of the reception and main administration area of the Institute.

Library Resources, Study and IT Facilities

The Institute is committed to provide high quality flexible education underpinned by relevant research. To achieve this, we recognise the importance of providing all the necessary reference materials for inter-disciplinary advanced teaching and research in the Study of Islam and Muslims. Shaikh Hamdan Library and Shaikh Muhammad IT Centre are just two examples of our dedication to encourage active scholarly activities within the Institute.

Both these facilities were built from scratch, and this obviously required a major injection of capital. The Shaikh Muhammad IT Centre now combines a room with ten fully networked PCs, complete with colour and mono printing facility and wireless access. The computer student ratio is very good indeed. The Library, on the other hand, contains books and manuscripts obtained from various sources around the world. We want to build a Library of international calibre and we have allocated a sizeable fund for this purpose.

The Institute's Shaikh Hamdan Library

Our aim to build a research led library of international calibre is well on its way to achievement. The Shaikh Hamdan Library contains a range of books and manuscripts and also journals and newspapers (both in Arabic and in English languages) which provide an excellent research tool.

The library collection started with my private library which he donated to build the Institute library. Since then, it has been greatly expanded from its relatively modest starting point. The past five years have seen very substantial financial investment in the library to which an annual fund was made available and to date a total of £100,000 have been spent on the collections since the Institute opened. This led to a more rapid growth of the Institute's library, and for example, subscriptions for a good number of peer-reviewed academic journals have been ordered. It also extended its journal subscriptions including purchases of back issues of selected journals. The library also has current journal subscriptions to:

- Journal of Islamic Studies (Oxford University Press) print & online
- Journal of Islam and Christian-Muslim Relations (Taylor and Francis) print & online
- Muslim World (Blackwells) print & online

- Journal of Muslim Minority Affairs (Taylor and Francis) print & online
- Journal of Qur'anic Studies (Edinburgh University Press)
- International Journal of Middle Eastern Studies (print & online)
- British Journal of Middle Eastern Studies (print & online)
- Journal of Islamicjerusalem Studies (Al-Maktoum Institute Academic Press)

These journals are a central part of the research of staff and students at the Institute, and the Institute Library and Information Committee is continuing to review whether further new titles should be added to its already extensive list of subscriptions.

The Institute has also continued to invest heavily in the purchase of reference resources. Major purchases for the library include the Encyclopaedia of Islam, Index Islamicus, the Oxford English Dictionary (20 volumes), the Encyclopaedia of Religion (15 volumes), and Encyclopaedia of Philosophy all very important multi-volume reference and research publications. In addition, the Institute also received over 1,000 Arabic language titles in a special order from Cairo in spring 2004 funded by the Al-Maktoum Foundation in Dubai, a further 150 titles purchased in Jordan in the summer of 2004, and a further 374 titles purchased from Cairo in January 2007. In the last few years, the main focus for the library has been in the continuing development of the English language titles for both teaching and research. The library now holds over 10,000 volumes in Arabic and English books, as well as a number of books in other languages.

Previous years saw two important organisational changes in the Institute library. The first was the upgrade of the library catalogue system to KnowAll, which allows a more sophisticated use of our records and users' data. Further to this, in a review of the system in June/July 2004, the Institute decided to adopt the classification system of the English books in the Library according to the Library of Congress system, while the Arabic books are classified on our home style. The Library of Congress system is an international standard system, and its introduction has greatly aided our students' and staff's use of the library catalogue, as has the recent introduction of the library catalogue as an accessible website.

In response to student feedback, the Library and Information Committee also decided to change the regulations for book loan of related to the taught courses. The library now operates a short loan lending system, enabling students to borrow high demand books for a four hour period, or overnight, thus ensuring good availability of key readings. It is expected that there will be at least two copies of all recommended course related books.

As a result of this continued investment in library materials, in spring 2006 it was recognised that the Institute was going to run out of shelving space within six months. In response to this the Library and Information Committee recommended the expansion of the current library space by moving some of the library collection into the room next door (at that time the Institute Office).

This move took place in August 2006, leading to the creation of two library rooms, one primarily for the Arabic language collection, which are mainly reference works of key sources for those whose research is focused on historical and religious texts (particularly hadith, fiqh, tafsir, and usul-al-fiqh literature). The second room contains the majority of the English language collection, including all the teaching related materials and reference works, including the Encyclopaedia of Islam, Encyclopaedia of Religion, and Index Islamicus. There is now more room for students to study with designated IT cluster consisting of six workstations complete with stations wireless network facilities. The library issue desk is located within the English text room.

Although it is a relatively small library at the moment, external visitors have commented that the Institute now has a collection of books within the field of the study of Islam and Muslims that rivals the libraries of other Scottish centres, such as St Andrews and Edinburgh Universities. The Institute plans to develop this further and our aim is that there will be further considerable expansion when the new library is created within the Al-Maktoum Multicultural Centre, to create the most extensive library in the field in Europe.

In short, the Al-Maktoum Institute has a fully functioning teaching and research library, with a system which can accommodates its ever-growing nature and which can also be adapted for future growth.

Study and IT Facilities

There are three separate study areas for students – the Shaikh Mohammad IT Suite for the PGT students, the Research Students' Room for PGR students, and the IT cluster in the library.

All students have an IT user account which gives them an email address, access to printing facilities, and file storage space. Students also receive a University of Aberdeen IT user account, which gives them not only access to the IT network facilities of the university, but also the online academic resources, such as databases, e-journals and resources.

The IT Suite has 11 networked desktop PCs, with standard software (Windows XP, MS Office, Internet Explorer and Outlook). It also has a laser printer and scanner. The Research Students' Room has 4 networked desktop PCs, with similar software. One PC has SPSS installed as a specialist facility for statistical data analysis. The room also has a printer and scanner. The IT cluster in the library has 6 newly purchased networked PCs, also with similar software. There is also a slightly older networked PC, which is dedicated to accessing the online library catalogue.

All these work areas – the IT Suite, the Research Students' Room, and the library, along with the conference hall – have wireless access points, to enable students to connect their own laptops to the Institute network wirelessly. The Institute is also exploring the possibility of extending this wireless networking to cover the whole of building in due course.

Students' Involvement

The Institute views students as partners in the process of producing the next generation of scholars in the field of the Study of Islam and Muslims. It is fully appreciated that students must to be involved in the endeavour to foster excellence at the Institute. Hence, students' participation was deeply encouraged from the start. Their presence in all the Academic Council committees helped to ensure that students actively participate in enhancing the quality of academic programmes at the Institute. Moreover, to ensure that students are aware of all the latest developments, a student representative is also invited to the Institute Council meetings.

Al-Maktoum Institute Students Society (ALMISS)

On 3 October 2002, the Al-Maktoum Institute Students Society was established. This is another serious attempt to ensure that students are represented by a body elected by the students themselves. It is hoped also that this will enable students to play an even more active role in developing the Institute.

The Interim Al-Maktoum Institute Students Society Executive put together a constitution that was passed on 19 June 2003 by the Annual General Meeting of the Students Society. At the elections on 22 October 2003, the first Executive of the Al-Maktoum Institute Students Society was elected[1] and consisted of:

---

[1]   The Executive of ALMISS during the academic year 2005/2006 consisted of: President: Abdallah M. Omar, PhD Student (Jordanian), Secretary:

President: Mohamed Roslan Nor, PhD Student (Malaysian)
Secretary: Alex Fowler, M.Litt Student (Scottish)
Treasurer: Lama Naasan M.Litt Student (Scottish Syrian)
Social & Cultural Officer: Rehab Imam, M.Litt Student (Egyptian)
Board Member: Aminurraasyid Yatiban, PhD Student (Malaysian)

The diversity of the Executive members' countries of origin is yet another reflection of the multicultural ethos fostered by the Institute. Bringing together the best of all worlds, the Students Society Executive brings to the Al-Maktoum Institute new dimensions of multicultural interaction, and add to the vibrant flavour and ambiance that has been created at the Institute.

Remembrance and Recognition of Senior Figures

HH Shaikh Zayed Bin Sultan Al-Nahyan

The staff and students of Al-Maktoum Institute mourned the death of Shaikh Zayed on 2 November 2004. The flag of the UAE was flown at half-mast outside the Institute for 40 days. A book of Condolence was opened at the Institute for signing for a week and it was then presented to HE Mr Easa Saleh al-Gurg, the UAE Ambassador in London.

Michael Adams

Michael Adams, a founding pillar and the first Director of the Council for the Advancement of Arab British Understanding (CAABU) died on 6 February 2005. He was key to putting out an alternative view of the Arab World to the British media. I sent a message to staff and students of Al-Maktoum Institute on 8 February 2005, informing them of Michael's death and expressing condolences to his family. Aisha and I also attended Michael's funeral in Exeter on 14 February 2005.

Fatimatuzzahra Abd Rahman, PhD Student (Malaysian), Treasurer: Rozita Ibrahim, MLitt Student (Malaysian), Social & Multicultural Officer: Pawel Bernat, MLitt Student (Polish), Board Member: Mohammed Habib, PhD Student (Pakistani). The Executive of the Al-Maktoum Institute Students Society during the academic year 2006/2007 consists of: President – Abdallah Omer (Jordanian), Secretary – Fatimatuzzahra Abd Rahman (Malaysian), Treasurer – Abdullah Siddiqui (Pakistani), Social and Multicultural Officer – Wiebke Wagner (Germany), Board Member – Fadi Al-Rabi (Palestine).

Michael's selfless and tireless efforts to encourage better understanding of the Arab world also received special mention at 2005 Shaikh Hamdan Bin Rashid Al-Maktoum Awards for Multicultural Scotland ceremony, where CAABU was also awarded the Arab-British Understanding Prize.

Michael Adams Seminar Room

In recognition of his contributions to Arab-British understanding, the Institute decided to establish and name a seminar room in honour of the late Michael Adams as the 'Michael Adams Seminar Room'. The room was officially opened on the first anniversary of his death on Monday 6 February 2006 by his widow Celia and son Paul Adams. Attending the opening were prominent figures from Dundee including the leader of Dundee City Council, Councillor Jill Shimi, Convener of Social Work, Baillie Helen Wright, and Mr Ernie Ross, a former MP for Dundee West.

The Michael Adams Seminar Room houses a large collection of journals and articles given to the Institute by CAABU.

HH Shaikh Maktoum Bin Rashid Al-Maktoum

On 4 January 2006, as the New Year dawned on the Institute we received the sad news that His Highness Shaikh Maktoum Bin Rashid Al-Maktoum, Vice President and Prime Minister of the United Arab Emirates and Ruler of Dubai, had passed away.

Staff and students mourned his passing and the flags were flown at half-mast outside the Institute for 40 days as a mark of respect. Messages of condolence were sent by many in Scotland. This included a letter of condolence from the First Minister, Jack McConnell on behalf of the people of Scotland to HH Shaikh Mohammed Bin Rashid Al-Maktoum. This letter was delivered during a visit to the Institute on 16 January by the Deputy First Minister Nicol Stephen. The Lord Provost of Dundee Mr John Letford and the Head of Administration, Jill Shimi for Dundee City Council extended condolences on behalf of the City of Dundee. A book of Condolences was opened at the Institute for people to sign. This was then presented to HH Shaikh Hamdan Bin Rashid Al-Maktoum. The Institute expressed thanks to the people of Dundee and Scotland through the local paper.

Shaikh Maktoum Garden

The internal courtyard of the Institute was redeveloped over the earlier part of 2006 and transformed into the 'Shaikh Maktoum Garden' in memory of His Highness Shaikh Maktoum Bin Rashid Al-Maktoum. A casual style landscape with a fountain as the centrepiece at the heart of the courtyard and a mixture of evergreen and deciduous plantings provides a calming atmosphere and a sanctuary for the senses of our staff and students. There are comfortable benches and a seating area around the fountain for reading and relaxing.

On Friday 17 July, the Garden was officially opened by the Institute Chairman Mr Mirza al-Sayegh, Lord Elder, Chancellor of the Institute, HE Mariam Al-Roumi, the Minister for Social Affairs in the UAE, and HE Dr Hanif Qassimi, Minister of Education in the UAE and this took place after the concluding ceremony of the Fourth Summer School. Many events have been held in the Garden during the summer season from the Tartan Tea Party to an informal Staff and Student gathering. The Institute is very proud that the Shaikh Maktoum Garden has created a peaceful space for all to enjoy.

We are also very proud that the Shaikh Maktoum Garden was awarded a Large Gold Medal Certificate as a Judge's Special Award for the Garden section of the Dundee in Bloom, Garden and Allotment Competition under category 8 – Business or Retail Premises. The Institute received this award at a ceremony on Tuesday 28 November 2006 in the Marryat Hall, Dundee.

Marketing and Recruitment

Following a brainstorming session on 9 June 2004 involving all members of staff at the Institute and a number of student representatives, the Institute started to develop its marketing and recruitment strategy. A draft strategy was produced and was examined and discussed at the various committees at the Institute before it was approved by the Institute Academic Council on 12 January 2005. The aims of this strategy are to contribute to the Institute's objectives by identifying key target markets towards which the bulk of recruitment resource should be directed and utilising available resources to the best advantage.

The strategy was developed further at the recruitment meeting on 3 March 2005, attended by all staff, to discuss its implementation. Staff held a further meeting on 24 May to report back on developments since the previous recruitment meeting. This resulted in the establishment of the Marketing and Recruitment Committee. To address the expansion in the Institute, the marketing of the Institute has been divided into three main areas:

1. The Marketing of the Vision, Mission and New Agenda
2. Student Recruitment and Admissions
3. Conference and Training Facilities

Corporate Identity

The Institute has continued to develop its corporate identity, in the form of logo colours and the style in which it presents itself in print. There is now a concentrated effort to focus upon a consistent approach to style and layout when designing any corporate information, including advertising and promotional materials.

It is through this consistent approach that our stakeholders will begin to recognise and be familiar themselves with the Institute more easily, and it will effectively raise our profile locally, nationally and internationally.

Publicity[2]

The Institute continues to benefit from the vigorous advertising campaign by the Al-Maktoum Foundation undertaken on a local, national and international scale. The cross-over of advertising for the Foundation Scholarships, along with the Institute's details, assisted with the strategic campaign to increase student numbers and raise the current profile of the Institute.

- *Herald*'s education supplement on Friday 10 March 2006
- *Birmingham Post* 16 March 2006
- *Dundee Courier and Advertiser* and *Evening Telegraph* for the Arabic Language Evening Classes, the Open Day, recruitment, and upon the death of HH Shaikh Maktoum Bin Rashid Al-Maktoum
- *Scotsman* 24 March 2006
- *Press and Journal* 10 March 2006
- *Stirling Observer* 15 March 2006
- *Herald* Graduate Fair Supplement 23 May 2006
- *Times* Higher Education Supplement 25 May 2006
- *Muslim Weekly* 5 May 2006.

---

2   In the past five years, the Institute has been advertising on Dubai TV several times a day at peak times. Our main activities were normally broadcast on Dubai TV and reported in the UAE newspapers. This was the case even from the beginning. For example, on 25 June 2002, I was interviewed live on Dubai TV on various issues relating to the establishment of the Institute and the academic programmes that we offer. There were also live questions from viewers. At the Scottish level, we have also advertised in The *Herald* (14 & 16 June 2002) and The *Scotsman* (21 June 2002). We received positive editorial comments in the *Scotsman* newspaper on Friday 21 June 2002.

- Dundee Directory, October 2006
- Islam Channel (TV) 3 – 25 October 2006

Postgraduate Exhibitions

The Institute took part in its first series of student recruitment exhibitions in 2006: London (25 January 2006), Glasgow (30 – 31 May 2006), Edinburgh (10 October 2006), and Dundee (1 November 2006).

Recruitment trip to the Gulf

As part of the Institute's recruitment strategy I travelled to the Gulf from 25 March to 7 April 2005. I delivered presentations at Qatar University, the University of UAE, Zayed University, Kuwait University, and the Arabian Gulf University in Bahrain. In addition to these visits I met senior members of these Universities where he discussed with them possible areas of joint academic co-operation to develop Islamic Studies into the Study of Islam and Muslims.

Recruitment trip to Malaysia

From 1 to 7 May 2005, the Depute Principal visited Malaysia to promote the Institute, and to recruit new students for our postgraduate programmes. During his visit he gave talks on postgraduate opportunities in Islamicjerusalem Studies and the Study of Islam and Muslims at Al-Maktoum Institute in the University of Malaya (Academy of Islamic Studies) and the British Council (in Kuala Lumpur). He also visited the University Putra Malaysia (UPM) and the Selangor International Islamic University College (KUIS).

5

DEVELOPMENT AND ENHANCEMENT OF RESEARCH CULTURE

The past five years have seen a number of very significant new events and initiatives at the Institute which are not only enhancing the research culture of the Institute as a centre for excellence, but are also establishing the Institute as a major innovative contributor to international academic debates on the study of Islam and Muslims.

Creating a Research Culture

As a research-led institution, the Institute has been very active in developing its research culture and in supporting the research activities of its staff and students. Along with the mechanisms for research training, the Institute has also given priority to the promotion of research through the areas of its two research centres: Centre for Islamicjerusalem Studies, and Centre for Research on Multiculturalism and Islam and Muslims in Scotland. Our new agenda for the Study of Islam and Muslims is also of great importance.

Research Development Fund

Research is the underpinning activity at the Institute. For that purpose, each and every member of our academic staff is strongly encouraged to conduct research in relevant areas within their expertise. In order to assist these scholars, the Institute's Academic Council decided in 2003 to establish a Research Development Fund to encourage, support and develop the Institute research culture.

The fund has been extended to be available for both staff and students, and in the past years it has been administered to fund a number of important researches and related activities. These include both staff and student attendance at academic conferences, as well as a major research project on research and teaching of the study of Islam and Muslims in the UK. The RDF funded staff participation at conferences in the US (the American Academy of Religion annual meeting in Atlanta, in November 2003 and San Antonio in November 2004) and London (the British Society for Middle-Eastern Studies annual conference at SOAS in June 2004). The RDF funded staff and student participation at conferences in Sofia, Cardiff, Switzerland, Kuala Lumpur and a panel from the Institute at WOCMES conference in Amman, Jordan in June 2006. It has also been used to fund fieldwork visits by PhD students to Vancouver, Canada and Switzerland.

Unique Research Centres
On 28 January 2002, the Institute Board resolved to establish unique research centres at the Institute under my leadership. These unique centres are part of the Institute's development strategy and they signify the Institute's commitment to the fields. The centres are:
1. Centre for Islamicjerusalem Studies
2. Centre for Research on Multiculturalism and Islam and Muslims in Scotland

Centre for Islamicjerusalem Studies
In the last five years, This Centre has organised a series of conferences and seminars on the following themes:

2003 International Academic Conference on Islamicjerusalem Studies

The 2003 International Academic Conference on Islamicjerusalem Studies was held on Monday 21 April 2003. The theme for this year's conference was 'Prophetic Temples and Al-Aqsa Mosque – Demystifying Realities and Exploring Identities'. This was the fifth time that a conference on Islamicjerusalem had been held by the Islamic Research Academy (ISRA) and the first time it was organised jointly with the Institute. The uniqueness of this conference is that it presented new and innovative theories in Islamicjerusalem Studies.

This was a highly successful conference which was attended by participants mainly from Scotland but also from as faraway as the USA, the United Arab Emirates, Egypt, Israel and Palestine. The conference was introduced by The Lord Elder of Kirkcaldy, Chancellor of Al-Maktoum Institute. Mr Ernie Ross MP, member of the Institute Council, read the Opening Speech on behalf of Mr Mirza Al-Sayegh, Chairman of the Institute Board. The Lord Provost John Letford also attended the Opening Session.

I presented an innovative paper entitled 'Exploring the Identity of Islamicjerusalem'. As the pioneer of this noble field of enquiry, I explained what he means by the term 'Islamicjerusalem'. I admitted that it took him three years to come to this definition and that it may take several years for it to be accepted by the wider public. I concluded that from his own research, Islamicjerusalem is a region that spans 40 miles by 40 miles with Al-Aqsa Mosque as the centre point. I also pointed out that Islamicjerusalem was built on the vision of inclusivity and plurality. Both led to the development of a peaceful and harmonious multicultural society in Islamicjerusalem. I indicated that Islamicjerusalem can be used as the model for the advancement of a multicultural, multi-religious society anywhere in the world. I also explained the 'Circle Theory', which is a new theory he developed based on new interpretations of the core Muslim sources and history.

The other main speakers were Professor George Wesley Buchanan, New Testament Emeritus Scholar (USA), and Mr David Sielaff from Associates for Scriptural Knowledge (USA). Professor Buchanan presented a paper on 'The Temple near the Spring of Siloan: Its Biblical Confirmation and Insights' while Mr Sielaff's paper was entitled 'The Jewish Temple Above the Gihon Spring: 1700 Years of Eyewitness Evidence.' Both speakers presented overwhelming evidence on the actual location of the Jewish Temple and they both confirmed that it is not the Al-Aqsa Mosque location of the Jewish Temple, as claimed by some. Both speakers also expressed disappointment at the claims that Al-Aqsa Mosque was built on the ruins of the Jewish Temple because there was no solid evidence to support these.

Dr Othman Al-Tel was announced as the winner of the prestigious Islamicjerusalem Prize for Young Scholars 2002. The award is issued by the Islamic Research Academy to young scholars who submit outstanding published or unpublished academic research related to Islamicjerusalem Studies. Additionally, Shaikh Raid Salah was announced as winner of the Al-Maqdisi Award for his outstanding work on Al-Aqsa Mosque.

2004 International Academic Conference on Islamicjerusalem Studies

To engage our postgraduate students in the activities of the research centres, several meetings have been organised for PhD and Masters students currently studying or researching the field of Islamicjerusalem Studies. These discussions led to the decision to organise the 2004 International Academic Conference on Islamicjerusalem Studies.

The 2004 International Academic Conference on Islamicjerusalem was held on 31 May and 1 June 2004. The theme for this year's conference was 'The New Field of Inquiry of Islamicjerusalem Studies: Background, achievements and the future'. This was the sixth conference organised on Islamicjerusalem Studies but the first one to be organised solely by the Centre for Islamicjerusalem Studies at the Institute.

The significance of this conference was that it evaluated the New Field of Inquiry of Islamicjerusalem and how to develop it in the future. The conference also acknowledged and celebrated the 10th anniversary of the establishment of the project on 4 August 1994. In addition, the founder of the field presented for the first time the concise definition of Islamicjerusalem Studies as 'a new branch of human knowledge which investigates all matters related to the Islamicjerusalem region and examines its various aspects with interdisciplinary and multidisciplinary approaches in order to understand the uniqueness of this region and its effect on the rest of the world'. During the conference, the speakers explored the past ten years of development and looked forward to the future developments to establish this new field of inquiry within specific international academic locations.

At the end of the conference, an important document was issued by the delegation of the conference, titled 'The future development of the New Field of Inquiry of Islamicjerusalem Studies' which stated that 'on the basis of the success so far in establishing this new field of inquiry in the UK, the Centre for Islamicjerusalem Studies is now looking towards promoting and expanding the new field on an international basis'. Indeed, the conference felt that teaching and research on Islamicjerusalem Studies should be encouraged and supported on an international basis.

To this end, it is proposed to develop three regional centres/hubs from which the field can be promoted: the Al-Maktoum Institute as a base for Europe; to establish a base in Malaysia for that country and for South East Asia; and a base within an Arab country.

A key part of the conference was ISRA's launch of its latest publication, a book by Aisha Al-Ahlas, entitled: Islamic Research Academy (ISRA): 1994 – 2004, Background, Activities and Achievements, with special reference to the New Field of Inquiry of Islamicjerusalem Studies. This book makes a significant contribution to the history of the development of the first ten years of Islamicjerusalem Studies, and is a piece of 'insider research' of the highest quality which clearly shows that Aisha Al-Ahlas is a serious scholar and researcher in her own right.

As part of the conference programme and as a series of events planned to celebrate the tenth anniversary of the establishment of the New Field of Inquiry of Islamicjerusalem Studies, the Institute hosted a 'Ten Years of Innovation Dinner' on 31 May 2004. The event, at Dundee Hilton, was attended by around 80 dignitaries, academics, politicians, religious leaders, business associates and friends of the Institute. A special gift of a beautiful stone from Islamicjerusalem inscribed with Umar's Assurance of Safety to the people of Aelia was presented to several individuals who were associated with, or supported the project. Amongst the guests were Sir Cyril Townsend and Lord Watson of Invergowrie, who have been involved with the project from the beginning.

2005 International Academic Conference on Islamicjerusalem Studies

On June 6 the 2005 International Academic Conference on Islamicjerusalem Studies entitled Islamicjerusalem: Definitions and Approaches was held at the Institute. The conference came as a response to an action point in the important document produced by the 2004 conference entitled 'The Future Development of the New Field of Inquiry of Islamicjerusalem Studies'. Accordingly, the conference was designed to review and explore the development of this new field of inquiry, looking in particular at the definition of the field produced by the Founder of the Field, Professor Abd al-Fattah El-Awaisi, along with examining the new research on the three interlinked elements of the definition of Islamicjerusalem: its geographical location and boundaries (land), their population (people) and its vision.

2006 International Academic Conference on Islamicjerusalem Studies

On 2 June 2006, the 2006 (eighth) International Academic Conference on Islamicjerusalem Studies entitled 'The Challenges of Islamicjerusalem' was held at the Institute. The Conference focused on the challenging issues presented in my latest monograph Introducing Islamicjerusalem. In the last paragraph of the conclusion of this newly published monograph, I argue that 'several supporting evidences have been provided to support the author's central argument that Islamicjerusalem is not exclusive but inclusive and should be opened up 'to everyone in the universe', Lil'alamin as stated in the Qur'an (21:71), 'so that you should get to know one another' Li ta'arafu (Qur'an, 49:13), not that you may despise each other. This unique global common space of openness and Barakah has made Islamicjerusalem an ideal Amal region where the one human family can make Li ta'arafu, live together in Aman and enjoy this Barakah'.

The topics of the conference included: the new concept and definitions of Islamicjerusalem and Islamicjerusalem Studies, the *Barakah* Circle Theory of Islamicjerusalem and the geographical location and boundaries of Islamicjerusalem, the new terminology, the land of *Amal* (Hope) and the Prophet's strategic plan which he himself drew up for Islamicjerusalem, the vision of Islamicjerusalem as a model for conflict resolution, and the vision of Islamicjerusalem as a model for multiculturalism and a unique global common space where *Lil'alamin* can make *Li ta'arafu*.

2007 International Academic Conference on Islamicjerusalem Studies

On 1 June 2007, the 2007 (ninth) International Academic Conference on Islamicjerusalem Studies entitled 'Mapping Islamicjerusalem: A Rediscovery of Geographical Boundaries' will be held at the Institute. To many contemporary scholars and academics Islamicjerusalem is merely a city with limits that do not go far beyond its ancient walls. Yet, in history, the existence of a region for Islamicjerusalem has been a long rooted concept. A region that, according to many accounts such as al-Maqdisi, extends to cover in addition to the ancient city, many other cities, towns and villages such as Hebron, Ramla, Zarnuqah, Jaffa, Nablus, Shuwaykah, Jama'in, Jericho, Karak, Zoar and Kuseifa. Other Qur'anic concepts namely the concepts of the Land of *Barakah* and the Holy Land have been long confused with each other and overlooked. This calls for the re-investigation of these Qur'anic concepts and their relationship with Islamicjerusalem. Contemporary understanding of the word *Hawlahu* (Qur'an 17:1) understood as 'surrounded by' sheds new lights on classical understandings of the extent of this area and the radiation of *Barakah* and has brought to life the Circle Theory of Islamicjerusalem.

The Conference will focus on the challenging issues presented in Khalid El-Awaisi's monograph *Mapping Islamicjerusalem: A Rediscovery of Geographical Boundaries*. scholars and researchers were invited to submit paper contributions including, but not limited to, the following themes: the boundaries of the region of Islamicjerusalem, the *Barakah* Circle Theory, the centre of *Barakah*: Al-Aqsa Mosque, the Land of *Barakah*, the Holy Land, the historical administrative boundaries, geography of the Qur'an with respect to Islamicjerusalem.

Islamicjerusalem Studies Research Seminars

In November and December 2004 the Centre for Islamicjerusalem held two research seminars at the Institute. The first one was held on 24 November on the future development of the new field of Inquiry of

Islamicjerusalem Studies. The second seminar, held on 7 December, focused on developing a plan for promoting of the field.

In the Autumn and Spring semesters during the academic year 2005/2006, the Centre for Islamicjerusalem Studies organised four research seminars at the Institute: The *Barakah* Circle Theory of Islamicjerusalem (28 November 2005), the Land of (Amal) Hope: Discussion of the Prophet Muhammad's Plan for Islamicjerusalem (12 December 2005), Islamicjerusalem as a Model for Conflict Resolution: a Muslim Theoretical Framework of Reference towards Others (20 March 2006), and Islamicjerusalem as a Model for Multiculturalism (3 April 2006).

Centre for Research on Multiculturalism and Islam and Muslims in Scotland

In spring 2004 the Academic Council approved two important developments for one of the Institute's leading research centres. The Centre for the Study of Islam and Muslims was renamed as the: Centre for Research on Multiculturalism and Islam and Muslims in Scotland. This change highlighted the key focus of research at the Institute on the study of issues on multiculturalism in the Scotland and the UK with reference to broad national, social, and political issues, as well as focusing on the particular issues facing British Muslims. The remit of this Centre is as follows:

- To establish itself as a centre of excellence for research on Multiculturalism and Islam and Muslims in Scotland
- To facilitate, encourage, and promote detailed ethnographic and sociological/anthropological research on particular Muslim communities and groups in Scotland
- To promote the analysis of wider social and cultural issues that structure and influence the experiences of Islam and Muslims in Scotland
- To monitor developments within the Scottish Muslim populations, through (for example) media reports and research projects
- Liaise with other research groups and centres with an interest or focus on Islam, Muslims and multiculturalism in minority contexts
- To participate in and develop networks of shared research interests in this field
- To develop and organise national and international research on political, social, economic, and cultural developments in Islam and

Muslim communities in Scotland, with a strong emphasis on recent and contemporary developments
- To be a leading European research centre for postgraduate research and training in issues related to Islam and Muslims in Scotland
- To develop an academic forum for scholars through publications, seminars, conferences, and workshops
- To promote the study and understanding of Islam and Muslims in multicultural Scotland

Further to this, the Academic Council also established within the Centre a special think-tank titled the Multiculturalism Research Unit (MRU). To further the Institute's role as a leading centre for research and debate on multiculturalism in contemporary society, this new think-thank will conduct research on the broad issues of multiculturalism and cultural and religious diversity, in particular to promote and contribute to national discussion in this area. The remit of the MRU is to further better understanding at local and national level of the development of a multicultural society based on mutual respect and co-operation. Among the activities to be undertaken by the Multiculturalism Research Unit will be:

- Organising roundtable discussions by leading scholars
- Issuing briefing papers and policy advice
- Conducting research on specific issues
- Producing reports, papers and information booklets

Together the Centre as a whole and the Multiculturalism Research Unit will work to promote research on the various Scottish Muslim communities and to engage with various bodies across Scotland to facilitate a greater knowledge and understanding of the needs of Scottish Muslims and the wider issues of a multicultural society. The Centre will also work to act as a focus for the research that is currently being carried out at the Institute on Scottish and British Muslim issues and the issues raised by a multicultural society.

Multicultural Symposium and Seminars
In the last five years, This Centre has organised symposium and a series of seminars on the following themes:

The 2006 International Academic Symposium on Multiculturalism

On 20 April 2006 the Centre organised a one-day International Academic Symposium on the theme 'The Challenges of Multiculturalism'. The symposium was attended by a wide cross-section of the local and national community, and involved fifteen speakers covering a variety of subjects, including experiences of multiculturalism in Islamicjerusalem, France, Russia, the United Arab Emirates, Malaysia, and the UK, and among other topics discussed were the role of Muslim women in multiculturalism, research on Muslims in Scotland, and Catholic approaches to multiculturalism. Feedback from the day was very positive and encouraging, and clearly demonstrated the important role for the Centre for developing research and discussion in this crucial area.

The Symposium was chaired by the Chancellor Lord Elder and I gave an opening presentation on the Vision for Multiculturalism of HH Shaikh Hamdan Bin Rashid Al-Maktoum. The symposium was opened by Mrs Margaret Curran MSP, Minister for Parliamentary Business, and in her opening address she recognised the importance of the work and the contribution of the Al-Maktoum Institute.

The 2007 International Academic Symposium on Multiculturalism

On 12 September the Centre will organise a one-day International Academic Symposium on the theme 'Multiculturalism, Education and Extremism: Facing the Challenges of the Twenty-First Century'. The contemporary debate over multiculturalism has been focused for several years on issues of religious extremism, particularly in the aftermath of 11/9 and 7/7 tragedies. Religion in turn has reoccupied the central stage in secular multicultural western societies, particularly with constant debates and issues relating to Islam and Muslims. Although overwhelmingly the public debates, academic discussions and media coverage have framed the issue around security/terrorism concerns, the viability and future of multicultural societies in Western Europe in particular has gained yet further significance. What is missing in such public debates is a comprehensive discussion on the role, relevance and task of education (or multicultural education) in responding to, and combating the threat of religious extremism in culturally and religiously diverse societies. Multiculturalism is a process, not an end product – this process is most often a challenging one, and sometimes may be unsuccessful. There are complex processes informing multicultural polity. Education is one of the most contested areas in multicultural societies as it brings diverse sometimes conflicting cultural, religious values into an inevitable interaction. Much debated social policy issues like integration, segregation, alienation and extremism are also related to educational inclusion or exclusion and different interpretations of multicultural education.

This symposium will bring together international practitioners, policy makers, and academics in the field of multiculturalism to explore the questions raised by the challenges of education and multicultural societies in a comparative international perspective. Potential topics for the symposium include: critical reflections on multicultural education, faith-based schooling in a multicultural society, multicultural and multi-faith societies in practice, religious tolerance/intolerance, education and multiculturalism, citizenship, integration, diversity and integration, models of presenting religion(s) in multicultural curriculum, religious extremism, youth and multicultural society, educational/social inclusion/exclusion in a multicultural society, and education and tackling extremism.

Multiculturalism Research Seminars

The Centre has internationally recognised expertise in this area and is working closely with a number of public bodies to spread awareness of how to promote a better knowledge and understanding of multiculturalism and cultural diversity. In addition, we are keen to see that academic research and debate on multiculturalism are developed alongside our work with communities.

Accordingly, the Centre for Research on Multiculturalism, and Islam and Muslims in Scotland launched a series of debates on the challenges of multiculturalism. The Institute held seminars on multiculturalism on 22 February, 22 March and 6 November 2006 with themes related to the discussion of multiculturalism in contemporary society, which were: Challenges of multiculturalism: taking stock (February 2006), Challenges of multiculturalism: integration or assimilation (March 2006), Minorities, identity, and integration (November 2006), National cultures, identity, diversity, and integration (December 2006), Multiculturalism, integration and education (January 2007)

The aim of these events was to involve participants from the Institute and also from the wider community including Dundee City Council's social work department, fire and rescue service, education, business, politics, health.

The debates proved to be lively and far reaching, focusing upon a number of issues on the challenges and opportunities presented by living in a multicultural society. These workshops were organised in the wake of many recent events, including the tragedy of the July 7th bombings in London, calls by politicians and leaders for a rethinking of the concepts of multiculturalism, and ongoing debates about issues of religious diversity, integration, mutual respect and cooperation.

We are extremely happy that these debates were so successful – not only did we have an excellent group of participants, but the debates were open and frank and addressed many of the challenges of our century. The questions of multiculturalism are on television every day of the week, and it is very important for Al-Maktoum Institute to take a lead in promoting and developing our understanding of where we are at the moment and where we might be going. It is the responsibility of a higher education institution such as ours to lead this debate and to be engaging with the wider community.

Research Seminars and Postgraduate Research Seminars

To further cultivate the thirst for knowledge and to strengthen the scholarly culture within the Institute, Research Seminars are regularly organised. These seminars are opportunities for academics from the Institute and also from outside the Institute to present and discuss their research with others interested in the same field. The Research Seminars are open to everyone within academia. Additionally, the Postgraduate Research Seminars provide opportunities for postgraduate students to discuss key monographs and their own work with colleagues and staff. In addition, in a series of research workshops, academic staff and students have been involved in discussing and debating the Institute's new agenda on the study of Islam and Muslims.

Visiting academics and scholars

In the first five years, the Institute hosted a number of scholars and speakers, including the following distinguished academics who gave research seminars for our staff and students:

- Dr Malory Nye, University of Stirling (24 April 2002)
- Professor Qasim Al-Samarrai, Leiden University, Netherlands (16 October 2002)
- Dr Hussein Abdul-Raof, University of Leeds (30 October 2002)
- Dr Ann-Sofie Rolad, Malmö University, Sweden[1] (13 November 2002)

---

[1]   Dr Anne-Sofie Roald's seminar paper was delivered as part of her two week return visit to the Institute from 22nd February to 5th March, which

- Dr Chris Davidson, University of St. Andrews (27 November 2002).
- Professor Yahya Michot, Oxford University (11 December 2002)
- Dr Gabriele Marranci, Queens University, Belfast (12 March 2003)
- Dr Jabal Buaben, University of Birmingham (23 April 2003)
- Dr Sean McLaughlin, University of Leeds (November 2003)
- Professor Jorgen Nielson, University of Birmingham (December 2003)
- Dr Anne-Sofie Roald, Malmo University, Sweden (March 2004)
- Dr Scott Reese, University of Arizona (April 2004)
- Dr Yassin Detton, University of Edinburgh (April 2004)
- Dr Haithem Al-Ratrout, Al-Najah National University, Nablus (June 2004)
- Dr Abdullah Sahin, University of Birmingham (June 2004)
- Dr Robert Hoyland, University of Andrews (26 Oct 2005)
- Professor Ulrich Sinn, University of Wurzburg Germany (5 Sep 2005)
- Dr Cheikh Mbake Gueye, International Academy of Philosophy Liechtenstein (19 October 2005)
- Professor David Kerr, University of Edinburgh (23 March 2005)
- Professor Alan Dobson, University of Dundee (28 April 2005)
- Dr Haithem al-Ratrout, An-Najah National University-Palestine (June 2005)
- Professor Fathiya Al-Nabarawi, Al-Azhar University, Egypt (June 2005)
- Dr Johan Rasanayagam, University of Aberdeen (22 Feb 2006)
- Dr Matteo Fumagalli, University of Edinburgh (1 Mar 2006)
- Dr Claire Heristchi, University of Aberdeen (29 Mar 2006)
- Professor Mustapha Pasha, University of Aberdeen (11 Oct 2006)
- Professor Robert Segal, University of Aberdeen (8 Nov 2006)
- Professor Gary Craig, University of Hull (15 November 2006)

was her second year as visiting scholar on the course Women in Islam for our postgraduate taught programmes.

Al-Maktoum Institute Academic Press

Another aspect of the Institute's development strategy is to foster intellectual discourse in the field of the Study of Islam and Muslims. The Institute believes that this can be achieved by encouraging publication of scholarly works and making them available to both the academic communities and the general public. To achieve this, the Institute has established Al-Maktoum Institute Academic Press.

Since its establishment, the Academic Press has published nine academic titles:

1. Exploring the Qur'an by Hussain Abdul-Ra'ouf
2. The First Islamic Conquest of Aelia (Islamicjerusalem): A Critical Analytical Study of the Early Islamic Historical Narratives and Sources by Othman al-Tel
3. The Architectural Development of Al-Aqsa Mosque in the Early Islamic Period by Haithem Al-Ratrout
4. Umar's Assurance of Safety (Aman) to the People of Aelia (Islamicjerusalem): a Critical Analytical Study of the Historical Sources, by Abd al-Fattah El-Awaisi
5. Introducing Islamicjerusalem by Abd al-Fattah El-Awaisi[2]
6. Time for Change: Report on the Future of the Study of Islam and Muslims in Universities and Colleges in Multicultural Britain by Abd al-Fattah El-Awaisi and Malory Nye
7. Executive Summary - Time for Change: Report on the Future of the Study of Islam and Muslims in Universities and Colleges in Multicultural Britain by Abd al-Fattah El-Awaisi and Malory Nye
8. Mapping Islamicjerusalem: A Rediscovery of Geographical Boundaries by Khalid El-Awaisi

---

[2]   On Monday 30 January 2006, the long awaited major Monograph by Professor Abd al-Fattah El-Awaisi entitled *Introducing Islamicjerusalem* was launched at the Scottish Parliament in Edinburgh organised by Richard Baker (MSP for the North East Region). In the evening there was a dinner reception held within the Apex Hotel to celebrate the launch of the Monograph with Institute family and friends attending.

The Monograph was similarly launched in the UAE at Zayed University on 25 December 2006 and Qatar University on 9 March 2006. It was translated and published by Dar al-Fikr al-Arabi in Cairo in December 2006, and is also in the process of being translated and published into another two languages: Malay and French.

9. Setting the New Agenda - A Unique Development of Innovation in
Cultural Engagement at Academic and Communities Levels - Seven
Years of Excellence: 2000 – 2007

Additionally, from spring 2004, the Al-Maktoum Institute Academic
Press also took over the publication of the *Journal of Islamicjerusalem Studies*
from the Islamic Research Academy (ISRA). The 2005 saw the Al-
Maktoum Institute Academic Press re-launch this Journal with a new
concept (Volume 6, Summer 2005, Number 1). It is an academic
refereed journal published in Arabic and English for the Centre for
Islamicjerusalem Studies by the Al-Maktoum Institute Academic Press.

The *Journal* has opened up a new area of specialisation in
Islamicjerusalem Studies with original articles addressing
Islamicjerusalem from a wide range of subjects in this area. Addressing a
gap in the published periodical literature, JIS especially seeks to
encourage research into specific historical, theological, empirical,
theoretical, conceptual or cultural themes and topics. As such, this new
journal will be essential reading for all those who are involved in the
Study of Islam and Muslim.

In addition to the nine titles, the *Journal of Islamicjerusalem Studies*, the
Poster of the *Barakah* Circle Theory of Islamicjerusalem, and the Poster
of Umar's Assurance of Safety to the People of Aelia (Islamicjerusalem)
are also available for purchase.

6 September 2006 also saw the Academic Press go on line
(www.almipress.com) with all the titles now available for purchase
globally. In addition, a new exhibition room (centre) was established at
the Institute.

6

INTERNATIOAL ACADEMIC LINKS AND COLLABORATIONS

We believe that academic excellence can be achieved partly by forging an international academic network and scholarship, particularly through working in partnership with other Higher Education establishments throughout the world. We also believe that we can contribute to the development of the study of Islam and Muslims worldwide. To this end, the Institute has created links and entered into partnerships with several institutions around the world to find practical ways in which the New Agenda for the Study of Islam and Muslims can be developed and implemented worldwide.

International Academic Network

The Institute's expansion strategy involves a vision of forming a worldwide network. This will bring the Institute into the international arena, especially in the provision of education in the field of the Study of Islam and Muslims in higher education.

In addition to the Institute's collaboration with the University of Aberdeen, we have to date signed Memoranda of Understanding with fifteen universities across the world. In the first two years, we entered into academic partnerships with five universities: Zayed University, UAE University, Ajman University (cancelled), University of Qatar and El-Gezira University in Sudan, in addition to the membership of the Islamic Universities League. In the academic 2003/2004, we continued to build this international network by signing Memoranda of Understanding with another six universities: Johann Wolfgang Goethe University in Frankfurt, Germany; Al al-Bayt University, Jordan; University of Jordan; University of Cairo and Al-Azhar University; and University of Malaya, Malaysia. In addition, we have signed a Memorandum of Understanding with four universities in the year 2004-2005: Higher Colleges of

Technology, UAE, Arabian Gulf University, the International Academy
of Philosophy, Liechtenstein, and the University of Wurzburg, Germany.
In the year 2005-2006 we signed a Memorandum of Understanding with
Abu Dhabi University on 7 November 2006.

Visit to United Arab Emirates in June 2002

My visit to the United Arab Emirates on 21 – 28 June 2002 was very
successful, and received good coverage in the media. I was honoured
with an opportunity to meet His Highness Shaikh Hamdan Bin Rashid
Al-Maktoum on 27 June 2002 where HH Shaikh Hamdan once again
showed very clearly that the Institute is very close to his heart.

Among the meetings organised during the trip, were the following:
with Mr. Tim Gore, Director of the British Council in Dubai, with Dr
Said al-Hassani, Undersecretary of UAE Ministry of Higher Education,
with Mr Lance De Masi, President of American University in Dubai,
with Dr Hanif Al-Qassimi, then Vice-President of Zayed University,
with Dr Hadef Jouan Al-Dhahiri, Vice-Chancellor of UAE University,
with Mr Mohamad Khalif Al-Murar, Executive Director of Zayed Centre
for Coordination and Follow-Up, and with Mr Simon Collis, then
Consul General British Embassy in Dubai.

There were also meetings with HE Mr Juma Al-Majid; Mr. Ahmad Al-
Qu'ud, Director-General of Dubai TV; the Cultural Attaché of UAE in
Jordan; and a visit to the Sultan Bin Ali Al-Owais Cultural Foundation.

1. Zayed University - UAE

The first Memorandum of Understanding was with Zayed University,
which was signed by Mr. Mirza Al-Sayegh, Chairman of the Institute
Board, and Dr Hanif Al-Qassimi, then Vice-President of Zayed
University, on 27 June 2002. The memorandum incorporates
understanding of various academic kinds of cooperation including
exchange of staff and students, cooperation on research projects, etc.
This Memorandum of Understanding was renewed on 26 March 2005.

Development of collaboration with Zayed University

Since the Institute's first Memorandum of Understanding was signed
with Zayed University in the UAE our relationship with this particular
university has developed and strengthened considerably over the past
five years.

The Institute received a visit by Dr Michael Owen, Dean of the
College of Business Sciences at Zayed University on 18-20 June 2003.
During the visit, Dr Owen spoke at the Annual Postgraduate Summer

Workshop and also attended the Al-Maktoum Institute Annual Lunch. Dr Owen expressed his admiration for the work of the Institute, especially for being able to achieve such a success in a very short time. He stated: 'You are all to be congratulated for getting the Institute off to an outstanding start! I wish you continued great success going forward.'

In autumn 2003, Zayed University invited Professor Malory Nye for a visit during the period from late December 2003 to early January 2004. In addition, I was also invited to spend the Christmas and New Year break there from 15 December 2005 – 6 January 2006. These were excellent opportunities for the Institute and Zayed University to build on their already close links. For the Institute, the aims of these visits were to raise the profile of the Institute and introduce the New Agenda in the Study of Islam and Muslims.

During their time at Zayed University, the two were based primarily on the Dubai campus, but visited the other campus in Abu Dhabi regularly. They gave lectures and seminars on both campuses. They also met with faculty staff and students on both campuses, in various departments and subject areas, including Islamic Studies, Sociology, Political Studies, History, and Anthropology. They also had opportunities to meet and hear feedback from the students who were in Dundee in summer 2003 and 2005. Whilst in the UAE, they also met a number of individuals and bodies in the UAE to discuss issues of further collaboration and research. At the conclusion of their visits it was agreed that the Institute and Zayed University should build further on these links, and that we would be working together to develop further both student and staff visits to Dundee and the UAE.

The Institute received several visits by Dr Hanif Al-Qassimi, then Vice-President of Zayed University. For example, he visited the Institute and participated in the Winter Postgraduate Research Training Workshop from 18 to 20 January 2006.

Since my first visit in April 1999, and my subsequent bi-annual visits to Zayed University, I have been hugely impressed with its vision, mission and leadership. I should admit that I have enjoyed every minute of my engagements, discussions, and debates at Zayed University. Indeed, I came out from these visits realising that we share several common intellectual goals, vision, aims and objectives, which are a great inspiration for us to work more closely together.

2. Qatar University
On 9 October 2002, Mr Mohammed Al-Kaabi, Cultural Attaché at the Embassy of Qatar in London, visited the Institute. Following a meeting

between Dr Abdulla Bin Salleh Al-Khulaifi, then President of Qatar University and myself at the Strategic Forum on Higher Education and the GCC in London on 12 September 2002, a delegation from the Institute visited Qatar University on 26 October 2002. The delegation comprised Mr Mirza Al-Sayegh, Mr Mohammad Obeid Bin Ghannam, and I. The delegation was very well-received by Dr Abdulla Bin Salleh Al-Khulaifi. Various possibilities for future collaboration were explored and as a result, a Memorandum of Understanding was signed on the same day. The memorandum incorporates understandings on, among others, various kinds of academic cooperation including exchange of staff and students, and cooperation on research projects. This is indeed another strategic step forward in expanding the Institute's relationship with major academic institutions in the Gulf region.

Since my first contact with Professor Sheikha Abdullah Al-Misnad, President of the Qatar University, in October 2003, and my subsequent two visits to Qatar University in 2005, and on 5 – 15 March 2006, I have been hugely impressed with the new vision, mission and leadership of Qatar University. I should admit that I have enjoyed every minute of my engagements, discussions, and debates at Qatar University. Indeed, I came out from these two visits realising that we share several common intellectual goals, vision, aims and objectives, which are a great inspiration for us to work more closely together.

3. University of Gezira, Sudan

Mr Mirza Al-Sayegh, Chairman of the Institute Board, signed a Memorandum of Understanding with Professor Ismail Hassan Hussain, Vice-Chancellor of University of Gezira on 8 February 2003 in Dubai. The memorandum incorporates understanding of various kinds of academic cooperation including exchange of staff and students, cooperation on research projects and exchange of educational material and resources.

On 2 April 2003, I visited El-Gezira University with Mr Mohamed Obeid Bin Ghannam to build upon the relationship already established. Several meetings were arranged including with the Principal, Vice and Deputy Principals, Dean of Faculties, Head of Departments, members of the University's Senate and the Governor of Medani. The welcome and reception given by El-Gezira University's officials were very warm and the visit certainly enhanced the cordial relationship between the parties.

In Khartoum, the Institute's delegation was entertained by the Minister of Finance and National Economy, Mr Azzubair Muhammad Al-Hassan, on behalf of the Sudanese President. The Institute's delegation also met Professor Mubarak Muhammad Ali al-Majzub, Sudan's Minister for Higher Education and Research.

4. UAE University in Al-Ain

I was invited to UAE University in Al-Ain on 19-20 May 2003 to meet students and staff at the university. The main purpose of this visit was to promote the Institute and to attract those who are currently at the UAE University pursuing their postgraduate studies at the Institute. I gave two main presentations at the UAE University to students and staff. Informal discussions were also held and there were many who showed interest in studying at the Institute.

A memorandum of understanding between the UAE University and Al-Maktoum Institute was signed in Al-Ain on 29 June 2003 and was attended by His Highness Shaikh Nahayan Bin Mubarak Al-Nahayan, UAE Minister of Higher Education. The memorandum incorporates understanding of various kinds of academic cooperation including exchange of staff and students and cooperation on research projects.

On 1 October 2003, the Institute hosted Dr Saeed Abd Allah Hareb Al-Muhairy, Deputy Vice Chancellor for Community Studies of the UAE University, and a full programme was organised for his visit. The aim of the visit was to discuss ways to implement the memorandum of understanding signed on 29 June 2003. The meeting included discussion on the possible and promising areas of joint academic cooperation and the drawing up of the next strategic step forward in strengthening the relationship between the two institutions.

A visit to Ninewells Hospital, the Medical School of Dundee University and Tayside Health Board was also arranged when Dr Hareb had the opportunity to view various departments and surgical technology units.

5. & 6. Jordan University and Al al-Bayt University, Jordan

During a visit to Jordan in December 2003, Memoranda of Understanding were signed with these two major universities in Jordan, which is the University of Jordan in Amman, and Al al-Bayt University in Mafraq.

The Memoranda of Understanding were signed by me as the Principal and Vice-Chancellor of the Institute, and Professor Salman Albdour, President of Al al-Bayt University on 21 December 2003; and Professor Abdullah Al-Musa, President of the University of Jordan on 23 December 2003. I was accompanied by Mr Mohamad Obeid Bin

Ghannam, Secretary General of the Al-Maktoum Foundation in Dubai
and Mr Zuhdi Al-Khattib, UAE Cultural Attaché in Jordan. HE Rahma
Hussein Rahma Al-Za'abi, UAE Ambassador in Jordan attended the
ceremony at the University of Jordan. Both Memoranda looked towards
developing further cooperation between the Institute and these two
universities.

7. Johann Wolfgang Goethe-University in Frankfurt, Germany

On 23 January 2004, the Institute signed its first Memorandum of
Understanding with a continental European university. This agreement
with the prestigious Johann Wolfgang Goethe-University in Frankfurt
followed a series of meetings involving senior staff from both
institutions.

The signing ceremony took place in the office of Mr Rudolph
Steinberg, President of Frankfurt University. He was accompanied by
Professor Andreas Gold and Professor Jurgen Bereiter-Hahn, his vice-
presidents, the University Chancellor Dr Wolfgang Busch, and Mr John
Skillen, head of the University's International office. Signing on behalf of
the Al-Maktoum Institute was Mr Mirza Al-Sayegh, Chairman of the
Board, who was accompanied by Mr Mohamed Obeid Bin Ghannam,
the UAE's Ambassador in Germany at the time, HE Mr Ali al-Zaruny,
and myself.

In the memorandum the two institutions agreed on exchanges of staff
and students. In addition they were to encourage joint research projects
and joint publications to 'promote advancement of Arabic and Islamic
studies', the use of staff as external examiners and work on joint
academic programmes that could see students from one institution sent
to the other as a recognised part of their course. The first step in this
cooperation was the announcement of the creation of two new
scholarships to allow graduates from Frankfurt to come to Dundee to
study for a Masters degree.

President Steinberg expressed the hope that the agreement would lead
to a fruitful relationship between the two institutions. He said Arabic and
Islamic studies had a high priority at Frankfurt, as the city was the most
international in Germany with a high percentage of Muslim residents.
The agreement with Al-Maktoum Institute would support their efforts to
expand teaching and research in Arabic studies. Mr Mirza Al-Sayegh said:
'We look forward to developing our research, course work and published
material in collaboration with our new colleagues from Germany. I am
confident that staff and students from both institutes will reap the

benefit and that this agreement will further assist our task of promoting multiculturalism.'

8. Cairo University

During the Al-Maktoum Institute delegation visit to Cairo, Mr Mirza Al-Sayegh, Chairman of the Institute Board, signed a Memorandum of Understanding with Professor Kamal El-Menoufi, Dean of the Faculty of Economics and Political Science at Cairo University on 3 March 2004. The memorandum established the formal framework for close cooperation between the two institutions and exchange of staff and students, cooperation on research projects and exchange of educational material and resources. During the signing ceremony which was attended by students from the faculty, it was agreed that the Institute would host five students where the Institute would organise a special programme to engage in dialogue with Scottish students. To strengthen this relationship, this institute offered two scholarships to graduates from Cairo University. These two students studied and completed their MLitt programme in Islamicjerusalem Studies at the Institute from September 2004 to September 2005.

On 19 September 2004, I visited Cairo University again with Mohammed Obeid Bin Ghannam to strengthen the relationship with the Faculty of Economics and Political Science.

9. Al-Azhar University - Cairo, Egypt

Discussions have been established with Al-Azhar University, the world's biggest and oldest Muslim University, which has a world-class international reputation in the field of various branches of Islamic Studies.. The initial discussions took place in June 2002. A delegation from the Institute comprised of Mr Mirza Al-Sayegh, myself, and Mr Mohammad Obeid Bin Ghannam, accompanied by HE Mr Juma Al-Majid, met Dr Ahmad Omar Hashim, President of Al-Azhar University, and his Deputy on 28 October 2002.

On 19 September 2004, I signed with Professor Ahmad Muhammad Ahmad Al-Tayib, President of Al-Azhar University, a Memorandum of Understanding between Al-Maktoum Institute and Al-Azhar University, working towards developing further cooperation. I was accompanied by Mr Mohamad Obeid Bin Ghannam, and HE Mr Ahmad al-Mil Al-Za'abi, UAE Ambassador to Egypt.

Al-Azhar University (Consultation on development of quality assurance systems)

During the signing Ceremony of the Memorandum of Understanding on 19 September 2004, Al-Azhar University asked if the Institute could help and advise them on introducing 'Quality Assurance' Systems and Procedures in Higher Education for Al-Azhar University. On that basis Professor Abd al-Dayim Nossair, Vice Principal for Academic Affairs and Research of Al-Azhar University, was invited to visit the Institute from 14 to 16 of September 2005.

His visit had four main elements:

- Meeting with Professor Abd al-Fattah El-Awaisi, Principal and Vice-Chancellor of Al-Maktoum Institute regarding issues relating to the Memorandum of Understanding between the two institutions
- Detailed discussion with Professor Malory Nye, Depute Principal for Academic Affairs, Al-Maktoum Institute on the topic of 'Al-Maktoum Institute: overview of quality assurance procedures and issues'
- Meeting with Dr Gillian Mackintosh, Deputy Academic Registrar (Teaching & Learning), University of Aberdeen on the implementation of quality assurance issues within the university
- Meeting with Dr Alan Davidson, from QAA Scotland, on 'the Scottish approach to quality in higher education: national policies and procedures for quality assurance and quality enhancement'.

Al-Maktoum Institute was delighted to be helping Al-Azhar University in this matter. Indeed we could be the bridge for Al-Azhar to reach the academic establishment of the western countries, because of its unique position as a Scottish higher education institution. It had been extremely useful for Professor Abd al-Dayim to make this visit to Al-Maktoum Institute, particularly to have the experience of talking with practitioners in quality assurance in the three different institutions. This had helped him to understand better the concepts of quality assurance and the methods of implementation.

From this, he would now be able to move from his theoretical understanding of quality assurance issues to a practical implementation of quality assurance within Al-Azhar University. Particular developments from this were:

- A better understanding by Professor Abd al-Dayim of the problems of the early stages of implementation of quality assurance, particularly the key problem of dealing with the resistance to QA from Al-Azhar academics and the wider university community.

- Al-Azhar University is not the only university that is currently seeking to introduce quality assurance. In fact, there are a number of European universities (for example in Italy and former Soviet countries) going through a similar transition and facing very similar issues.

- Considerations by Al-Azhar University of the introduction of specific mechanisms for implementation of quality assurance, including the use of questionnaires for both staff and students to enable the review of course delivery each semester – using as a template the forms for such review employed by the Al-Maktoum Institute and the University of Aberdeen.

- The establishment at Al-Azhar of a university Academic Standards Committee to oversee and develop quality assurance issues, using the models of the ASC of the University of Aberdeen and the Teaching Quality Committee of Al-Maktoum Institute.

- The development of models for the structure of training courses for academic staff.

- The importance of scholars in Al-Azhar University to have experiences of working and studying outside the university, to enable them to develop a broader viewpoint to use as a basis for facing the challenges and opportunities of the twenty-first century.

- The discussions also helped to clarify for Professor Abd al-Dayim some of the key practical experiences of implementation of quality assurance matters, in particular the need to develop an approach that combines acceptance from the senior management of the need for QA (and with that the pressure for change within the system), whilst also encouraging ownership and engagement with the quality assurance agenda at the grassroots level. That is, the approach needs to work at both levels, and methods of implementation have to engage with both to prepare the ground for successful outcomes.

- It was also noted in our discussion that Al-Azhar University will be teaching a new course this coming year in Shari'ah through the medium of English language. This is a very important step for the development of the agenda for Islamic Studies in the University.

In a final meeting with Al-Maktoum Institute staff and students, Professor Abd al-Dayim said that this meeting brought a good conclusion to the excellence of Al-Maktoum Institute'.

Action Points
- The two scholarships for graduates of Al-Azhar University to come to Al-Maktoum Institute to do the MLitt in Islamic Studies or Islamicjerusalem Studies would need to be implemented for entry in the future. Al-Azhar would now widen the search for these two nominations to include students in the areas of humanities, social sciences, arts, and languages as well as within Islamic Studies.
- As one way to spread the concept of quality assurance in Al-Azhar University, and to assist senior people of the university, Professor Abd al-Dayim extended an invitation for the Principal and Depute Principal of Al-Maktoum Institute to visit the university to give a public lecture and/or seminar to explain and develop the agenda for quality assurance.
- In addition, one or more visiting scholars from Al-Azhar University should come to the Institute for a month, when they could give some classes and talks, and could share the Institute's new agenda for the study of Islam and Muslims. Such visiting scholar would have to good English language.

Visit to Malaysia and Brunei
I visited Malaysia on 18 – 30 July 2002. During this visit, meetings were arranged with the Vice-Chancellors with almost all the Universities offering Islamic Studies at their institutions. These include the University of Malaya, Universiti Kebangsaan Malaysia, Kolej Universiti Islam Malaysia, International Islamic University Malaysia, Universiti Teknologi Malaysia, International Institute of Islamic thought and Civilization and Universiti Teknologi MARA. All these visits have helped tremendously in introducing the Institute to academic institutions in Malaysia, thus opening up the doors to future academic cooperation and student recruitment.

I also visited University Brunei Darussalam in July 2002 and met the late Professor Dr Haji Mahmud Saedon, former Vice-Chancellor of the University. This initial relationship with Brunei was boosted further when I visited HE Pengiran Haji Yunus, High Commissioner of Brunei to the United Kingdom, at the Brunei High Commission on 22 July 2003. Various issues were discussed, focusing on academic matters and also introducing Dundee to Brunei. During the meeting, HE Pengiran

Haji Yunus accepted my invitation to visit Dundee on 25-26 September 2003. However this visit had to be postponed.

10. University of Malaya

I visited University of Malaya during my first visit to Malaysia between 18 to 30 July 2002 and the discussion continued to develop between the two institutions. ISRA offered two scholarships to the University of Malaya for students to come to study Islamicjerusalem Studies at the Institute in September 2002 and 2004.

The first Memorandum of Understanding outside Europe and the Arab world was signed with the University of Malaya on 24 September 2004. This University is Malaysia's oldest, largest, and most prestigious university, and is a major university within the whole region of South East Asia.

I travelled to Malaysia to sign the Memorandum of Understanding, accompanied by Lord Elder, the Chancellor of the Institute, and Mr Mohamad Obeid Bin Ghannam, we were joined for the signing by HE Mr Nasser Salman Al-Aboodi, UAE Ambassador to Malaysia and Mr Edward Hobart, Head of Political, Economic and Public Diplomacy Section at the British High Commission. Dato' Professor Hashim Yaacob signed the Memorandum, as the Vice-Chancellor of the University of Malaya.

In my speech at the signing ceremony, I presented the Institute's new agenda for the future development of the study of Islam and Muslims, and ideas were discussed for future collaboration between the Institute and both the Institute of Islamic Studies and the Centre for Civilisational Dialogue of the University of Malaya.

Following the ceremony, I also delivered a Public Lecture on 'Islamicjerusalem as a model for Multiculturalism'. The lecture was well received and great interest was shown for this new field of inquiry of Islamicjerusalem Studies.

The Signing of the Memorandum of Understanding with the University of Malaya was another major step forward in the Institute's quest to build and foster links with Higher Education establishments throughout the world.

We should mention that the Institute always had a high proportion of Malaysian students. In September 2004 we had eleven postgraduate Malaysian students and a number of them were graduates of the University of Malaya.

A joint Symposium with the University of Malaya and Al-Maktoum Institute on Islamic Studies

On 4 to 5 May 2005 a joint symposium between the Centre for Civilisation Dialogue and Academy of Islamic Studies at the University of Malaya and the Al-Maktoum Institute took place at the University of Malaya. The aim was to present the New Agenda on the Study of Islam and Muslims. The symposium was officially opened by Tan Sri Dato' Dr Abdul Hamid Othman, Religious Advisor to the Prime Minister of Malaysia. The symposium was attended by a delegation from the Institute including Professor Abd Al-Fattah El-Awaisi, Mr Mohammed Obeid Bin Ghannam, Professor Malory Nye, and Mr Aminurraasyid Yatibian.

During the delegation's visit to Malaysia there were several senior engagements including a meeting with the Malaysian Minister of Higher Education, Dato' Dr Haji Shafie Mohd Salleh, and Tan Sri Dato' Dr Abdul Hamid Othman, Religious Adviser to the Prime Minister of Malaysia.

11. Arabian Gulf University
A Memorandum of Understanding was signed during a visit to the Arabian Gulf University in Bahrain on 2 May 2004. It was signed by Dr Rafia Gubash, President of the Arabian Gulf University and myself.

12. Higher Colleges of Technology, UAE
A Memorandum of Understanding was signed in Dubai on the 26 March 2005 by Mr Mirza Al-Sayegh, Chairman of the Institute Board, on behalf of Al-Maktoum Institute and the Higher Colleges of Technology (HCT). The memorandum was signed on behalf of the Higher Colleges of Technology by Dr Howard Reid, Director of the Colleges.

13. International Academy of Philosophy, Liechtenstein
On 30 June 2005 a Memorandum of Understanding was signed in Dundee between the International Academy of Philosophy, Liechtenstein and the Institute. It was signed by Professor Malory Nye, Depute Principal for Academic Affairs on behalf of the Al-Maktoum Institute and Dr Cheikh Gueye, Assistant Researcher on behalf of the Academy, in the presence of HH Prince Philipp von und zu Liechtenstein, Lord Elder, Chancellor of the Institute, myself, and the students attending the 2005 Summer school.

14. University of Wurzburg, Germany (Dundee's twin city)

During a visit to the Institute on 5 September 2005, a Memorandum of Understanding was signed between the University of Wurzburg and the Institute, by Professor Ulrich Sinn, Vice President of the University of Wurzburg and myself, as the Principal and Vice-Chancellor of the Institute.

Professor Sinn invited me to visit the University of Wurzburg to talk to students and staff on the New Agenda of the Institute. Accordingly I visited from 12 – 13 of October 2005 where I discussed with Professor Sinn and other senior members of the University areas of possible collaboration between the two institutions.

15. Abu Dhabi University

A Memorandum of Understanding was signed in Abu Dhabi on 7 November 2006, by Mr Mirza Al-Sayegh, Chairmen of Al-Maktoum Institute Board on behalf of Al-Maktoum Institute. The Memorandum of Understanding was signed on behalf of Abu Dhabi University by Mr Ali Saeed Bin Harmel Al-Dharari, Chairman of the Executive Board of Governors.

International Academic Network

EUROPE		
No.	**University Name**	**Date of Signing**
1	University of Frankfurt, Germany	23 January 2004
2	University of Aberdeen, Scotland	26 May 2004
3	International Academy of Philosophy, Liechtenstein	30 June 2005
4	University of Wurzburg, Germany	05 September 2005

AFRICA		
1	University of Gezira, Sudan	08 February 2003
2	Cairo University, Egypt	03 March 2004
3	Al-Azhar University, Egypt	19 September 2004

THE GULF STATES		
1	Zayed University, UAE	26 June 2002
2	Qatar University, Qatar	26 October 2002
3	United Arab Emirates University, UAE	29 June 2003
4	Arabian Gulf University, Bahrain	02 May 2004
5	Higher Colleges of Technology, UAE	26 March 2005
6	Abu Dhabi University, UAE	7 November 2006

ASIA		
1	Al-al Bayt University, Jordan	21 December 2003
2	The University of Jordan, Jordan	23 December 2003

SOUTH EAST ASIA		
1	University of Malaya, Malaysia	24 September 2004

These Memoranda of Understanding are a formal development in the process of the Institute and these Universities working together to a shared common goal. In addition, all these links will help the Institute to achieve our aims of building bridges and providing a meeting point between the western and Muslim worlds of learning and to encourage scholarship and academic co-operation at this crucial time.

Indeed, we are playing an important role in enhancing the understanding of a multicultural world, helping to bring together the Muslim and western people and to build bridges of understanding and co-operation between different cultures and religions that live together in today's world.

Al-Maktoum Institute Academic Network: Student Forum

On 12 December 2006, the Institute Academic Council approved a proposal to organise a Forum from 31 May to 2 June 2006 at the Institute in Dundee, for an invited international body of students from nine of our universities partners. The aim is to disseminate the New Agenda for the study of Islam and Muslims, as set out in the Dundee Declaration and developed by the Institute. The main points for discussion and implementation will be:

- The New Agenda for the Study of Islam and Muslims (as developed from Dundee Declaration)
- The Major Research Report on 'Time for Change: Report on the Future of the Study of Islam and Muslims in Universities and Colleges in Multicultural Britain'
- The New Field of Inquiry of Islamicjerusalem Studies.

The Forum will bring together the next generation of scholars and leaders from many different countries: Al al-Bayt University (Jordan), University of Jordan (Jordan), University of Cairo (Egypt), Al-Azhar University (Egypt), University of Malaya (Malaysia), Johann Wolfgang Goethe University in Frankfurt (Germany), International Academy of Philosophy (Liechtenstein), University of Würzburg (Germany), and

University of Aberdeen (Scotland). Two students and one academic of staff from each university will represent their universities. The two students will be at least towards finishing his/her undergraduate studies (i.e. 3rd or 4th year) or at the postgraduate level and may be studying in any discipline within the Study of Islam and Muslims, which includes any subject areas within humanities, social sciences, as well as Islamic Studies.

The Forum will be made up of: formal presentations by speakers from the Al-Maktoum Institute, discussion and debate sessions, and attending the 2007 International Academic Conference on Islamicjerusalem Studies.

Other International Academic Links and Collaborations

British University in Dubai

As part of my visit to the UAE in June 2002, I met, on 21 June, Mr. Tim Gore, then Director of the British Council in Dubai, who informed me and Mr Mohamad Obeid Bin Ghannam, Secretary-General of Al-Maktoum Foundation in Dubai and a member of the Institute Board, about the intention to establish a British University in Dubai. I registered an interest in being part of the new University especially in the field of the Study of Islam and Muslims. This was then followed by a meeting with Mr Simon Collis, then Consul General of the British Embassy in Dubai on 24 June 2002. Mr Collis, on 4 July 2002, also met with Mr. Mirza Al-Sayegh, Director of the Office of HH Shaikh Hamdan and Chairman of the Institute Board, to gain HH Shaikh Hamdan's support for the concept to establish the British University in Dubai.

The initial discussions were then followed by a visit by Mr Mirza Al-Sayegh, Mr Mohammad Obeid Bin Ghannam, and myself to the University of Edinburgh on 17 September 2002. The meeting with senior officials at the University of Edinburgh was to further discuss the concept and the proposal for the British University in Dubai. On 21 October 2002, Mr Mirza Al-Sayegh, Chairman of the Institute Board, was made the leading figure in Dubai to pursue the establishment of that University.

HH Shaikh Maktoum Bin Rashid Al-Maktoum, the late Ruler of Dubai issued a decree on 19 May 2003 to establish 'The British University in Dubai' with a capital of Dhs 11.7 million. His Highness Shaikh Ahmad Bin Saeed Al-Maktoum was announced as Chancellor and Chairman of the Board of Trustees. His Highness Shaikh Ahmad is also Chairman of

Emirates Airline. The Chairman of Al-Maktoum Institute's Board, Mr Mirza Al-Sayegh, was appointed as a member of the Board of Trustees.

The founders of the university were Al-Maktoum Foundation in Dubai, Dubai Development and Investment Authority, Rolls-Royce PLC, National Bank of Dubai and British Business Group. The idea of the educational system of the university would primarily be based on cooperation with distinguished educational institutions, first with the University of Edinburgh, and subsequently with other British universities, institutions and colleges.

The Institute, through its Chairman Mr Mirza Al-Sayegh, is working to bring other Scottish universities into this project. Once it is decided to establish the field of the Study of Islam and Muslims at the British University in Dubai, Al-Maktoum Institute will be responsible for setting up this field at the University.

Strategic Forum on Higher and Further Education and the GCC

I attended the Strategic Forum on Higher Education and the GCC in London on 12 September 2002 and 11 September 2003. The Forum was organised by International Trade and Investment Mission, and focused on the possible strategic relationship between higher education establishments in the UK and those in the Gulf countries.

The Forum was attended by senior representatives from Gulf States. However, in 2003 it was also attended by two representatives of Iraq, one from the private Higher Education Sector and one from the Government University. The Forum widened the Institute's network of contacts especially with the British Council.

In 2003, both Dr. Hanif al-Qassimi and myself presented Al-Maktoum Institute to the audience as a model of cooperation and partnership between the Gulf States and the UK. Three main aspects of this cooperation were highlighted: the British University of Dubai, Al-Maktoum Institute Summer school, and Al-Maktoum Institute's 'Books for Baghdad' Project.

International Strategies Forum for Higher and Further Education – the Middle East and the UK

On 25 November 2005, I attended the International Strategies Forum for Higher and Further Education at the Institute of Civil Engineers in London. Delegates from 14 countries attended the forum, heard and discussed presentations focused on the education strategies of Saudi Arabia, Qatar, Kuwait, the United Arab Emirates, Jordan, Iraq, Egypt and the UK's new international strategy for education.

The Strategic Forum's objectives were to develop practical co-operation between higher education establishments in the Gulf and Mashriq countries and the UK in the fields of teaching, research and academic systems and standards. Another aim was to identify obstacles to co-operation and how to deal with them, as well as finding areas of progress for further future development.

Dubai Internet City

A Memorandum of Understanding was signed with Dubai Internet City on 4 November 2002. The Memorandum of Understanding was signed by the Chairman of the Institute, Mr Mirza Al-Sayegh, and the Chief Executive Officer of Dubai Internet City, Dr Omar Bin Sulaiman.

Ajman University of Science and Technology (AUST Network)

The Institute received a visit by a delegation from AUST Network led by their President, HE Dr Saeed Abdullah Salman, President of AUST Network, on 4 – 8 January 2003. HE Dr Salman is also President of the Association of Arab Private Institutions for Higher Education and President of Euro-Arab Research Network.

On Tuesday, 7 January 2003, the delegation held an Approach Seminar[1] hosted by the Al-Maktoum Institute. The seminar was connected with other participants from seven locations around the world including Jordan, Bahrain and the UAE via videoconference. In addition to Dundee University, it was attended by several senior representatives of organisations and companies involved in healthcare and biomedical industries in Dundee. The Seminar discussed ways in which the Al-Maktoum Institute could act as a bridge between Dundee and the AUST Network.

In addition, a Memorandum of Understanding was signed between Al-Maktoum Institute and AUST Network. Since the AUST Network is particularly interested in the biomedical and healthcare related industries, the Institute was hoping that the signing of this understanding would enhance the relationship with Dundee and Scotland. But, regrettably, HE Dr Saeed Abdullah Salman, President of AUST Network requested the

---

[1]   During the seminar, Al-Maktoum Institute asked to join the Association of Arab Private Higher Education Institutions and the Euro-Arab Research Network which is chaired by HE Dr Saeed Abdullah Salman. The Euro-Arab Research Network provides its members with opportunities to exchange experience, expertise, data and information so that they can update and upgrade their capacities through the linkages.

cancellation of this Memorandum of Understanding. It is worth mentioning that this was for the Institute the only memorandum of understanding which was cancelled at the request of the other partner.

Islamic Universities League
On 3 June 2003, the Executive Council of the Islamic Universities League accepted the Institute as a member of the league. We are the first British higher education institution to be part of this international league. Membership will indeed help the Institute to achieve our aim of providing a meeting point between the Western and Muslim worlds of learning and encouraging scholarship and academic co-operation.

Cambridge University
On 25 August 2005 the Institute was invited to the University of Cambridge to meet the Deans of Peterhouse College (Dr Ben Quash) and Jesus College (Dr Tim Jenkins), along with a representative of the International Academy of Philosophy, Liechtenstein (Dr Cheikh Gueye). The Depute Principal represented the Institute at this meeting which discussed, in particular, areas of collaboration between the Cambridge Interfaith Programme, and the work and research that the Institute is doing in the areas of Islamicjerusalem studies, multiculturalism and religious and cultural diversity.

Arts and Humanities Research Council
In August 2005, the Depute Principal was invited to sit on the Arts and Humanities Research Council Commissioning Panel for their scheme for research on Diasporas, Migration and Identities. The AHRC is the government's funding council for research in these areas, and it is a measure of considerable academic esteem to be invited to play such a prominent role in the allocation and award of prestigious grant funding to scholars across the UK. It is a significant marker of Al-Maktoum Institute's leading role in the development of research in this important area of multiculturalism.

Research House for Islamic and Heritage Revival – Government of Dubai, UAE
On 2 June 2006 during the (eighth) International Academic Conference on Islamicjerusalem Studies held at the Institute, the Institute and the Research House for Islamic and Heritage Revival – Government of Dubai, UAE signed a Memorandum of Understanding. I signed the Memorandum of Understanding with Dr Mohammad Ahmad al-Qurashi, Director General of the Research House. The aim of the

Memorandum of Understanding is to promote cooperation between the Institute and the Research House.

United Nation Educational, Scientific and Cultural Organisation (UNESCO)

During my trip to Paris in early June 200 to visit HE Mr Zuhdi Al-Khatib, the UAE Cultural Attaché in Jordan, we met with Dr Omar Massalha, Director of the Division of Relations with International Organisations Sector for External Relations and Cooperation (UNESCO). During that meeting, we discussed the possibility for the Institute to become a member of UNESCO. Accordingly, I sent a letter, dated 1 September 2006, to Mr Koichiro Matsuura, the Secretary General expressing our keen interest in working and establishing official relations with UNESCO and to identify areas of cooperation.

On 31 October 2006, a positive response was received from Mr. Ahmed Sayyad, Assistant Director-General for External Relations and Cooperation on behalf of the Director-General, noting our work on "promoting dialogue and multiculturalism through education". He requested the Institute to complete an application form for the establishment of official relations with UNESCO, which was submitted to the Chief, Section of International Non-Governmental Organisations and Foundations at UNESCO on 28 November 2006.

In short, all these partnerships and links certainly helped to enhance our teaching and research capabilities and ultimately benefit our staff and students. They also helped to promote Dundee and Scotland as home to a centre of excellence in the Study of Islam and Muslims.

7

ACHIEVEMENTS: ACHIEVING ACADEMIC EXCELLENCE

As the Institute aims to promote excellence in research, teaching, and consultancy in the field of the Study of Islam and Muslims, all aspects of teaching at the Al-Maktoum Institute are delivered according to the teaching quality criteria of the British Higher Education system. In the past five years, the Institute has continued to develop its activities in teaching, learning and research and to seek enhancement in all matters of quality assurance. In addition the Institute has provided consultation to other international universities on the development of quality assurance systems.

External approval
Through partnership with our Scottish partner, the Institute implements the National Quality Assurance framework that ensures consistency and maintenance of teaching quality standards.

External Examiner's comments
As part of this, all our taught Masters programmes courses are externally monitored and examined by senior academics who are appointed by the University as external examiners. The role of these examiners is to verify academic standards within the taught degree programmes by monitoring the whole assessment process, from the setting of assessment on individual courses to the formation of judgements on courses grades and programme awards. To achieve this, external examiners are asked to scrutinise exam and essay questions, to read coursework written by students, and to attend the exam board meetings.

Feedback received from both our external examiners has been very positive. The minutes of the exam board meetings in February 2003 recorded that:

- Both External Examiners were generally happy with student performance and have considered it to be on a par with other similar institutions. Dr Hussain Abdul-Raof, senior lecturer in the Department of Arabic and Middle-Eastern Studies at the University of Leeds, stated that he is impressed by the approach taken by the Institute in combining traditional and contemporary modules in teaching Arabic and Islamic Studies. (Subject Assessment Board)
- Dr Bustami Khir, senior lecturer in the Department of Theology at the University of Birmingham, informed the Board that he was pleased with the performance of the students. He further stated that the level of teaching and the assessment profile of the modules are comparable with other institutions. (Course Assessment Board)
- Dr Hussain Abdul-Raof informed the Board that he is pleased with the breadth and balance of the programmes. In particular, Dr Abdul-Raof stated that Al-Maktoum Institute should be credited for using traditional and modern approaches to Islamic studies as it is innovative. (Course Assessment Board)

A letter from Dr Hussein Abdul-Roaf dated 19 February 2003 indicated a high level of satisfaction with our procedures and quality, and indeed outlined a ringing endorsement of the Institute: 'I strongly believe that your Institute is credited for the variety of courses offered which cover a unique combination of both traditional and modern approaches to Islamic Studies. I believe it is a unique approach which has made your institute distinguished among other British and international academic institutions. This is what students need in the 21st century.'

In his report to the University of Abertay Assessment Boards in September 2004, Dr Bustami Khir of the University of Birmingham stated that he was very happy with our procedures and that the standards and quality of our teaching were comparable with those expected in the British higher education system.

In his report dated 28 August 2005, Dr Jabal M Buaben, our external examiner who was appointed by the University of Aberdeen, stated: 'The whole programme is of a very high standard. The quality of work produced by the students is indicative of a sound teaching and learning experience. There was enough evidence that students are familiar with the relevant classical and contemporary sources in the relevant subject areas and are able to make use of these critically in their work. They have shown awareness of the basics of research methods. The quality of work meets all the requirements of national frameworks and compares favourably with other institutions in the United Kingdom offering similar programmes.'

In addition, during the examiners meeting on 10 October 2005, he also stated that he was very pleased with the products which he had looked at, dissertations and other materials. He noted the quality of work saying that 'something good is happening here – keep it up.' He commented that Al-Maktoum Institute coursework and results compare very favourably with other similar institutions both at home and abroad.

He suggested that the Institute should consider the possibility of developing an undergraduate programme in the near future. He also suggested doing some market research within the immediate catchment area in Dundee. Undergraduates would help 'catch the vision' of the Institute and help distinguish the philosophy behind it from other academic institutions.

At the final examiners' meeting for 2005-06, on 3 October 2006, Dr Jabal Buaben, of the University of Birmingham expressed overall satisfaction with the delivery of the programmes, the standards of assessment, and the Institute's overall quality assurance standards. He did, however, make two proposals for further development, which were as follows:

i. To assist dissertation supervisors, and to encourage dissertation students to take their supervision meetings more seriously, the external examiner recommended that a written record of all supervision meetings should be taken by the supervisor. This suggestion was subsequently implemented at the next meeting of the Institute's Academic Affairs Committee, and from spring/summer 2007 onwards all dissertation supervisors will be expected to use a meeting record form, based on the existing meeting record form for PGR supervision.

ii. Dr Buaben's second proposal recommended that dissertation also be given specific training in the writing of an introduction to the dissertation. Following this up, the Academic Affairs Committee invited Dr Buaben to attend the PG Research Training Workshop at the Institute on 17-18 January 2007, to run a training session for all students on the writing of an introduction.

Visiting Scholars

Since starting the teaching on the MLitt programmes, the Institute has had a number of distinguished visiting scholars participating in its activities. For example, in autumn semester 2002, Dr Anne-Sofie Roald took up a position in the Institute for two months during which time she taught a course on 'Women and Islam'. Dr Roald is an Associate Professor at Malmö University, Sweden and is Programme Director at the Christian Michelson Institute, Bergen, Norway, and has published the book *Women in Islam* with Routledge. At the end of her visit she wrote a report on her experiences which said: 'I found that many of the students had a very high profile... The atmosphere among the students and the staff was also one of harmony and good humour...The staff would have an open door to students and other staffs' requests, thus creating an including atmosphere at the Institute. The non-academic staff's, such as the reception, played an important role in the creation of a good atmosphere on the Institute and the caretakers were always helpful when asked for help. I always received good treatment from the head of the Institute and the assisting manager... I have been given full academic freedom to teach in the manner I want and I have appreciated this very much. All in all I had a very pleasant stay both intellectually and personally speaking.'

Student Enrolment

The Institute plans to further enrich the cultural diversity within the City of Dundee by continuing attracted both national and international students. We believe that by having a pool of intellectuals of various cultural backgrounds and nationalities all under one roof, the quality of scholars produced by the Institute would be even higher as a result of the exposure that they had had while studying and researching here. To this end, we aim to have 50 per cent of our student population from within the United Kingdom and Europe and the other 50 percent from the international communities.

It was truly inspiring to see the steady increase in the number of students walking the halls of the Al-Maktoum Institute. In November 2002, there were 17 students undertaking the taught Masters programme. Nine were doing Masters in Islamicjerusalem Studies and eight in Islamic Studies. Additionally, there were another ten students registered for a research degree at the Institute. This brought the total number of registered students at that time at the Institute to 27. Seven more students were registered between October 2002 and March 2003, bringing the total to 34. In November 2003, there were 38 students at the Institute, 16 attending the taught courses and another 22 conducting research in various specialisations within the Study of Islam and Muslims.

With all the major restructuring work, and the change of the awarding university just before summer 2004, the Institute succeeded in recruiting the same number of postgraduate students as in the previous year. However, we continue to develop our recruitment and marketing strategies which have resulted in securing highly qualified, nationally and internationally, students.

Students Enrolment Statistics

Academic year	Taught Students			Research Students			Total
	New	Return	Total	New	Return	Total	
2001 - 2002	7	0	7	5	0	5	12
2002 - 2003	11	6	17	12	5	17	34
2003 - 2004	12	3	15	9	14	23	38
2004 - 2005	12	3	15	3	21	24	39

We feel very pleased with the steady increase of student intake since the Institute's inception in 2001 which started with only one student.

First Student to Complete PhD

History was made on 7 October 2002 when the first student completed his PhD thesis at the Institute. On that day, Othman Al-Tel had an oral examination on his thesis entitled 'The First Islamic Conquest of Aelia (Islamicjerusalem): a critical analytical study of the early Islamic historical narratives and sources.' Al-Tel successfully defended his thesis in front of a panel of examiners, thus resulting in the panel's recommending that he be awarded a PhD subject to only minor amendments. Othman Al-Tel graduated on 29 November 2002. Al-Tel then took up a Post-Doctoral Studentship at the Centre for Islamicjerusalem Studies by Islamic Research Academy (ISRA) from 1 November 2002 until 30 June 2003.

The First Concluding Ceremony for the Al-Maktoum Institute Summer School and to mark the end of the Academic Session 2002-03

On 9 July 2003, a ceremony was held in Shaikh Rashid Conference Hall to mark the end of the 2002-03 Academic Session. This was combined with the conclusion of the 2003 Al-Maktoum Institute Summer School.

The ceremony was attended by both Mr Mirza Al-Sayegh and Lord Elder of Kirkcaldy as well as many senior officials from Dundee. It was a memorable day for students and staff alike as this was the first such celebration in the first two years that the Institute had been operating. During the ceremony, awards were presented to students who had achieved distinctions in their studies and certificates were also presented to all those who helped in organising the 2003 Al-Maktoum Institute Summer School.

The First Al-Maktoum Institute Annual Recognition of Achievement Ceremony (28 November 2003).

Following the success of the Concluding Ceremony to mark the end of the Academic Session 2002-03, the Academic Council in its meeting on 2 October 2003 decided to organise an annual 'Recognition of Achievement Ceremony' to celebrate the achievements of the Al-Maktoum Institute students.

At the first such ceremony at the Institute on 28th November 2003, we were very pleased to mark the graduations of our first group of students from the Institute. It was attended by the graduate students, their families and friends, as well as by a host of local dignitaries and invited guests. This ceremony was scheduled to take place around the time of the University of Abertay November graduations, and so our graduating students attended the Recognition of Achievement Ceremony in the morning, prior to their receiving their graduation certificates from the University of Abertay later in the afternoon.

The calibre of students graduating was very high, with 7 students receiving passes with distinction. In addition, our second student to receive a PhD from the Institute, Maher Abu-Munshar, also graduated that day.

My address to an audience of around 100 highlighted that our greatest enemies are ignorance and extremism and education is the key to combating these to establish a greater understanding between communities locally, nationally and internationally. A very positive atmosphere with an air of great achievement was created in the Institute.

The 2004 Recognition of Achievement Ceremony (26 November 2004)

The Recognition of Achievement Ceremony took place on Friday 26 November 2004 at the Institute to recognise and congratulate the excellent achievements of our students. We were very pleased to mark the graduation of our students of 2003-04 from the Institute. As in the previous year, it was attended by students, their families and friends, as well as by a number of local dignitaries and invited guests.

The Institute was extremely delighted with the continuing success of our students. We were also very pleased at the continuing success of our MLitt students. Autumn 2004 saw 11 students complete the MLitt Programme. Two new prizes for distinction were introduced for our MLitt students: Shaikh Hamdan Bin Rashid Al-Maktoum Prize for Academic Distinction in the Master Dissertation and Shaikh Hamdan Bin Rashid Al-Maktoum Prize for Academic Distinction in Masters Programme. The two 2003 – 2004 prizes were awarded to Fatimatuzzahra Abd Rahman. One of these prizes was for her dissertation titled 'Political, Social and Religious Changes in Islamicjerusalem from the First Islamic Conquest until the end of Umayyad period (637 to 750CE): An Analytical Study.' She gained a distinction at the highest possible grade.

In addition two Honorary Fellowships were awarded to the Bishop of Brechin, the Rt Revd Neville Chamberlain and Mr Ernie Ross (then MP for Dundee West since 1979). Both men have served as members of the Institute Council and have long demonstrated their commitment to multiculturalism.

The First Graduation Ceremony (1 December 2005)

The first Al-Maktoum Institute Graduation Ceremony was held at the Institute on 1 December 2005 to celebrate the graduation of the Institute students during the academic year 2004/2005. It was presided over by Lord Elder, the Chancellor of the Institute, and it was attended by Professor Steven Logan, Senior Vice-Principal of the University of Aberdeen. It was also well attended by students, their friends and families, dignitaries and invited guests. The graduation marked one of the Institute's many notable milestones since opening its doors.

The Graduation Ceremony also marked the award of the two prizes for distinction for our MLitt Students. Shaikh Hamdan Bin Rashid Al-Maktoum Prize for Academic Distinction in the Masters Dissertation was awarded to Sara Hassan, for her dissertation titled 'Women: Active Agents in Islamising Islamicjerusalem from the Prophet's Time until the End of Umayyad Period'; and Shaikh Hamdan Bin Rashid Al-Maktoum Prize for Academic Distinction in Masters Programme was awarded to Abd Allah Omar. His dissertation was entitled 'Towards the Conquest of Islamicjerusalem: The Three Main Practical Steps Taken by Prophet Muhammad - Analytical Study.' At the Ceremony, the Chancellor also conferred two new Honorary Fellowships on Councillor Jill Shimi and Rev Erik Cramb.

The 2006 Graduation Ceremony (1 December 2006)

The second Al-Maktoum Institute Graduation Ceremony was held at the Institute on 1 December 2006 to celebrate the graduation of the Institute students during the academic year 2005/2006. It was presided over by Professor Abd al-Fattah El-Awaisi, the Principal and Vice-Chancellor of the Institute; and it was attended by Professor Steven Logan, Senior Vice-Principal of the University of Aberdeen. As in the previous year, it was also well attended by students, their friends and families, dignitaries and invited guests. With the 14 graduates this year, this will brought the total of PhD and Masters Graduates to 54. These students are to be highly commended for their hard work. They are truly an asset to the Institute. At the Ceremony, I also conferred two new Honorary Fellowships on Baillie Helen Wright and Alan Harden.

GRADUATE STUDENTS OF AL-MAKTOUM INSTITUTE (From July 2003 to December 2006)

Degree of Doctor of Philosophy in Islamicjerusalem Studies

1.   **Othman Al-Tel (Palestine)**
     For a Thesis entitled *The First Islamic Conquest of Aelia (Islamicjerusalem); a Critical Analytical Study of the Early Islamic Historical Narratives and Sources* (July 2003)

2.   **Maher Younes Abu-Munshar (Jordan)**
     For a Thesis entitled *A Historical Study of Muslim Treatment of Christians in Islamic Jerusalem at the Time of 'Umar Ibn al-Khattab and Salah al-Din, with Special Reference to Islamic Value of Justice* (Nov 2003)

3.   **Mohamad Roslan Mohamad Nor (Malaysia)**
     For a Thesis entitled *The Significance of Islamicjerusalem in Islam: Qur'anic and Hadith Perspectives* (Dec 2005)

4.   **Aminurraasyid Yatiban (Malaysia)**
     For a Thesis entitled *Muslim understandings of the concept of Al-Siyada (sovereignty): an analytical study of Islamicjerusalem from the first Muslim conquest until the end of the first Abasid period* (16-264AH/637-877CE) (April 2006)

5. **Ra'id Fathi Jabareen (Israel)**
For a Thesis entitled *Muslim Juristic Rulings of Islamicjerusalem with special reference to Ibadat in Al-Aqsa Mosque: A Critical Comparative Study* (April 2006)

6. **Khalid El-Awaisi (Scotland - UK)**
For a Thesis entitled *Mapping Islamicjerusalem: The geographical extent of the land of Bayt al-Maqdis, the Holy Land and the Land of Barakah* (Aug 2006)

Degree of Doctor of Philosophy in Islamic Studies

1. **Faris Ahmad Keblawi (Israel)**
For a Thesis entitled *Motivational Orientations, Attitudes, and De-motivation: A Case Study of Muslim Arab Learners of English in Public Schools in Northern Israel* (Mar 2006)

2. **Ibrahim Hashim (Malaysia)**
For a Thesis entitled *An integrated concept of Islamic Education: A study on Islamic Education in Muslim religious secondary schools in Selangor, Malaysia* (June 2006)

3. **Mohammed Khalid (Pakistan)**
For a Thesis entitled *A Muslim Understanding of the Development of the Events in the Early Muslim History (11 A.H/632 C.E. – 40 A.H/622 C.E.) in the Light of the Principles of the Governance in Islam: An Analytical Assessment* (Oct 2006)

Degree of MLitt in Islamicjerusalem Studies

1. **Mohamad Roslan Mohamad Nor (Malaysia)**
Malaysian Muslim Non-Governmental Organisation's Awareness Towards Islamic Jerusalem: Muslim Scholars Association of Malaysia (PUM) - as a case study (July 2003)

2. **Maimon Herawati (Indonesia)**
Islamicjerusalem under the Latin Kingdom: The Life of Muslims during the period 1099-1187 AD (July 2003)

3. **Amanullah De Sondy (Scotland – UK)**
Religio/ Intellectual activities of Muslims in Islamicjerusalem from 7th – 11th Century AD (July 2003)

4. **Aminurraasyid Yatiban (Malaysia)**
   The Islamic Concept of Sovereignty: Islamicjerusalem during the First Islamic Conquest as a Case Study (Nov 2003)

5. **Khalid El-Awaisi (Scotland – UK)**
   Geographical Boundaries of Islamicjerusalem (Nov 2003)

6. **Raja Hisyamudin B. Raja Sulong (Malaysia)**
   The Development of Islamicjerusalem under the Mamluks Sultanate with Special Reference to the Urbanization and Constructional Activities in the Walled City (Nov 2003)

7. **Aisha Muhammad Ibrahim Al-Ahlas (Scotland – UK)**
   Islamic Research Academy (ISRA) 1994-2003; Background, Activities and Achievements with Special Reference to the New Field of Inquiry of Islamic Jerusalem Studies (Nov 2003)

8. **Fatimatuzzahra' Abd Rahman (Malaysia)**
   Political, Social and Religious Changes in Islamicjerusalem from the First Islamic Conquest until the end of Umayyad period (637 to 750CE): An Analytical Study (Nov 2004)

9. **Hany Mohamed Aly Beshr (Egypt)**
   The European Union and the Jerusalem Question: Analytical Study of the Official EU Position and Role (Nov 2004)

10. **Paezah Binti Sabli (Malaysia)**
    The Fall of the Walled City of Islamicjerusalem to the Crusaders: A Comparative Study between Muslim's and Christians Accounts (Nov 2004)

11. **Mohammed Herbawi (Palestine)**
    Umar's Administration System in Bilad al-Sham with Special Reference to Islamic Jerusalem (Nov 2004)

12. **Rizwan Masaud Ahmed (England - UK)**
    Authentication of the Hadith of the Virtues of Bayt al Maqdis and al Masjid al- Aqsa – Complete Translation with Annotated Commentary (Nov 2004)

13. **Rehab Sayed Mohamed Emam (Egypt)**
    The Umayyad Dome of the Rock in Islamicjerusalem with Special Reference to its Calligraphy (Nov 2004)

14. **Ramona Ibrahim (Egypt)**
Islamicjerusalem as a Model of Conflict Resolution: A Case Study of the Negotiations between Salah al-Din and Richard 1 the Lionheart (Dec 2005)

15. **Sarah Hassan Mohamed (Egypt)**
Women: Active Agents in Islamising Islamicjerusalem from the Prophet's Time until the End of Umayyad Period (Dec 2005)

16. **Abdallah Ma'rouf Omar (Jordan)**
Towards the Conquest of Islamicjerusalem: The Three Main Practical Steps Taken by Prophet Muhammad - Analytical Study (Dec 2005)

17. **Akhmal Bin Ayob (Malaysia)**
Islamicjerusalem as a Model for Multiculturalism: With Special Reference to the Time of 'Umar āb to the Time of 'Umar Ibn 'Abd al-'AziztIbn Al-Khat (Dec 2005)

18. **Burhan Che Daud (Malaysia)**
The Vision of Nur al-Dīn Mahmud b. Zanki Towards Liberating Islamicjerusalem: A Historical Analysis (Dec 2005)

19. **Najah Nadiah Amran (Malaysia)**
The Concept of adīth Literature: A Study of al-Bukhārī, Muslim and AbūBayt al-Maqdis in H Dawūd's Approaches and Understandings (Dec 2005)

20. **Rosalind Anderson (Scotland - UK)**
An investigation into the significance of Jerusalem for those of Jewish, Christian and Islamic Faith and a detailed study on how the significance awarded to Jerusalem in these faiths affects any views, interpretations and comprehensions of the term IslamicJerusalem/Islamicjerusalem and accompanying definition (Dec 2005)

21. **Ahmad Irfan Bin Ikmal Hisham (Malaysia)**
The early stages of liberating Islamicjerusalem from the crusaders (1099 CE-1174 CE): An analytical study on Muslim juristic perspectives (Dec 2005)

22. **Mahmoud Mataz Kazmouz (Syria)**
The Ottoman implementation of the vision of Islamicjerusalem as a model for multiculturalism with a special reference to Sultan Suleiman I, the Magnificent (1520 – 1566) (Sep 2006)

23. **Rana Al-Soufi (Jordan)**
    Treatment of non-Muslims in Islamicjerusalem under Fatimids rule (Sep 2006)

24. **Ashinida Aladdin (Malaysia)**
    Intellectual activities in Islamicjerusalem under the Mamluks 648-923 AH / 1250-1517AD (Sep 2006)

Postgraduate Diploma in Islamicjerusalem Studies
1. **Alexander Fowler (Scotland – UK) (Nov 2004).**

Postgraduate Certificate in Islamicjerusalem Studies
1. **James Allinson (Scotland – UK) (July 2003)**

Degree of MLitt in Islamic Studies
1. **Faris Ahmad Keblawi (Israel)**
    Socio-Cultural Aspects in the Teaching of English as a Foreign Language to the Arab Learners in the Arab Schools in Israel (Nov 2003)

2. **Amina McKerl (Scotland - UK)**
    The Implementation of Culturally Aware, Faith Sensitive Healthcare in the National Health Service in Scotland (Nov 2003)

3. **Samia Abdulla A.M. Ali Al-Shamisi (UAE)**
    English Law and the Islamic Shari'a: The Dichotomy Experienced by Muslim Minorities, with a Special Focus on Divorce (Nov 2003)

4. **Mark Alexander Brash (Scotland - UK)**
    British and Muslim Identity in the works of Hanif Kureishi and Salman Rushdie (Nov 2003)

5. **Shaniza Shafie (Malaysia)**
    Halal Slaughter of Animals: To Stun or not to Stun? A response to the FAWC's Recommendation to ban slaughter by religious method (Nov 2003)

6. **Muhamad Rafiq Habib (Pakistan)**
    Minhaj-ul-Qur'an International Movement (Nov 2004)

7. **Ayesha Ebrahim Al Moutawa (UAE)**
   Electronic Commercial Contracts in Islamic law: A study on Dubai experience as a case study (Nov 2004)

8. **Fawaz Al-Ajmi (Kuwait)**
   Education in Islam with a Special Reference to Ibn Sina, Al Gazaly and Ibn Kaldoon (Nov 2004)

9. **Yasmin Nomura Kotyashi (UAE)**
   The Wearing of Hijab by Contemporary Muslim Women (Nov 2004)

10. **Noor-Ul-Islam Fazel-Ul-Haq (Pakistan)**
    Study of Hukm Shari according to the Methodology of the Scholars of Usul (Nov 2004)

11. **Mohamad Naser Alam (Bangladesh)**
    Ethno-Religious Conflict: Mapping the Scottish Executive's Policy on Ethno-Religious Conflict Resolution (Dec 2005)

12. **Lama Naasan (Scotland - UK)**
    The Role of Schools – Separation or Integration (Dec 2005)

13. **Zeena Al-Hafidth (Scotland - UK)**
    Mixed-faith marriages in Islam, conversions, and bringing up children in a Scottish context (Feb 2006)

14. **Rozita Ibrahim (Malaysia)**
    Single professional women: a case study of the Malay Muslims in Malaysia (Sep 2006)

15. **Pawel Bernat (Poland)**
    The meaning and importance of the notion of repentance for Al-Ghazali's moral theology (Sep 2006)

Postgraduate Diploma in Islamic Studies

1. Khalda Abd Allah (Sudan) (July 2003)

Postgraduate Certificate in Islamic Studies

1. Suzan El-Morabie (Egypt) (Nov 2004)
2. Andrew Richardson (Scotland - UK) (Dec 2005)
3. Amal Abu-Khrais (Libya) (Feb 2006)

GRADUATE STUDENTS OF AL-MAKTOUM INSTITUTE STATISTICS
(From July 2003 to December 2006)

Degree of Doctor of Philosophy					
Nationality	Male	Female	IJS	IS	Total
Pakistan	1			1	1
Palestine	1		1		1
Jordan	1		1		1
Malaysia	3		2	1	3
Israel	2		1	1	2
Scotland (UK)	1		1		1
TOTAL	9	0	6	3	9

Degree of MLitt in Islamicjerusalem Studies & Islamic Studies

Nationality	Male	Female	IJS	IS	Total
Bangladesh	1			1	1
Egypt	1	3	4		4
England – UK	1		1		1
Scotland – UK	3	5	4	4	8
Indonesia		1	1		1
Israel	1			1	1
Jordan	1	1	2		2
Kuwait	1			1	1
Malaysia	6	6	10	2	12
Pakistan	2			2	2
Palestine	1		1		1
Poland	1			1	1
Syria	1		1		1
United Arab Emirates		3		3	3
TOTAL	20	19	24	15	39

Scotland – UK	1		1		1
Sudan		1		1	1
TOTAL	1	1	1	1	2

Egypt		1		1	1
Scotland – UK	2		1	1	2
Libya		1		1	1
TOTAL	2	2	1	3	4

TOTAL GRADUATES					54

	MALE	FEMALE	IJS	IS	TOTAL
TOTAL GRADUATES	32	22	32	22	54

Legend:

IJS	Islamicjerusalem Studies
IS	Islamic Studies

Al-Maktoum Institute Alumnus Network (Amian)

On 15 February 2006 the Al-Maktoum Institute Alumnus Network (AMIAN) was established. The aims of the Alumnus Network are to enable former students to keep in touch with the Institute and with one another, and to provide opportunities for graduates to support the Institute, to promote and facilitate lifelong links between the Institute and its graduates, and to maintain an up-to-date database of former students of Al-Maktoum Institute. This database forms the mailing list for publications such as bulletins, the Institute brochures and Annual Reports, and offers a range of services.

Graduates become members of the Alumnus for free and it is open to all graduates of the Institute. We see our graduates as very important ambassadors for the Institute and our aims and vision.

Honorary Fellowship of Al-Maktoum Institute

To recognise individuals who have made a significant contribution both to the development of the Institute and to further its mission, aims and objectives, the Institute decided to award them Honorary Fellowships of Al-Maktoum Institute. Their contribution may be in any area of the Institute's activities either at the academic or the communities' levels, and they will have demonstrated their commitment to the multicultural vision that is at the heart of Al-Maktoum Institute.

In the last three years, the Institute has awarded six Honorary Fellowships which were conferred on the recipients during the Recognition of Achievements Ceremony in 2004 and in the Graduation Ceremonies in 2005 and 2006:

- The Bishop of Brechin, the Rt Revd Neville Chamberlain (2004)
- Mr Ernie Ross, MP for Dundee West since 1979 (2004)
- Councillor Jill Shimi, Dundee City Council Head of Administration (2005)
- Rev Erik Cramb, Scottish Churches Industrial Mission (2005)
- Baillie Helen Wright, formal Dundee Lord Provost (2006)
- Mr Alan Harden, Chief Executive of Alliance Trust (2006)

PART THREE
SETTING THE AGENDA FOR
CULTURAL ENGAGEMENT AT THE
COMMUNITIES LEVEL

8

SERVING THE LOCAL AND NATIONAL COMMUNITIES

In the last five years, we have been actively working to serve the local, national, and international communities. The main aim is to set the agenda for cultural engagement at the communities levels through providing practical beneficial relationships to develop the relationship between all communities.

As part of setting the new agenda in cultural engagement, I was aiming and working hard, from the first day of the Institute's birth in Dundee, to become an integral part of Dundee and Scotland fabric society through serving its communities and contributing to the regeneration of the City. Various steps have been taken to solidify our connections with the communities. This includes the Institute's decision to invite leaders of the local communities onto the Institute Council. The Institute also has adopted a policy of giving priority to local businesses whenever there is need for procurement of goods or services.

Institute Council

To ensure that the link with the local Scottish communities is well established, the Institute Board formed the Institute Council to advise and make recommendations to the Board. Indeed, the Council is a reflection of the very powerful commitment the Institute has to serving the communities.

The Institute Council is chaired by the Chancellor and meets twice annually. The first meeting was held on 26 April 2002. Membership of this Council includes many respected and leading figures from the communities and churches and this ensures a strong link with the communities. The current members of the Council are[1]:

1. Lord Elder, Chair
2. Professor Abd al-Fattah El-Awaisi, Vice-Chair
3. Professor the Lord John Sewel
4. Professor Malory Nye
5. Mr Ernie Ross (now former Member of Parliament for Dundee West)
6. Rt Rev Erik Cramb (now former Co-ordinator of Scottish Churches Industrial Mission)
7. Rt Rev Neville Chamberlain (now former Episcopalian Bishop of Brechin)
8. Rt Rev Vincent Logan (Bishop of Dunkeld)
9. Councillor Jill Shimi (Leader of Dundee City Council)
10. Baillie Helen Wright (formal Dundee Lord Provost)
11. Mr Alan Harden
12. Ms Denise Holmes
13. Mrs Mary Hanlon
14. Mr Harry Terrell
15. A student representative from Al-Maktoum Institute Student Society.

Arabic Language Evening Course

Another programme offered by the Institute in order to serve, and for the benefit of, the local communities is the Arabic Language Evening Course. Since the first class took place in March 2002, classes have been held every Thursday evening, each course lasting for ten weeks. During the second year (2003), the format of the course was changed slightly to ensure that the students received maximum benefits from the lessons. Rather than having only one lesson per week as was the case previously,

---

[1]   The first members of the Institute Council were: Professor Abd al-Fattah El-Awaisi, Mr Mirza al Sayegh, Mr Mohammed Obeid Bin Ghannam, Mrs Aisha Al-Ahlas, Dr Muhammad Branine, A representative of the University of Abertay Dundee (Professor Mike Swanston), Dr Hanif Al-Qassimi, Mr Ernie Ross MP, Rt Rev Erik Cramb, Rt Rev Neville Chamberlain, Rt Rev Vincent Logan, Dr Sue McAllion, Councillor Jill Shimi, Ms Jennifer Adams, Ms Ann Murray, Mr William Spence.

all students attended twice per week. The lessons on Tuesday focused on conversation while the lessons on Wednesday focused on reading.

Community Education Unit

The response from the public to the Arabic Language Evening Course has always been very good. The success of this class, and the high demand from the local communities, prompted the Institute's Academic Council on 9 May 2003 to set up a Community Education Unit with the aim of providing even better educational services and serve a wider portion of the local communities. Indeed, the Community Education Unit has continued to develop its role in providing education at the community level beyond the specifically academic/HE provision in the taught and research programmes of the Institute.

The main activity of the unit has been Arabic evening classes which were well attended and received very positive feedback from the students. For example, the spring 2004 Arabic evening classes ran from February through to May, and with a total of 22 students two separate class groups were organised, both meeting on a Thursday evening from 7-9pm. The 2005 Arabic evening classes ran from September through to December and with three separate class groups were organised, both meeting on a Tuesday evening from 7-9pm. The Community Education Unit agreed to run two levels of Arabic evening courses, one at 'beginners' level for students with no background in the subject, and another at 'basic' and intermediate level which was principally aimed at those students who had previously studied with us in the evening class.

In the past five years, the classes normally were divided into either two or three levels – beginners, basic, and intermediate. However, in Autumn 2006, the classes divided into two levels – beginners and intermediate with an additional third class in 'holiday Arabic'.

The Community Education Unit of the Institute is clearly meeting a strong demand for the teaching of Arabic at this level, and we are currently exploring possibilities for extending this further. One option that has been explored is evening classes that give a basic academic introduction to the question 'What is Islam?' The Unit is also exploring the idea of introducing a new course specifically designed as 'Arabic for Business'.

Dundee City Council

We believe that it has a significant role to play in helping to build a multicultural Dundee and Scotland. For that reason, various efforts have taken place to strengthen its links with Dundee City Council, and this is not limited to the Education Department only. Several constructive meetings have taken place between senior officials from Dundee City Council - including the Lord Provost, Head of Administration, and Chief Executive – and the Institute to strengthen links between the two establishments. The successful visit to Dubai organised by the Institute for the Dundee delegation in October 2002 certainly helped to forge a more solid relationship with the City Council.

Dundee City Council Education Department

On 30 October 2001, I met the Director of Dundee City Council Department of Education, Mrs Ann Wilson. This meeting was followed by another discussion with the Chief Executive of Dundee City Council, Mr. Alan Stephen, and the Lord Provost of the City of Dundee, Mr John Letford JP, on 21 March 2002. The relationship was built and developed to benefit all parties with particular emphasis on ways in which the Institute can further serve the needs of the local communities.

The link was made stronger by the signing of a Memorandum of Understanding between the Institute and Dundee City Council Education Department on 3 May 2002. This memorandum put on paper the commitment of both the Institute and the Department in building a fruitful and mutually beneficial working partnership, especially with regard to establishing and developing links with schools in Dundee. The memorandum also sets out the Education Department's conviction that the Institute can provide access to a wide range of information, materials, facilities and events, which will enrich various aspects of teaching and learning related to Islam and Muslim cultures, to teachers and pupils of primary and secondary schools in the city.

The Institute continued its discussion with the Department to enhance their relationship and work together. For example, I met with Councillor Fraser McPherson and Mrs Anne Wilson, Director of Education at Dundee City Council on 6 February 2004.

In discussion with the Department of Education, we identified the need for provision of information and support to teachers in Dundee in issues related to Islam and Muslims. The first outcome of this effort was a Teacher Seminar held on 25 April 2002 at the Institute which attended by thirty five teachers.

Several other developments took place in strengthening the relationship with Dundee City Council Department of Education. The Institute hosted a Network Meeting of Head of Religious Education Departments from secondary schools in Dundee on 4 September 2002. I was invited to give a short presentation about the Institute before the meeting started. A representative of the group expressed how the group admires the Institute's real sense of belonging to the community of Dundee and the emphasis on multiculturalism. The Institute also actively participates in the continuous development of teachers across the local areas. In the academic year 2002 - 2003, we organised a series of lectures for teachers in local areas covering topics such as fundamentalism, women in Islam and multiculturalism in Scotland.

On 24 February 2004, Professor Malory Nye gave a talk and discussion at the Institute on the topic of One Scotland, Many Cultures, Understanding Diversity for Dundee City Council Education Department. The event was attended by around 40 people, including a number of teachers, plus individuals from across the Education Department, and also from other parts of the council. Professor Nye explored some of the issues raised by our living in a multicultural society today – including some of the challenges that we must face, along with how it presents us with issues that we cannot ignore in all aspects of contemporary life. The talk stimulated a very lively debate among the teachers and other attendees present, and there was strong feedback from the group that this sort of event should be organised more regularly in Dundee for teachers and others working in similar fields.

In addition to this, the Institute also hosted two different visits of school children that year. The Institute was visited on 23 March 2004 by a group of 55 pupils from the Morgan Academy in Dundee for a talk and discussion on studying Islam and Muslims. Professor Malory Nye and some of our postgraduate students delivered the talk and answered questions from the students.

And from Tuesday 11 to Thursday 13 May 2004, the Institute hosted a three-day event involving over 150 pupils from eight of Dundee's Secondary Schools. The pupils were taking part in workshops aimed at teaching how people of different faiths can learn to live together. The events were organised by the Religious Education Movement in Scotland (REMS), as a pilot project on 'The Same but Different' theme sponsored by A Company of Speakers, and were run in conjunction with Dundee City Council. The Institute were very happy to make our facilities available for this very interesting work. During their day of activity the pupils, from first and second year classes, took part in a number of classes including drama, drumming and story telling. The schools taking part were Harris Academy, Braeview Academy, Lawside Academy, Grove Academy, Menzieshill High School, Craigie High school, St John's High School and Morgan Academy.

In August 2006, the Institute extended an invitation to the Principals of every high school in Dundee to make contact with the Institute if they were interested in bringing a group of pupils to visit us, with the available option of organising a debate on multiculturalism here at the Institute.

I was also invited to sit at the top table of the Dundee City Council Education Department's, Focus of Achievement Awards on 14 September 2006 at the Caird Hall. First Minister Jack McConnell opened the ceremony with Councillor Jill Shimi, Head of Dundee City Council Administration, and the Director of Dundee City Council Education Department, Mrs Anne Wilson.

In 2005, I proposed to Dundee City Council Education Department to add another category to their Focus of Achievement Awards, which was launched in 2004. I am pleased that the Department has added this category 'Award for Multicultural Education' for the 2007 awards which will be sponsored and presented by the Institute during the Focus of Achievement Awards Ceremony to be held on 13 September 2007. The Award will be presented to a school in Dundee that is judged to have made the most substantial contribution to multicultural education in Dundee.

Dundee City Council Social Work Department

On 2 November 2005, I was invited as the keynote speaker to address an awards ceremony given by Dundee City Council Social Work Department to recognise the achievements of staff personal development and the gaining of educational qualifications.

As part of the Institute's commitment to build partnerships with the local communities in Dundee, the Institute signed a Memorandum of Understanding on 11 January with the Social Work Department of Dundee City Council to develop a mutually beneficial practical relationship between the Institute and the Social Work Department.

The signing of this Memorandum of Understanding with the Social Work Department is another example of our commitment to the citizens of multicultural Dundee. The Institute looks forward to building upon the early initiative with the Social Work Department to establish and develop links with staff and services in Dundee and to strengthening the relationship between the Social Work Department and the Institute.

On 27 January 2006, the Institute provided conference and meeting facilities to the Social Work Department, for 30 senior managers. In addition, the Fourth Summer School students were very fortunate to take part in a specially prepared all-day event with the Dundee City Council's Social Work Department. The intention of the programme was for the students to grasp a basic understanding of the department's activities, including their aims and objectives. Members of staff who participated in the day event also attended the evening lecture and dinner held on the 11 July 2006 at the Hilton Hotel.

Dundee City Council Leisure and Communities Department

The relationship between the Institute and Dundee City Council was further enhanced in 2006 with the signing of a Memorandum of Understanding with the Leisure and Communities Department on 6 July 2006 at the Institute during the Fourth Summer School.

The Fourth Summer School students were also very fortunate to take part in specially prepared half day events with the Leisure and Communities Department. The intention of the programme was for the students to grasp a basic understanding of the Leisure and Community Department's activities, including their aims and objectives. The opportunity was given to all students to visit some of the facilities of this department.

Tayside NHS Health Board

On 25 March 2002 the Institute received a visit from Mr Peter Bates, Chairman of NHS Tayside Health Board, and Professor Tony Wells, its Chief Executive. This visit gave birth to a desire to develop a firmer relationship, which then led to the signing of a Memorandum of Understanding between the Institute and NHS Tayside Health Board on 3 May 2002. The memorandum articulates the commitment of both parties to promote greater understanding of Islamic tradition and culture by developing a modular training programme for public sector staff, including Health Service staff. This training will allow the NHS to provide an enhanced level of care and service to members of the community.

Following this signing the Institute has organised the delivery of three workshops for cultural, religious and spirituality awareness training for NHS front-line staff. The pilot workshops have been delivered at Stracathro Hospital (Brechin), Murray Royal Hospital (Perth) and Ninewells Hospital (Dundee). Feedbacks from the participants of these workshops have been very positive.

Dundee United Football Club

The Institute is also building a strong relationship with Dundee United Football Club (DUFC). This started with a visit by Mr Scott Carnegie, Chairman of DUFC on 13 August 2002. I was then invited to a hospitality lunch and was offered seats in the Director's box for a match on 14 September 2002. This was followed closely by an invitation to visit Tannadice Park to Mr Mirza Al Sayegh, Chairman of the Institute Board, and Mr Mohamad Obeid Bin Ghannam on 16 September 2002. The visit received good media coverage and it also strengthened the relationship even further.

Being committed to serving the community, the Institute assisted in introducing DUFC to leading football clubs in the UAE by ensuring that Mr Scott Carnegie, then Chairman of DUFC, was invited to be part of the Dundee Delegation to Dubai on 20 – 25 October 2002. The Institute has also taken up two perimeter boards at Tannadice Park. The two boards advertise the cooperation between the Institute and DUFC and they read 'Serving the Communities' and 'Arab United Working with the People of United Arab Emirates' respectively.

Tayside Police

On 14 March 2006, Professor Malory Nye, Depute Principal for Academic Affairs, participated in the Police Diversity Training workshop on Islam and Muslims. His presentation focused on 'Multiculturalism, diversity and the Study of Islam and Muslims'.

During my meeting with Mr John Vine, Chief Constable of Tayside Police, on 6 February 2007, we discussed the possibility of the Institute providing training to Tayside Police Force in areas relating to Islam and Muslims. This was followed up by another meeting with Wilma Canning, Tayside Policy Equal Opportunities and Policy Adviser and Sergeant Norrie McPherson, Staff Development Unit on 14 February 2007. We are now in the process of developing tailored training programmes to address the needs of Tayside Police at the executive, middle management, and grass roots levels.

Dundee Civic Trust

I met Jack Searle, Chairman and Tom Devaney, Public Relations Officer of the Dundee Civic Trust on 14 June 2006 to introduce the Civic Trust to the Institute and discuss membership options. The Institute became a corporate member of the Dundee Civic Trust on 15 June 2006.

Community Links

I have seen our links with external institutions, whether nationally or internationally, as part and parcel of our efforts to serve the communities. The benefits from all the relationships that we form will ultimately be channelled back to the communities in one way or another.

For example, as a result of the very good relationship the Institute has with Dubai, Dundee as a City has benefited from a twinning arrangement between the two cities, where the Institute was the catalyst for the process.

Religious Education Movement in Scotland

I have accepted the invitation to become Honorary Vice-President of the Religious Education Movement in Scotland. The movement is a Scottish Charity which has developed from an older charity called the Christian Education Movement. It exists to challenge young people to reflect on shared human experience and living faith traditions in order to be responsible members of our pluralist society. It also aspires to challenge the educational community with a vision of education which is committed to the development of integrated persons in the context of a just and open society. The Institute hosted the Religious Education Movement in Scotland AGM and Council meeting on 6 December 2003.

Moderator of the General Assembly of the Church of Scotland

On 12 March 2004, the Institute was visited by the Right Reverend Professor Iain Torrance, in his capacity as the Moderator of the General Assembly of the Church of Scotland. The Moderator had just returned to Scotland from several days visiting British troops in Iraq and the visit to the Institute was his first public engagement in Scotland since.

During his visit the Moderator attended a lunch at the Hilton Dundee with senior figures from the city. Before welcoming the Moderator, I called for a minute's silence as a mark of respect for those who have been murdered in the terrorist atrocity in Madrid. My speech highlighted the efforts being made by the Institute to provide a platform on which cultures and religions can be shared to foster a better understanding between them.

In a very reflective speech to an invited audience, Professor Torrance drew attention to the need for more academic debate and discussion on all aspects of our understanding of Islam and Muslims in the contemporary world. He also spoke about Christian-Muslim intellectual dialogue and interaction and how it can serve to benefit the wider society. He strongly commended the Institute for the work that it is pioneering. In his opening address he stated: 'I am honoured to be present as Moderator of the General Assembly, and thus publicly to support your institution and the initiative of the Scottish Executive in promoting One Scotland, Many Cultures.'

Professor Torrance is not only a senior churchman, he is also a senior academic Christian theologian, and at that time he held a Chair in Divinity at the University of Aberdeen. On retiring from his position as Moderator, in summer 2004 Professor Torrance took up the position of President of Princeton Theological College. Although the Institute is disappointed that we did not have the opportunity to work with him at the University of Aberdeen, we wish him very well in this new post.

Relationship with Leaders of the Communities

I have also taken the initiatives to present ourselves to all MSPs. In fact, several have already visited the Institute and they have all expressed their admiration of the efforts put in by the Institute on building bridges between the Muslim world and the Western world. Indeed our endeavour is not only to produce future scholars in the field of the Study of Islam and Muslims but also to provide a meeting point between the Western and Muslim worlds and to encourage scholarship and academic co-operation between the two worlds. In our efforts to achieve this, we aspire to act as a national resource in the Scottish and UK context for consultation by government bodies, public organisations, industry, business and the media. This is being appreciated by everyone, academics and politicians alike.

John Swinney MSP, then the National Convener of the Scottish National Party, visited the Institute on 17 June 2002. he expressed his belief that the Institute provides an excellent facility for the students and academics, as well as helping to build strong bonds within the diverse communities of Scotland. Ian Luke MP, Member of Parliament for Dundee East, also visited the Institute on 22 August 2002. Similarly, Mr Luke stated that he believes the Institute is a very important step in the regeneration of the City of Dundee.

Other politicians who have visited the Institute include Mr Tom McCabe (MSP), Scottish Minister for Finance and Public Service Reform, Mrs Margaret Curran(MSP), Minister for Parliamentary Business, Sir David Steel (MSP), former Scottish Parliament's Presiding Officer, Mr Nicol Stephen (MSP), the Scottish Deputy First Minister, Councillor Fraser Macpherson (14 January 2002), Mr John McAllion (MSP) (15 April 2002), Mrs Shona Robison (MSP) (22 April 2002 and a number of times), Brian Adam (MSP) (30 April 2002), Richard Baker (MSP), and Ms Kate McLean. Mr Ernie Ross former MP has also visited the Institute several times.

Following a debate in Dundee City Council regarding the signing of the Sister Cities Agreement between Dubai and Dundee, I invited

Dundee SNP Councillors to a meeting at the Institute. On 18 February 2004, eleven local SNP Councillors came for two meetings, one in the morning and the other in the early evening. At the end of those meetings it was felt by all the SNP councillors that the visits were very important and informative and helped develop bonds of mutual understanding and friendship. Lord Elder and I also met with Labour Councillor Julie Sturrock and Marlyn Glen MSP on the same issue on 19 February 2004.

Religious Communities

The Institute received a visit from the participants of the Churches' Commission on Mission (CCOM) Africa Forum Consultation on 17 April 2002. This large delegation, consisting of representatives from various churches in the UK, Africa and Europe, was extremely pleased to see the development of this Institute. The comments they expressed were very positive.

On 8 May that year, I participated in a seminar at St Mary's Episcopal Church, Newport-on-Tay, at which another panellist was the Reverend Neville Chamberlain, Episcopalian Bishop of Brechin and member of the Institute council. The seminar was chaired by Professor Alan Dobson of Dundee University. I also led a training forum organised by CAIRS in Dunblane on 21 May.

The Institute organised an open evening for the local Muslim communities on 23 May 2002. I then on 13 July 2002 led a forum organised by the Fellowship of Reconciliation of Scotland at St John's Kirk, Perth. Later in the year, I attended a dinner hosted by the Lord Provost of Dundee in honour of the Rt Reverend Riah Abu El-Assal, Bishop of Jerusalem, on 5 October 2002. Additionally, I have participated in a seminar on 'Justice and Peace: Jewish and Islamic perspectives' organised by Leckie Church in Peebles on 8 October 2002. Another panellist was Rabbi Peter Tobias of Glasgow New Synagogue.

Visit by Church Group

The Institute received a visit by a group of Ecumenical Officers from the Church of Scotland on 7 May 2003. The Ecumenical Officers, from various places around Scotland, were attending a consultation meeting in Dundee and Rev Erik Cramb, a member of the Institute Council, introduced the group to the Institute.

A training Seminar for Ministers of the Church of Scotland

Following discussions initiated by Rev Erik Cramb, 7 February 2007 Professor Malory Nye and Dr Alhagi Manta Drammeh gave a training seminar for ministers of the Church of Scotland at their annual in-service training conference at Gartmore House, Aberfoyle. The training focused on understanding Islam and Muslims in a multicultural society, under the heading of 'Preaching in a multicultural society: the big picture'. In total 19 ministers and deacons took part in the training, from many different parts of Scotland. The participation of staff from the Institute was very well received, and feedback highlighted that they considered the issues of multiculturalism and understanding Islam and Muslims to be something of great importance to the work of the church today.

Dundee Arab Intellectuals Meeting

As part of the efforts to serve the various communities in Dundee, the Institute initiated an informal get-together for several Arab intellectuals currently based in Dundee. The event, held on 14 May 2003, was attended by approximately 15 intellectuals. The event succeeded in ensuring that the Institute is always open to the local communities.

Mass of Thanksgiving

On 24 February 2006, I attended the Mass of Thanksgiving in the Caird Hall to mark the Silver Jubilee of the Episcopal Ordination of the Rt Rev Vincent Logan, Bishop of Dunkeld, to celebrate a quarter of a century since his ordination.

Scottish Churches Industrial Mission

On 13 February 2006, I met Reverend Gareth Jones of Scottish Churches Industrial Mission at the Institute. We discussed the work of the Institute and that of SCIM. It was with sadness that I learnt of the Reverend Jones recent death.

Rotary Clubs

On 10 November 2003 the Institute was visited by North Fife Rotary Club. The club had shown an interest in the Al-Maktoum Institute, and decided to hold their annual trip to the Institute for a guided tour of the building and to hear more about our activities.

On Tuesday 25 April 2006, I gave a talk on the Institute's vision and New Agenda to the Claverhouse Rotary Club at their weekly lunch-time meeting held at the Queens Hotel in Dundee. I also welcomed Dr Nesbitt Torrance of Fife Rotary Club, who arranged an introduction to the Institute for the Reverend Ian Patton, of the same Club and a former Minister in Jerusalem.

Public Relations Activities

Public relations activities continue to be undertaken with various stakeholders on group and one to one basis. These are mainly through meetings, and invitations to host or give talks. The Institute takes all public relations activities seriously and endeavours to build upon our past success by utilising the public relations tools that are most aligned to meeting and achieving our strategic objectives.

We are extremely keen to engage with the local community and regularly attend the West End Community Council Meetings, keeping them informed of the Institute activities and plans for the Multicultural Centre.

West End Community Council

On 14 February 2006, I attended the West End Community Council meeting and gave a verbal presentation regarding the Institute and the forthcoming Al-Maktoum Multicultural Centre, with a question and answer session at the end of the talk.

In 2006, many members of the West End Community Council have shown their support for the Institute by attending numerous events including the Open Day, 7 July Memorial, Tartan Tea Party, DVD launch, and the Fourth Summer School Concluding Ceremony in July 2006. I also met Anne Prescott on 9 August 2006 to discuss the top soil on the site of the Al-Maktoum Multicultural Centre.

I was again invited to give a presentation regarding the Al-Maktoum Multicultural Centre to the WECC on 12 September at the Logie St Johns Cross Church. WECC members were given an informative and interesting presentation on the Centre and each individual was given a Newsletter detailing the purpose and facilities of the Centre.

Receipt of the 1998 Poem for Scotland

On 17 March 2003, the winner of the 1998 Poem for Scotland competition, Scott Martin, presented me an illustrated copy of his prize winning poem 'The Ploughman'. The poem, whose main themes embrace reconciliation and the future in the aftermath of war, was translated in Arabic language by the Institute.

'The Ploughman' has been translated into several languages including Gaelic, and is now on display on various locations around Scotland and even abroad. Mr Martin, a local poet who lives on Blackness Road, was kind enough to dedicate the Arabic translation of the poem to the children of Palestine, past, present and future.

Peter Adamson's Book on Dundee

I was approached by photographer, Peter Adamson regarding the Institute's being included in a book of photography about the City of Dundee which would reflect the importance of the Institute to the City. The book focuses on different aspects of Dundee such as jute, architecture, churches, leisure etc. The Institute is placed in the 'Higher Education Institutions' Chapter. Mr Adamson took some images around the campus including shots of students and the Principal, and these images now form two pages of the 208 page hardback book which was published on 7 October 2006

The First Open Day 2006

As part of the strategy to raise the profile of the Institute, an Open Day was organised on Saturday 18 March 2006. It proved to be a success, with the number of visitors reaching approximately 130. The Open Day received coverage on the local radio station Wave 102 three times in the morning prior to the event. The response by visitors suggests that the day was a clear success, resulting in further exposure for the Institute and a continued rise in profile locally.

The Open Day was supported by the Al-Maktoum Foundation and also Emirates Airlines. Emirates Airline was kind enough to provide a return economy flight from Glasgow to Dubai as the prize for the Open Day Prize Draw. This was won by Lorna Drummond from Dundee and was presented to her on 5 April 2006. Denise Holmes, the Sales Manager for Emirates Scotland, attended the Open Day on behalf of Emirates, operating a stand with information for visitors to the Institute.

Remembering 7 July London Bombings

The students from the Fourth Summer School along with the Lord Mayor of Wurzburg, Dr Pia Beckmann, and members of Institute Staff, Students, Council and the local community took part in the national two-minute silence to remember victims of last year's July 7 bombings. As part of the remembrance ceremony there was a balloon launch at the end of the two-minute silence that took place at 12 noon. There were fifty-two balloons, one for each person who died, each with a card attached with the name of one of the victims. The local evening newspaper led with a photograph of the remembrance on the evening of 7 July.

Sponsorship and Support to Local Institutions, Clubs and Societies in Dundee

We actively seek to work with organisations that share our aspiration to serve the local communities. Thus, we have provided funding and sponsorship to several institutions and organisations in Dundee during the course of the last five years.

University of Abertay Dundee

To help the University of Abertay Dundee enhance its research capacity, Al-Maktoum Foundation of Dubai, through Al-Maktoum Institute for Arabic and Islamic Studies, has donated a sum of £100,000 to fund a research project in image analysis. The project was chosen following an internal competition run by Abertay. The funds were given to Abertay in January 2003.

Rep Theatre Production

Sponsoring the Shakespearean comedy *Twelfth Night* at Dundee Rep Theatre is just one of the Institute's many contributions to the communities. There is so much that the world of arts and theatre can offer in terms of educating the public and the Institute is proud to be the sponsor of this play.

This great Shakespearean comedy portrays the desperate ends people go to for love. *Twelfth Night* is a farcical tale of misplaced passions and mistaken identity, with a splendid array of riotous characters, razor sharp wit and yellow-gartered seduction. This was a very well-received production, highly praised by critics and audiences alike, with a very high media profile and playing, over the three weeks, to in excess of 4,700 theatregoers. We were pleased that the sponsorship was announced in the *Courier* newspaper twice, the *Evening Telegraph*, the *Forfar Dispatch*, and the *Perthshire Advertiser*, and were particularly pleased with the *Independent*'s review which also credited the Institute.

Shakespeare's *Twelfth Night* was shown at Dundee Rep Theatre on 3 September – 20 September 2003. 25 complimentary tickets were used by the Institute guests at performances of their choice.

Lochee Freestyle Karate Club

Lochee Freestyle is an active club that trains children and young adults from all backgrounds. The members are from a diverse cultural and religious upbringing and the Institute believes that helping the club would help foster a multicultural environment in the local communities.

The club received a cheque from the Institute in a simple ceremony on 20 June 2003.

Fun Factory Out-of-School Club, Park Place Primary School

The Fun Factory received their cheque from the Institute on 20 June 2003 to help with the running of the club. The out-of-school club had been trying to obtain donations from other organisations around Dundee and the Institute was happy to assist in this matter. Similar to the Karate Club, the Fun Factory is also another Dundee-based organisation that shares the Institute's vision of multiculturalism. The children who attend the Fun Factory are from diverse backgrounds and different ethnicities.

Al-Maktoum Multicultural Garden for Dundee Fun Factory after School Club

The Al-Maktoum Institute sponsored the creation of a new multicultural garden in a formerly barren area of land within Park Place School. The idea to create a garden space out of waste ground came from Valerie Lynch, the coordinator of the Fun Factory. The Fun Factory and Park Place Primary School cater for a large number of children from Dundee's multicultural communities and do a marvellous job of encouraging integration and multiculturalism.

On my visit to the club on 9 July 2004, I presented a £2000 cheque to the Out-of-School Club based at Park Place Primary School. I was accompanied by a number of students from the UAE who were attending the Institute summer school. The Club coordinator, Valerie Lynch, said, 'Thanks to the generosity of the Al-Maktoum Institute and the hard work of the staff and children, we will be able to create a green space that will have plants, shrubs, flowers, a special seating area and art work that will reflect the multicultural diversity of the children who attend the club and who attend Park Place primary School.' The Institute is delighted to continue its support for the Fun Factory Out-of-School Club.

On 8 July 2005, I formally opened the Garden at a special ceremony attended by the fifty female students from the Summer School, Lord Provost John Letford and Dundee City Council Head of Administration, Councillor Jill Shimi.

Iftar for Muslim Students in Dundee during the month of Ramadan

As part of building bridges with communities in Dundee, the Institute sponsored Iftar dinners for Muslim students in Dundee during the month of Ramadan. Dundee University Islamic Society provides Iftar to over one hundred Muslim students, including those at Ninewells Hospital. Al-Maktoum Institute was pleased to be able to help and sponsored DUIS for thirteen days' Iftar. Similarly, Abertay University Islamic Society (AIS) makes Iftar provision for Muslim students studying at the University. The Institute sponsored seventeen days of Iftars for twenty to thirty students.

At the Institute itself, our twenty to twenty-five Muslim students, most of whom are from overseas, enjoyed Iftars at the Institute three days a week sponsored by the Institute and provided by the Al-Maktoum Institute Students Society. In Ramadan 2004, the Institute sponsored Iftar for staff and students at the Institute during the month of Ramadan through the Al-Maktoum Institute Students Society.

Hajj

Through the generosity of HH Shaikh Hamdan Bin Rashid Al-Maktoum, the Institute administered the Hajj trips twice in 2004 and 2005. The Hajj trip in 2004/1424 was possible for a delegation of ten staff, students and Institute Council members to perform Hajj (pilgrimage to Makkah). The ten names were chosen at random publicly by Professor Malory Nye from all those who were eligible and had applied to go on Hajj. The main stipulation was that this must be the first time that all applicants would perform Hajj. The group left from the Al-Maktoum Institute on 22 January 2004 and returned safely on 10 February 2004.

In 2005, ten individuals from the British/Scottish Muslim communities within Dundee were selected to perform this Muslim duty. The ten names were chosen at random publicly from all of those who were eligible and applied to go on Hajj. The main stipulation was that this must be the first time that all applicants would perform Hajj. The group left from the Al-Maktoum Institute on 12 January 2005 and returned safely on 2 February 2005.

The two trips were hailed a big success and the groups expressed their deep appreciation to HH Shaikh Hamdan Bin Rashid Al-Maktoum for his generosity in sponsoring, what was an unforgettable trips of a lifetime.

New Criteria for our Sponsorship Scheme

To promote multiculturalism at all levels, the Institute sponsorship scheme, from 2004, was only provided to organisations and institutions that have demonstrated their commitment to multiculturalism and for projects to further this aim.

Al-Maktoum Foundation

The Al-Maktoum Foundation was created on 18 March 2005 to achieve the following objectives:

i. To promote, for the benefit of the public, equality of opportunity and good race, religious and cultural relations between persons of different racial/religious groups and to advance the religion of Islam and to support and promote a better understanding of Islam and Muslims and to advance public education in the history, languages, traditions, customs and heritage of the various communities, nationalities and races;

ii. To promote for the benefit of the inhabitants of the United Kingdom and its environs without distinction of sex, sexuality, political, religious or other opinions by associating the local statutory authorities, voluntary organisations and inhabitants in a common effort to advance education and to provide facilities or assist in the provision of facilities in the interest of social welfare for recreation and other leisure-time occupation so that their conditions of life may be improved.

These objectives will be pursued particularly through the administration of projects in the United Kingdom and the rest of Europe including the Al-Maktoum Cultural Centre in Dundee. The Foundation will provide financial grants and funding to support local organisations sharing the Foundation's objectives, i.e. promoting multiculturalism. Examples of such funding include:

1. Scholarships to students to pursue their postgraduate studies at a Masters and PhD level in the study of Islam and Muslims at Al-Maktoum Institute. These scholarships have previously been funded and administered by the Al-Maktoum Institute.
2. Sponsorship of local projects at various community levels. Previous projects sponsored in this way by the Al-Maktoum Institute include the following: the Fun Factory Out-of-School Club, Dundee; Dundee Rep Theatre's production of the play *Twelfth Night*; the Lochee Karate Club, Dundee; and the Multicultural Garden at Park Place Primary School, Dundee. Responsibility for such sponsorship will now be with the Al-Maktoum Foundation.
3. Facilitate British/Scottish citizens who cannot financially afford to go for Hajj, i.e. Muslim pilgrimage to Makkah.

Following the establishment of the Al-Maktoum Foundation, all these activities which were in the past funded by the Al-Maktoum Institute will now be the responsibility of the new Foundation.

Scholarships

In order to encourage students to pursue postgraduate studies at the Institute, His Highness Shaikh Hamdan Bin Rashid Al-Maktoum has generously funded many scholarships which have given great benefits to young postgraduate students from around the world. Postgraduate students from the Arab world, Far East, and Europe as well as the United Kingdom are studying under the schemes. This prestigious scholarship scheme is another serious effort on the part of Al-Maktoum Institute for Arabic and Islamic Studies and Al-Maktoum Foundation to serve the local, national and international communities, and a great human investment to prepare an academic team of young scholars as specialists in the field of the Study of Islam and Muslims. Winners of the scholarship undertake the taught full-time MLitt programme in either Islamic Studies or Islamicjerusalem Studies, according to the scheme they apply for.

Al-Maktoum Multicultural Centre in Dundee[2]

Following the agreement of HH Shaikh Hamdan Bin Rashid Al-Maktoum in December 2003 to build Al-Maktoum Multicultural Centre in Dundee, on 13 May 2004, Al-Maktoum Foundation concluded the Missive to purchase the site of the former Harris Academy Annexe from

---

[2]   The following is a short summary of the progress made so far towards the building of the Al-Maktoum Multicultural Centre in Dundee from December 2003 to July 2006:

15 January 2003 During the Al-Maktoum Institute's Formal Dinner to announce the appointment of Lord Elder as the Chancellor of Al-Maktoum Institute, Mr Mirza Al-Sayegh announced that the Al-Maktoum Foundation would be building a Cultural Centre in Dundee.

29 August 2003 A letter sent from Mr. Douglas Grimond, Director of the Economic Development Department at Dundee City Council, to Mr Mirza Al-Saygeh identifying a site for the Cultural Centre.

15 December 2003 Lord Elder, Chancellor of the Al-Maktoum Institute, presented a letter to HH Shaikh Hamdan Bin Rashid Al-Maktoum regarding the proposed Cultural Centre, to which HH Shaikh Hamdan gave his approval and full support. The approval of HH Shaikh Hamdan Bin Rashid Al-Maktoum was reported in the newspapers in both the Emirates and Scotland.   —

Dundee City Council to house the Centre. We had worked with Dundee City Council's Economic Development Department to identify the site for the centre.

This site has been derelict since fire destroyed the building a number of years ago. Local Councillor Jim Barrie was quoted as saying he was keen to see the site developed into a centre which would enhance the whole area. In addition, he said he 'would certainly welcome any proposal to develop the site sympathetically for the benefit of all of the community of the Blackness area. The ward, at present, has no leisure or sports facilities, nor a hall of any size that can be used by the local residents.'

The vision is that the complex will create a better understanding between the communities in Dundee, and serve as a model for Scotland and the United Kingdom. Needless to say, this significant project will also create jobs for the local people both in the short term and the long term.

In order to take the project a step further, I visited the Islamic Cultural Centre of Ireland on 29 May 2003 to explore the concept and design of the centre to be built in Dundee. I talked to the architect of the Dublin Islamic Cultural Centre and was also given a tour. It is envisaged that the Multicultural Centre in Dundee will be different in concept and design for the one in Dublin and on a smaller scale.

–   Mr Mirza Al-Sayegh replied to Dundee City Council' letter confirming the purchase of the site.

10 April 2004 Mr. Mirza Al-Sayegh appointed the design team to build the Cultural Centre. The team included four firms.

1 Feburary 2005 Mr. Mirza Al- Sayegh also appointed Mr Philip Hodson as Project Manger for building the Centre. Since that date, the Institute's involvement was limited and the Project Manager was dealing directly with both Mr Mirza Al-Sayegh and the design team.

18 March 2005 Al-Maktoum Foundation was registered in Scotland as a company limited by guarantee and a charity to administer the Al-Maktoum Multicultural Centre in Dundee.

26 August 2005 The application for planning permission to build the Al-Maktoum Multicultural Centre was submitted to Dundee City Council.

23 January 2006 Dundee City Council granted the planning permission to build Al-Maktoum Multicultural Centre.

17 July 2006 At the concluding ceremony for the 4th Summer School, Mr Mirza Al-Sayegh in his speech reassured both the Scottish Executive and the citizens of Dundee that we are not building only a mosque or a facility for Muslims, but a centre for all the communities, which will start very soon.

On 10 April 2004, the project of building Al-Maktoum Cultural Centre, which will be a landmark for the City, took a significant step forward with the selection of the design team responsible for managing the project. I meet the Design Team on 11 May 2004. The team is led by Mr Fred Stephen of James F Stephen Architects and Interior Designers, based at Glamis, Angus. It consists of Mr David Stephen, James F Stephen Architects and Interior Designers; Mr Bruce Rae and Mr Doug Patterson, D I Burchell & Partners Quantity Surveyors; Mr Alan Driscoll, Ove Arup & Partners, Structural Engineers; and Mr Bob Hopkins, David Elder & Partners, Mechanical & Electrical Engineers. As the policy of the Al-Maktoum Institute is always trying to generate economic activity locally, the design team was chosen from the expertise available in the local area. On 23 April 2004, Mr Fred Stephen visited the Centre in Dublin.

On 8 October 2004, I meet Councillor Jim Barrie, local councillor for the Blackness area and two members of the Blackness residents' association. It was also attended also by James F Stephen, head of the design team. The purpose of the meeting was to shed some light on the Cultural Centre, as local residents were asking for more information regarding the architectural and practical plans. Both the councillor and the two members of the residents' group were very impressed with the concept and the proposed design for the Al-Maktoum Cultural Centre, and indicated that this will be a great resource for the local people.

On 26 October 2004, I also met Alan Ball and Charlie Ward of Dundee Texol Stars Ice Hockey Club, who explained that their club would like to use the facilities at the Centre when it is built. On 28 October 2004, I meet Ben Gibson and Simon Bain from Hillcrest Housing Association who expressed also an interest for their tenants to use the facilities at the Cultural Centre when it is built.

To develop this important project, Mr Philip Hodson was appointed on 1 Feburary 2005 as the project manager. He held several meetings with the design team and the application for planning permission was lodged with Dundee City Council on 26 August 2005. To present the project to the local residents I attended the Blackness Area Residents Association Annual General Meeting on 16 March 2005. My open and informative discussion on the Centre received a favourable response from those present.

Dundee City Council granted permission for the Multicultural Centre on Monday 23 January 2006. The Al-Maktoum Foundation hopes to see work begin on the building in 2007.

The Main Facilities of Al-Maktoum Multicultural Centre

The design of the building reflects the concept of openness. It is to be a multi-purpose building, and will be three storeys high. The main facilities of the Multicultural Centre will include, among others, the following:

Ground Floor Level: An Internet Café for the use of the wider communities, in particular the youth and senior members of the communities. A large Exhibition Hall will be for the benefit of the whole communities to exhibit and to use this open space to promote good relations between people, nations, cultures, and religions. There will be a Public Conference Hall for the use of agencies, institutions, community groups, charities and businesses. Providing this facility will hopefully address the gap in the available conference facilities market in Dundee. A Small Prayer Hall (Mosque) within the Multicultural Centre will form a small part of the building, and will incorporate traditional design features including a domed roof and a non-functioning minaret. It is going to be a public worship space which will be open to all communities to visit.

First Floor Level: A Public Library will house a substantial collection in the field of the Study of Islam and Muslims for research purposes and public use. It is intended that the library will in time house a leading collection in this area in the whole of Europe and will be an educational facility for the people of Dundee and Scotland.

Second Floor Level: Flexible Meeting (Rooms) this space could be used by local community groups, charities, and families for functions, meetings and celebrations.

In short, Al-Maktoum Foundation is building a Multicultural Centre and not an Islamic cultural centre. It is not building a mosque or a facility available only to Muslims in the City, but a Multicultural Centre which will be a facility for all the communities of the City of Dundee and of Scotland, and a model for multiculturalism in Scotland. It will work to promote understanding and bring communities together

9

SERVING THE INTERNATIOAL COMMUNITIES

In addition to our work with the local and national communities, have been actively working to serve the international communities. The main aim is to continue setting the agenda for cultural engagement at the communities' levels through providing practical beneficial relationships to develop the relationship between these communities.

Hosting One of the Most Senior Delegations from the Muslim World Ever to Visit Dundee

In spite of the hectic schedule at the foundation stage of the Institute's history, we successfully organised a major event. The Institute went a step further in building bridges between the Muslim and the Western Worlds by hosting a dialogue with one of the most senior delegations from the Muslim world ever to visit Dundee. On Saturday, 9 March 2002, the Institute organised a meeting to discuss 'The Role of Islam and Muslims in the West'. Not only was the event a great success, it also raised the profile of the Institute and helped to establish good relationships locally, nationally and internationally. The meeting was attended by a delegation of Muslim scholars and dignitaries led by HE Dr. Abdullah bin Abdul Mohsin Al-Turki, Secretary General of the Muslim World League. The delegation included, among others, HE Dr Kamil Al-Sharif, former Minister of Islamic Endowment and Islamic Affairs of Jordan, Shaikh Hussain Aale-Sheikh, Imam of the Prophet's Mosque, and HE Dr Surin Pitsuwan, former Foreign Secretary of Thailand and current member of Thai Parliament. Academics, politicians, representatives of nearly all the main churches in Scotland, and many communities' leaders took part as well.

The delegation was extremely impressed by our links with academics, politicians and community leaders. Although at the initial stage the delegation had not been planning to visit Dundee at all, they did so after my last minute persuasion. Members of the delegation said that the visit to the Institute was the best during their visit to the United Kingdom which had included Oxford University, London, Birmingham University and the House of Lords. This meeting received excellent coverage by the media both locally and abroad, especially in the Arab world.

As a result of the meeting, it was agreed that Al-Maktoum Institute for Arabic and Islamic Studies and the Islamic Universities League would organise a joint international symposium on Islamic Studies. This symposium was hosted by the Institute in Dundee on 17-18th March 2004.

Books for Baghdad

The Institute's commitment to serve the communities is not just confined to the surrounding areas. Our commitment to promote learning and support scholarly works benefited Iraq and the people of Iraq. On 29 May 2003, I flew to Dublin to meet Dr Nooh Al-Kaddo, Director of Ireland's Islamic Cultural Centre in Dublin, for discussions about the immediate purchase of books to replace those lost in the looting and burning during the invasion of Iraq. Following that discussion, Dr Al-Kaddo departed for Iraq on 4 June 2003 to work with the universities there to identify their needs.

This extremely important project enabled libraries at the universities in Baghdad, Basra and Mosul to replace at least part of the valuable books and manuscripts that have been lost. HH Shaikh Hamdan Bin Rashid Al-Maktoum decided to donate $300,000.

Dr Al-Kaddo came to meet me in Dundee on 16 September 2003 when it was agreed that it would be the responsibility of Ireland's Islamic Cultural Centre, Dublin, to purchase the Arabic titles from Egypt. It was also agreed that the Al-Maktoum Institute would be responsible for the purchasing of the English titles from Scotland. The Institute received a book list from the Universities of Baghdad, Mosul and Basra.

This was a tremendous cause and the Institute was very proud to be able to play a significant part in rebuilding the education systems in Iraq. We have been applauded by librarians worldwide for this effort, including from Harvard University.

Malaysian High Commissioner Visit

The Malaysian High Commissioner to the UK, HE Dato' Abd Aziz Mohammed, visited the Institute on 27 May 2005. He brought with him a delegation of senior officials from the High Commission, representing academic, tourism and business interests. The Malaysian delegation consisted of HE Dato' Abd Aziz Mohammed, Malaysian High Commissioner to UK, Mr C Mathialakan, Director, Malaysian Industrial Dev Authority, Ms Wan Norma Wan Daud, Trade Commissioner, Malaysia External Trade Dev Corp, Ms Hasanah Abd. Hamid, Minister Counsellor, Malaysian High Commission, Dr Syed Raisudin Syed Abdullah, Director, Malaysian Student Dept, Mr Mohmed Razip Hasan, Director, Malaysian Tourism Promotion Board, Mr Sharipudin Kasim, Education Attache, Public Services Department, and Mr Mohamad Libra Lee Haniff, Deputy Director, Malaysia Tourism Promotion Board.

The Malaysian delegation was briefed about the Vision and Mission of the Al-Maktoum Institute. They were also briefed about the latest developments in the Institute's relationship with Malaysia, especially with the University of Malaya, the Malaysian Prime Minister's Office and the Malaysian Minister of Higher Education. The delegation was given a tour of the facilities available at the Institute and met the Malaysian students studying here.

At the end of the visit the Institute organised a business lunch with various senior representatives of Dundee's business community and with politicians including the Lord Provost and all of Dundee's parliamentary representatives.

Liechtenstein

One of the countries with which Al-Maktoum Institute has developed links recently is Liechtenstein. This small European state has much in common with Dubai, both in its size and in the role of its royal family, which has responsibility for economic matters. They are keen to develop links with Dubai, and have therefore made contact with Al-Maktoum Institute.

Following the visit to the Institute by Ghayth Armanazi the former Arab League Ambassador for the UK, and Daniel Morler of LGT Bank, I was invited to Liechtenstein to meet Prince Philipp. Prince Philipp is the second brother of the Ruling Prince Hans-Adam II, and is also the Chairman of the Board of Trustees of LGT Foundation. On 28 January 2005, I visited Liechtenstein where I met Prince Philipp in the LGT Bank. I was warmly welcomed by Prince Philipp at the beginning of the meeting where a brief introduction to Liechtenstein was given, highlighting in particular the country's financial system in addition to the Higher Education System, and the International Academy of Philosophy. During the meeting I met Sir Roger Tomkys, and Richard Muir, and Daniel Morler and Ghayth Armanazi once more.

I, then, briefed the Prince Philipp in full about the Vision of Shaikh Hamdan and Dundee Declaration. Prince Philipp was impressed and intrigued to learn about the project, praising Shaikh Hamdan and his practical model. Sir Roger Tomkys and Richard Muir, both former diplomats, were also overwhelmed to hear about the practical model.

I extended an invitation to Prince Philipp to visit the Institute. In addition to accepting the invitation, Prince Philipp said he would consider establishing a scholarship programme for European students to come and study at the Institute, in line with his contribution to support the Dundee Declaration for the Future Development of the Study of Islam and Muslims. During the trip, I visited the International Academy of Philosophy, which has resulted in co-operation between the Academy and the Institute.

The outcome of my visit to Liechtenstein was that Prince Philipp visited the Institute in June 2005, and a Memorandum of Understanding was signed between the Institute and the International Academy of Philosophy in Liechtenstein.

HH Prince Philipp von und zu Liechtenstein's Visit to Al-Maktoum Institute

Al-Maktoum Institute in Dundee, Scotland, played host to several high level visitors on 30 June 2005, including HH Prince Philipp von und zu Liechtenstein and Mr Tom McCabe MSP, Minister for Finance and Public Service Reform of the Scottish Executive. During their visits, both dignitaries met with the 54 female UAE students at Al-Maktoum Institute for the 2005 Summer School on Multiculturalism and Leadership.

HH Prince Philipp spent a day at Al-Maktoum Institute, on the invitation of the Institute. He headed a delegation from the Principality, including Daniel Morler of LGT Bank (Middle Eastern section) and Dr Cheikh Gueye of the International Academy of Philosophy, Liechtenstein. During his visit, HH Prince Philipp met the staff of the Institute, with whom he had a discussion on HH Shaikh Handam Bin Rashid Al-Maktoum's Vision for Multiculturalism. He expressed a strong interest in HH Shaikh Hamdan's vision and the implementation of this vision through Al-Maktoum Institute.

Whilst in Dundee, Al-Maktoum Institute arranged a series of meetings for HH Prince Philipp, including one at the Diocesan Offices of The Right Reverend Vincent Logan, Bishop of Dunkeld, where he met the leaders of the Christian communities in Dundee. In the afternoon he visited the historic Dundee City Chambers, meeting Councillor Jill Shimi,

Leader of Dundee City Council, and other senior councillors and officials. This was followed by a visit to the offices of the Alliance Trust investment group, to meet their Chief Executive Alan Harden and Chairman Ian Goddard and other senior staff.

HH Prince Philipp then returned to Al-Maktoum Institute for an extended meeting with the 54 UAE Summer School students. He made a presentation on Liechtenstein, which was followed by a lengthy question and answer session, covering a range of topics including the development of financial and other links between the UAE and Liechtenstein and the role of women as leaders in both countries. This meeting concluded with a public ceremony for the signing of a Memorandum of Understanding between Al-Maktoum Institute and the International Academy of Philosophy, Liechtenstein, to establish cooperation between the two centres of learning, through joint research and the exchange of staff and students.

In conclusion to his visit, Al-Maktoum Institute hosted HH Prince Philipp at a dinner in Dundee, which was attended by a number of senior dignitaries including Mr Tom McCabe, Jill Shimi, Lord Elder (Chancellor of Al-Maktoum Institute), Dr Hanif Al-Qassimi (Vice-President of Zayed University), and Professor Steve Logan (Senior Vice-Principal of the University of Aberdeen), along with the UAE Summer School students.

In a speech to the invited guests, Tom McCabe spoke of the Scottish Executive's pleasure with Al-Maktoum Institute, both at hosting HH Prince Philipp in Dundee, and for their work to develop links between Scotland and the UAE. Mr McCabe passed on to HH Prince Philipp and to Al-Maktoum Institute the best wishes of the First Minister of Scotland, Mr Jack McConnell MSP. Mr McCabe also said how proud Scotland are to have Al-Maktoum Institute, particularly for the work that the Institute is doing, as an example for the rest of the world, to promote multiculturalism and religious tolerance. This point was reiterated also by Jill Shimi, who spoke of how extremely proud the city of Dundee is to be the home of Al-Maktoum Institute, as the gateway to Dubai not only for Scotland but also for Europe.

HH Prince Philipp in turn spoke of how much he had enjoyed his visit to Al-Maktoum Institute and Dundee, and how he had found the Institute to be very impressive. He was equally impressed by the UAE students, whom he had found to be excellent ambassadors for their country and who would surely become very able leaders of the UAE. He looks forward to developing this new link between Liechtenstein and both Al-Maktoum Institute and the UAE.

Potential collaborations with Rotterdam Municipality

On 1 September 2004, Mr Mirza al-Sayegh, Chairman of the Institute Board, and Professor Malory Nye, Depute Principal for Academic Affairs of the Institute, visited the City Hall, Rotterdam, along with Dr Noor al-Qaddo, Director of the Dublin Islamic Cultural Centre, and representatives from the city of Rotterdam, there they met Ivo Opstelten, Mayor of Rotterdam. At the meeting they discussed possible academic collaboration between the Institute and Rotterdam Municipality, and also with a local university, to see how the Institute's expertise in the area of multiculturalism, cultural and religious diversity, and the study of Islam and Muslims, can be utilised to enable the city of Rotterdam to face and develop some of these major issues.

Advice on multiculturalism to Rotterdam Municipality

From 19 to 21 May 2005, the Depute Principal was invited by the Rotterdam Municipality to participate in a three day forum involving a small specialist group of academics, policy makers, and politicians from across Europe to discuss the development of issues of multiculturalism and integration within Rotterdam. Professor Nye's expertise in these areas was used to help to develop a strategy for the municipality to develop their policy for the city, and to draft a 'Rotterdammers Charter' to encourage effective integration and cultural dialogue amongst all its citizens.

Visit of HE Sairaan Kadar, MP of Mongolia

The Former Mongolian Ambassador to Egypt and UAE gave a presentation on Mongolia: History, Religion, and Muslim minority to students and staff which was organised by the student society Al-Maktoum Institute Student Society on 24 March 06 in the Michael Adams Seminar Room.

Visit of Cecil Shea – US Consul General – Scotland

Cecile Shea, US Consul General in Edinburgh, visited the Institute on 28 March 2006, when I met her with the Depute Principal for Academic Affairs, Professor Malory Nye. She was very interested to learn of the aims and mission of the Institute and in particular the New Agenda for the Study of Islam and Muslims. During her visit, at her request, the Institute also arranged for her to meet a number of our current students to find out more about our programmes and the diversity of our student and research community. Ms Shea emphasised her considerable interest in the agenda of the Institute and was keen to make sure that her successor at the Consulate in Edinburgh (who is soon to take over from her) should visit the Institute in the near future.

Presentation at the Royal Danish Consulate, Dubai

On 10 April, the Depute Principal for Academic Affairs, Professor Malory Nye, made a visit to Dubai where he gave a short presentation at the Royal Danish Consulate and Trade Commission of Denmark on the 'Vision of the Al-Maktoum Family', talking in particular about the diverse activities of the Al-Maktoum Foundation, in Dubai and across the world. He showed how the Al-Maktoum Foundation is a practical implementation of the Vision of HH Shaikh Hamdan Bin Rashid Al-Maktoum, through various areas of humanitarian work in particular social needs and support, education as investment in human potential, community needs, emergency support and relief, and academic investment and development (especially through the Al-Maktoum Institute in Dundee)

International Association of Community Development

On 21 June 2006, I was invited to talk to the International Association of Community Development (IACD) Board meeting at their annual board meeting at Glasgow University. My presentation on 'Promoting Multiculturalism with a New Agenda' focused on our vision, mission and new agenda. Through this meeting the Chairman of the IACD Professor Gary Craig, a Professor of Social Justice at the University of Hull, visited the Institute in November 2006 and delivered a research paper to students and staff.

Visit of the Lord Mayor of Wurzburg – Germany

On the 7 July 2006, during the Fourth Summer School, the Lord Mayor of Wurzburg, Dr Pia Beckmann, visited the Institute and gave two lectures to the Summer School students. One was on How to become and to be a Lord Mayor as a woman, and the other was on New ways of marketing, example of Wurzburg, Germany. On a more poignant note, the Lord Mayor attended the memorial service for the Seventh of July London Bombing held by the Institute on the site of the Al-Maktoum Multicultural Centre.

I also invited Dr Beckmann to assist in the Presentation of Al-Maktoum Tartan to the Institute staff in recognition of their hard work over the past year at a Tartan Tea Party held in the Shaikh Maktoum Garden on 7 July 2006. On 24 August 2006, Councillor Eva Maria of Wurzburg also visited the Institute.

SDOA Scuola Di Direzione e Organizzazione Aziendal, Salerno Italy

On 22 September 2006, I met Maria Pia Paravia, Alessandro Paravia, and Dr Benedetta Paravia of the SDOA, a higher educational institution based in Salerno, in the south of Italy in order to explain the activities, vision, mission and new agenda of the Institute and also the role the Institute plays in the already existing relationship between the UAE and the UK

10

THE UNITED ARAB EMIRATES AND SCOTLAND AS AN EXAMPLE

As part of setting the agenda for cultural engagement, the Institute was in particular playing a key role in building strong links between the UAE and Scotland. The aim was to help to promote a two way traffic for educational, cultural, and business links between the UAE and Scotland.

In the last five years, we have worked on a series of practical steps for a model of co-operation that is bridging Scotland and the UAE. This has led to a number of important achievements in a short space of time.

The First Scottish Delegation of Al-Maktoum Institute to the UAE

His Highness Shaikh Hamdan Bin Rashid Al-Maktoum was very impressed with Dundee and Dundonians during his visit to officially open Al-Maktoum Institute for Arabic and Islamic Studies on 6 May 2002. Following on from that historic and successful visit, HH Shaikh Hamdan invited a senior delegation representing the City of Dundee to visit Dubai on 20 – 25 October 2002. The delegation was led by Lord Provost John Letford, as the Civic Head of the City. Al-Maktoum Institute for Arabic and Islamic Studies played a key role in catalysing this historic and successful visit which has demonstrated its commitment to serve Dundee and to help promote Dundee at both national and international level.

In addition to Lord Provost John Letford and myself, the Dundee Delegation included Professor Malory Nye (Al-Maktoum Institute for Arabic and Islamic Studies), Professor Tony Wells (Chief Executive, Tayside Board), Professor Bernard King (Principal and Vice-Chancellor, University of Abertay Dundee), Mr Ernie Ross (then Member of Parliament for Dundee West), Mr Doug Grimmond (Director of Economic Development, Dundee City Council), Mr Mervyn Rolfe CBE (then Chief Executive, Dundee and Tayside Chamber of Commerce and Industry) and Mr Scott Carnegie (then Chairman, Dundee United Football Club).

The visit was extremely well covered by the media in United Arab Emirates, both on the TV and in the newspapers. The very positive coverage indeed raised Dundee's profile in the UAE as a whole. The delegation also had an audience with His Highness Shaikh Hamdan Bin Rashid Al-Maktoum. In the discussions, the delegation proposed that Emirates Airline should introduce a regular direct flight from Dubai to Scotland.

The aim of the visit was to explore and make stronger the business and economic connections that had been initiated during HH Shaikh Hamdan's visit to Dundee. To achieve this, the delegation had meetings with, among others, His Highness Shaikh Nahayan Bin Mubarak Al-Nahayan (UAE Minister of Higher Education), the Director General of Dubai Municipality, Director General of Dubai Economic Development Department, and Director General of Dubai Chamber of Commerce and Industry. Various issues were discussed. For example, this high powered delegation to Dubai brought back the possibility of twinning arrangements between Dundee and Dubai.

The delegation also attended the Award Ceremony for 'His Highness Shaikh Hamdan Bin Rashid Al-Maktoum Award for Medical Excellence'. These prestigious awards are made annually to outstanding scholars in the field of medical sciences. That year, two of the winners were from Scotland.

Second Scottish Delegation of Al-Maktoum Institute to the UAE

Following the first Scottish Delegation of Al-Maktoum Institute to Dubai, HH Shaikh Hamdan Bin Rashid Al-Maktoum extended, once again, his kind invitation for another senior delegation to visit Dubai from 14 – 18 December 2003. To prepare for the visit Lord Elder invited the members of the delegation to a meeting at the Institute on 28 November 2003, where several issues were discussed on how to strengthen the link with Dubai and how to make this second delegation a successful one.

The delegation was led by Lord Elder, Chancellor of Al-Maktoum Institute. I acted as Vice-Head of the delegation. In addition, the delegation comprised Professor The Lord Sewel (then Senior Vice Principal, University of Aberdeen), Ernie Ross (then Member of Parliament for Dundee West), Doug Grimmond (Director of Economic

Development, Dundee City Council), David Smith (Director of Europe, Middle East and Africa, Scottish Development International), and Professor Malory Nye, then Head of Department from Al-Maktoum Institute.

The aim of the visit was to widen and strengthen the initial contact which had been established in the first delegation and to strengthen the business and economic connections between the two nations as part of implementing HH Shaikh Hamdan's vision of building the relationship between Scotland and Dubai.

To achieve this, the delegation had meetings with, amongst others, His Highness Shaikh Hamdan Bin Rashid Al-Maktoum, HH Shaikh Ahmad Bin Saeed Al-Maktoum, Chairman of Emirates Airline and Chancellor of the British University in Dubai, HE Mr Saeed Al-Kindy, then the Speaker of the Federal National Council of UAE, HE Mr Saif Al-Ghurair, HE Mr Qasim Sultan, then Director General of Dubai Municipality, HE Mr AbdulRahman Saif Al-Ghurair, first Vice President of Dubai Chamber of Commerce and Industry, HE Mr Qadhi Saeed Al-Murooshid, Director General of Dubai Department of Health and Medical Sciences, HE Dr Hanif Al-Qassimi, then Vice President of Zayed University, Hadef Bin Jouan Al-Dhahiri, Vice Chancellor of UAE University, Mohammed Al-Abbar, Director General of Dubai Department of Economic Development, Simon Collis, then British Consul in Dubai, and the Dean of Dubai Medical College. In addition, there was a visit to DUGAS (Dubai National Gas Company). Accordingly, there were opportunities for delegates to make and enhance business links with a number of senior officials involved in higher education and medicine, business, trade and industry, and culture.

During the audience with HH Shaikh Hamdan on 15 December, Lord Elder presented two letters to His Highness. The first one dated 11 December 2003 was from the Rt Hon Jim Wallace (MSP), Deputy First Minister and Minister for Enterprise and Lifelong Learning of the Scottish Executive, thanking Shaikh Hamdan for inviting this senior delegation from Scotland which had been organised by the 'well regarded Al-Maktoum Institute'. He also thanked him for his support in securing the Emirates Airline new Glasgow to Dubai air service, and adding that 'Emirates Airline has shown significant commitment to Scotland with this year's round daily [daily round] service.'

The second letter was from the Al-Maktoum Institute inviting HH Shaikh Hamdan to lay the foundation stone for Al-Maktoum Multicultural Centre in Dundee, which he accepted. In addition, Lord Elder briefed Shaikh Hamdan on the success of the Institute in its activities and the fundamental role that it is playing to strengthen the link between the two countries.

During a Press Conference held at Zayed University on 18 December 2003, before the delegation departed for Scotland, it was announced that:

1. HH Shaikh Hamdan agreed to the establishment of Al-Maktoum Multicultural Centre in Dundee. This included the purchase of the former Harris Annexe in Blackness Road to build the Centre.
2. HH Shaikh Hamdan agreed to launch Shaikh Hamdan Bin Rashid Al-Maktoum Awards for Multicultural Scotland.
3. HH Shaikh Hamdan extended an invitation to Lord Elder as the Chancellor of the Al-Maktoum Institute to organise the third Scottish delegation for Al-Maktoum Institute to visit Dubai in early April 2004, so that the delegation could return on the first flight of Emirates Airline from Dubai to Glasgow on 10 April 2004.
4. The second Al-Maktoum Institute Summer School for female UAE students would in 2004 include ten female students each from Zayed University, UAE University and Dubai Women's College.

In addition, on 17 December, Zayed University and Aberdeen University signed a Memorandum of Understanding. The visit also received excellent media coverage in the UAE, as well as being well highlighted in the local press in Dundee and Aberdeen throughout the visit.

In short, this visit succeeded in widening and strengthening the links at all levels and it is hoped the parties involved in the delegation will develop this opportunity by working very closely with the Institute.

Third Scottish Delegation of Al-Maktoum Institute to the UAE

During the second Scottish Delegation of Al-Maktoum Institute, HH Shaikh Hamdan Bin Rashid Al-Maktoum once more issued a kind invitation for a third Scottish delegation of Al-Maktoum Institute to visit Dubai from 6 to 10 April 2004.

This delegation was again led by Lord Elder, Chancellor of Al-Maktoum Institute. I once more acted as Vice-Head of Delegation. In addition, the delegation consisted of Professor The Lord Sewel (then Senior Vice Principal, University of Aberdeen), Lord Provost of Dundee John Letford and Joyce McVarrie (Lead Official, Church, State and Faith Issues, Scottish Executive). The visit to the UAE again received excellent media coverage in the UAE as well as being well covered in the local press in Dundee and Aberdeen.

The Inaugural Emirates Flight to Glasgow

The intention was for the delegation to return to Scotland on the inaugural flight of Emirates Airline flying direct to Glasgow from Dubai. I think the Institute can claim that we have some influence on Emirates deciding to have a daily non-stop flight between Dubai and Scotland. Indeed, the Al-Maktoum Institute is particularly pleased that our presence in Scotland further enhanced the relationship between Scotland and Dubai and helped by proposing the revitalisation of the idea to bring about this prestigious new service to Scotland. The idea was first discussed during the first delegation's visit in October 2002.

Sister Cities Agreement between Dubai and Dundee

Another important outcome of this visit was that a Sister Cities Agreement between Dundee City and Dubai was signed on 7 April 2004. The Institute played a major role to achieve this significant agreement for Dundee and to help Dundee City Council to promote Dundee at the national and international levels.

Dubai has built a worldwide network of sister cities – eleven in all – in countries such as China, Japan, Australia, the United States, Switzerland and across the Arab and Muslim countries. Dundee is the only one in the UK. Indeed, the presence of the Institute in Dundee certainly led to Dundee's being invited to become a sister city.

To celebrate the signing of the Sister Cities Agreement, the Institute, during the signing ceremony in Dubai, presented to HE Mr Qasim Sultan, then Director General of Dubai Municipality one of a pair of especially distinctive commissioned paintings. The second painting is displayed in Shaikh Rasid Conference Hall at the Institute. The paintings are the work of local artist, Eddie Lange whom the Institute commissioned to create something that would symbolise the new relationship between the two cities. The paintings illustrate both cities' links with the sea. It shows the famous RRS *Discovery* and an Arab Dhow sailing towards each other with the Institute logo outlined in the water between them. In the background is the skyline of both cities showing the Tay Bridge, the Dundee Law, Discovery Point and Al-Maktoum Institute building alongside the Burj al-Arab Hotel, a traditional house and the Emirates Towers.

Dubai Sister City Forum

On 11 May 2004, I met the Dundee City Council Delegation to the Dubai First Sister City Forum (15-17 May 2004): Dundee City Council Leader Jill Shimi (Head of Delegation), Mr Doug Grimmond, Director of Economic Development, Stan Ure, Business Development Manager, Jennifer Casewell, Team Leader, Economic Development; and Gaynor Sullivan, Business Development Officer. The meeting aimed to answer any questions about this important Forum and other custom and cultural issues related to Dubai. The Dundee Delegation was very well received by senior officials in Dubai.

Emirates Airline

Emirates Airline invited me and the members of the Third Al-Maktoum Institute Scottish Delegation to a Gala Dinner on 27 May 2004 in the Hilton Glasgow to celebrate its new service between Glasgow and Dubai.

On 14 September 2004, a meeting was held in the Institute with Laurie Berryman, Emirates Manager UK North and Denise Holmes, Sales Manager of Emirates Airline. The meeting was to discuss how the Institute and Emirates Airline could work together to strengthen the relationship between Dubai and Scotland, following the introduction of the direct daily Dubai Glasgow flights on 10 April 2004. It was agreed with Emirates that they could use Al-Maktoum Tartan for any promotion of the link between Dubai and Scotland.

The Emirates Airline' daily direct flight between Dubai and Glasgow which was inaugurated on 10 April 2004 was so successful that Emirates boosted the number of seats on this route by more than 50% (from 15 December 2005, 278 to 427 seats). This came less than a year after the introduction of the daily direct service and was, according to Mr Sheppard, Emirates Vice-President for the UK, a 'direct response to increasing demand from Scottish travellers'. This was a great achievement which represented, said Stephen Baxter, Managing Director of Glasgow Airport, a 'real success story... Not just in terms of passenger numbers, but in an economic sense too. This expansion of Emirates represents a major economic boost for Scottish exporters.' This direct link with the major global economic centre of Dubai is a tremendous advantage for Scottish business development with the UAE, and of course beyond, to other potential partners such as India and China. It is worth noting that Scotland does not have direct air links with many of these countries, but does have direct links with Dubai. This successful young airline celebrated its 20th Anniversary on 25 October 2005.

BAA Glasgow

I meet Mr Stephen Baxter, Managing Director and Mr Malcolm Robertson, Head of Public Affairs, from BAA Glasgow during their visit to the Institute on 14 April 2004 and discussed possible cooperation between the Institute and BAA Glasgow following the inaugural flight between Dubai and Glasgow.

Shaikh Hamdan Bin Rashid Al-Maktoum Awards for Multicultural Scotland

HH Shaikh Hamdan's commitment to multiculturalism has been shown in particular by the launch of these new prestigious Awards. At a press conference held in Edinburgh City Chambers on 24 May 2004, the Chancellor of the Institute Lord Elder, together with Mary Mulligan (MSP), the Scottish Executive Deputy Minister for Communities, and myself, launched the Shaikh Hamdan Bin Rashid Al-Maktoum Awards for Multicultural Scotland. At another press conference at the Al-Maktoum Foundation in Dubai on 27 September 2004, Lord Elder, Mr Mirza Al-Sayegh, and myself, re-launched the Awards in the UAE.

These new awards are a very significant development both for the Institute and for Scotland. They are designed to recognise and encourage individual and institutional contributions to multicultural Scotland in which religious diversity, cultural equality, social justice, and civilisational dialogue flourish. Scotland is a diverse, multicultural, and multireligious society, and the Al-Maktoum Institute commends the Scottish Executive for its pro-active campaign to promote the concept of 'One Scotland, Many Cultures'.

Through the Shaikh Hamdan Bin Rashid Al-Maktoum Awards, the Institute aims to promote further work and to reward the achievements of individuals and organisations in the development of good multicultural practice at all levels of Scottish society. Through its efforts the awards seek to identify and encourage the efforts of many people in Scotland who share the Al-Maktoum Institute's vision for greater tolerance, understanding and engagement between people of different cultures, religions, and nations.

The selection process emphasises the activities of individuals and organisations in many areas of contemporary Scottish life, including education, sport, healthcare, the media, and business. Further to this, the awards seek to recognise progress that has been made in relations between Scotland and the UAE, British-Arab understanding, and, more broadly, civilisational dialogue. Selection for the awards was based on nominations made to the Institute on a two yearly basis. The award panel was chaired by the Chancellor of the Al-Maktoum Institute.

The Shaikh Hamdan Bin Rashid Al-Maktoum Awards are made up of a principal award combined with seven smaller awards to recognise a number of key areas of contemporary Scotland: The principal award is for a Major Contribution to Contemporary Scotland; and the seven other awards were: Multicultural Education, Multicultural Healthcare, Multiculturalism in the Media, Multicultural Sport, Civilisational Dialogue, Scottish-Emirates relations, and Arab-British Understanding.

The 2005 Awards scheme was strongly promoted through the autumn of 2004, including high profile advertisements in the *Herald*, the *Scotsman*, the *Press and Journal*, and the *Courier*, together with a mailing campaign that sent out over 2,000 brochures and posters. The closing date for nominations to this awards scheme was on 17 December 2004. The Awards Panel sub-committee met on 11 January to short-list the nominations, and the full panel, chaired by Lord Elder, met on 4 March to select the winners of the awards.

These new awards clearly show the commitment of the Institute to this vision for multiculturalism, as well as its particular commitment to Scotland and Scottish society. These also are a key element of the work of the Al-Maktoum Institute, not only to promote and encourage international research and teaching in the field of multiculturalism, but also to implement this multiculturalism in practical ways.

The Awards were presented for the first time on 15 August 2005 at a high profile event at the Apex Hotel in Dundee. The awards were a certificate, a cash prize (£500 for each awards), and a piece of artwork specially commissioned to express the vision for multiculturalism. The winners of the Awards were as follows:

- Award for Multicultural Healthcare: NHS Fife (5 nominations, 3 short-listed)
- Award for Multicultural Education: Eastwood School (5 nominations, 3 short-listed)
- Award for Multiculturalism in the Media: Channel 4 (3 nominations, one short-listed)
- Award for Multicultural Sport: No award (2 nominations, none short-listed)
- Award for Civilisational Dialogue: The Interfaith Council (2 nominations, 2 short-listed)
- Award for Scottish-Emirates Relations: Zayed University (1 nomination, 1 short-listed)

- Award for Arab-British Understanding: CAABU (1 nomination, 1 short-listed)
- Principal Award: No award this year (no specific nominations, no category winners outstanding enough to win the Principal Award)

The Institute Award Ceremony was attended by senior dignitaries from Dundee, Scotland and the UAE including Margaret Curran, Minister for Parliamentary Business (Scottish Executive), Mirza Al-Sayegh, Chairman of the Institute Board, and Lord Elder, Chancellor of the Al-Maktoum Institute.

The Re-Launch of Al-Maktoum Tartan

A tartan first designed almost 30 years ago for HH Shaikh Rashid Bin Saeed Al-Maktoum for use in his pipe band was rediscovered and unveiled in a ceremony held at the Institute on 22 March 2006.

This discovery was made when I was thinking of ideas for new corporate colours. Wanting something to reflect the links between Dubai, home of Shaikh Hamdan Bin Rashid Al-Maktoum, the Institute's Patron and Scotland, I investigated the possibility of designing a new tartan. An old sample of the original tartan was found by the Strathmore Woollen Company Ltd within the archive of the Scottish Tartan Authority.

The Tartan is based on the colours of the Cameron tartan and was designed in 1977 by Pipe Major Stallard for Dubai's pipe band which was the pride and joy of the then Ruler, the late Shaikh Rashid Bin Saeed Al-Maktoum. This was a wonderful discovery that the Institute was delighted to have been able to bring back into production. The new tartan is now the official colours of the Al-Maktoum Foundation - Scotland.

At the re-launch Tom McCabe MSP, Scottish Executive Minister for Finance and Local Government, unveiled the tartan. He said, 'This wonderful Al-Maktoum tartan perfectly symbolises the links which exist between Scotland and Dubai. I've been extremely impressed by the ambitious work the Al-Maktoum Institute has been undertaking. I was delighted to be asked to unveil the tartan to underline the importance the Scottish Executive attaches to strengthening our links with Dubai. I believe this is a win-win scenario for Scotland. We've much to offer Dubai, but the incredible economic growth Dubai is experiencing has huge potential for Scottish businesses'.

Also in attendance was Brian Wilton the Administrator of the Scottish Tartan Authority who presented me with a copy of the Certificate of

Registration for the Tartan. The re-launch was attended by many prominent figures from Dundee's political, business and local community. It also received excellent coverage both in the local papers and from BBC Scotland on line and radio.

As part of the ongoing planning and development of the re-launch of Al-Maktoum Tartan I had met Brian Wilton of the Scottish Tartan Authority (STA) on 8 February 2006 to discuss the registration process of the Tartan. Mr Brian Wilton attended the re-launch of the Tartan at the Institute on 22 March 2006. The registration document along with the tartan can be viewed in the waiting area and the Majilis Meeting Room of the Institute.

Scottish Council for Development and Industry conference: 'The World We're In'

I was invited by the Scottish Council for Development and Industry (SCDI) to deliver a key-note speech at their annual conference in St Andrews in 17-18 March 2005. My speech highlighted the current opportunities for trade with Dubai to an audience of Scotland's business and political leaders. I pointed out the practical steps which have been achieved in developing the relationship between Scotland and Dubai since the establishment of Al-Maktoum Institute as Scotland's Gateway to Dubai, and said that Dubai is keen that Scotland reciprocates by making more of the opportunities.

I stressed the importance of direct air links in developing trade relationships, and pointed out the success of the direct Emirates route between Glasgow and Dubai, which shortly afterwards expanded capacity by 50%; Scotland doesn't have direct links with major emerging markets such as China and India – on which the conference focused – although these destinations are also serviced via Dubai. I presented HH Shaikh Hamdan Bin Rashid Al-Maktoum's Vision and the New Agenda for the Study of Islam and Muslims and focused upon Dubai – Scotland relations. I emphasised that 'this relationship should be a two way traffic' and added 'the best way for Scotland to do business with Dubai is to establish a Scottish House in Dubai where multiple agencies would work together to promote Scottish business and industry.' Other speakers at the conference included Lord Robertson, Ex-Secretary General of NATO, and First Minister Jack McConnell.

Women as Global Leaders Conference, Zayed University

UAE's Zayed University held its First Annual International Student Leadership Conference from 14 to 16 March 2005, under the title,

'Women as Global Leaders'. Al-Maktoum Institute worked closely with the organisers to recommend a Scottish representative at the conference; Wendy Alexander MSP was suggested as a head for the Scottish delegation, and as a keynote speaker at the conference.

The Institute sponsored the students from Scottish universities who made up the main body of the delegation. Ruth Wishart, a prominent Scottish journalist, was the ninth member of the delegation, and was also sponsored by Al-Maktoum Institute. The participating students and universities were: Sarah Hassan (Al-Maktoum Institute), Ramona Ibrahim (Al-Maktoum Institute), Rosalind Anderson (Al-Maktoum Institute), Marie-Louise Morcos (Dundee University), Mandy Yilmaz (Dundee University), Mhairi Laidlaw (University of Aberdeen), and Anne Bachman (University of Aberdeen).

The students gave a presentation on their experiences at the conference to their colleagues at Al-Maktoum Institute on 20 April 2005.

By participating in the Women as Global Leaders conference in Dubai we have been given the opportunity to explore places and people and future pillars of global leadership in the conference. We hope to realise Al-Maktoum Institute's vision of bridging gaps between cultures, and understanding of diversity through dialogue. We hope to come back to Dundee reflecting on the ongoing learning experience we arranged in Dubai. (Rosalind Anderson, Ramona Ahmed, Sarah Hassan: Al-Maktoum Institute).

It is an honour for us to represent the University of Dundee at this historic event which will undoubtedly be a pillar of the ongoing empowerment of women around the world. We are proud to be part of the growing relationship between Scotland and Dubai, and hope to increase tolerance and build bridges and cultures. (Mandy Yilmaz, Marie-Louise Morcos: University of Dundee).

We feel privileged and excited to have the opportunity to represent Aberdeen University and Scotland in this important event aimed at furthering the position of women around the world. We are looking forward to experiencing first hand the culture of Dubai, so that our understanding of different cultures can be based on knowledge rather than ignorance. (Mhairi Ritchie, Anne Bachman: University of Aberdeen)

The Women as Global Leaders conference held in Dubai is a rich experience to each one of us. The conference is one of the founding steps towards women's empowerment and leadership. Dubai can be considered as one of the practical models of Shaikh Hamdan Al-Maktoum's vision for multiculturalism. The discussions that took place among more than 400 students from all over the globe were directed towards dialogue rather than clash, and bridging gaps rather than widening them. The conference centred on women's education and giving them equal opportunities like those given to their male peers and colleagues. These aims perfectly coincide with the aims of Al-Maktoum Institute for Arabic and Islamic Studies in Dundee. The Institute works on promoting its female students to become 'Women as Global Leaders'. (Sarah Hassan: Al-Maktoum Institute)

I also represented the Institute at the Women as Global Leaders Conference organised by Zayed University in Abu Dhabi from March 12-14 2006.

UAE University Medical School Visits to Aberdeen and Dundee

In 2005 the Institute had two visits from UAE University Medical School, arranged through Al-Maktoum Institute. The impetus for these visits came when the Chancellor of the Institute, Lord Elder, visited UAE University in April 2004 with Lord Sewel and myself. From the discussions between Lords Elder and Sewel and myself with UAEU Medical School, there arose the possibility of formal contacts for collaboration between the university and the medical schools of Dundee and Aberdeen. Following on from this, the Dean of the UAEU Medical School, Professor George Carruthers, visited us from 20 to 22 April 2005, and together with the Depute Principal they visited the Medical Schools of University of Aberdeen and University of Dundee to explore possible areas of cooperation in both the teaching of medicine for UAEU students and for research. This visit was followed up in August (from 24 to 26 August) by a visit from the Associate Dean of UAEU Medical School and the Head of the Gynaecology and Obstetrics Department, to meet specific Dundee and Aberdeen medical school staff to plan practical projects of collaboration.

Alliance Trusts - Al-Maktoum Institute Postgraduate Internship in Financial Services

The Institute worked in partnership with the Alliance Trust to provide the opportunity to create a working internship for one female student from UAE. The internship is for a period of 12 months in Financial Services for graduates of Zayed University. The intern will be based within the Alliance Trust in Dundee in order to develop her skills for a career in financial services in other financial markets. The internship programme is in line with the Institute's own agenda to provide training for future female leaders. However, due to personal circumstances, the candidate decided at the last minute not to take up the internship.

Dubai International Arab Racing Day Exhibition, Newbury

From 12 to 14 August 2005, and from 22 to 23 July 2006, Al-Maktoum Institute had a stand at the Dubai International Arab Racing Day Exhibition, a major event held at Newbury Racecourse. The Institute's stand presented the new agenda of the Institute for teaching and research in the study of Islam and Muslims and demonstrated HH Shaikh Hamdan Bin Rashid Al-Maktoum's commitment to developing the areas of education and multiculturalism. The exhibition is a major event for the promotion of Dubai, and included many other participants, including Jumeirah Hotels, Emirates, Dubai Global Village, Dubai Shopping Festival, and the British University in Dubai. The exhibition was opened on Sunday 14 August 2005 by HH Shaikh Hamdan Bin Rashid Al-Maktoum. The Chancellor Lord Elder and myself attended this opening and met HH Shaikh Hamdan. In 2006, it was opened on Sunday 23 July by HH Shaikh Hamdan Bin Rashid Al-Maktoum. I had the privilege of attending this opening and meeting with HH Shaikh Hamdan once more.

Dubai Economic Development Delegation to Scotland

A delegation from Dubai Economic Development Department arrived in Scotland from 13 – 17 November 2005 in order to:

- Sign a Memorandum of Understanding between the Dubai Government Economic Development Department and the Institute
- Investigate the two ways in which economic activities between Dubai and Scotland can increase
- Enhance the research and knowledge base of Dubai's strategy for economic development

The Delegation comprised: Mr Khalid Al-Kassim, Deputy Director-General of Planning and Development (Delegation Leader), Mr Saeed Al-Suwaidi, Director Planning and Studies Division and Dr Ibrahim Kursany, Economic Development Adviser, Planning and Studies Division

I had arranged an extensive programme for the delegation during their brief visit to Scotland: in Dundee on 14 November, in Aberdeen on 15 November, and in Glasgow on 16 November. During this brief trip, the delegation met Dundee, Aberdeen and Glasgow City Councils, Scottish

Enterprise Tayside, Grampian and Glasgow. There were meetings held with the Scottish, Aberdeen and Grampian Chambers of Commerce and the Scottish Council for Development and Industry in Glasgow. Each meeting began with a briefing session on the background of the delegation visit to Scotland, followed by me giving a brief background on Al-Maktoum Institute for those who had not been aware of the Institute. This was followed by the hosting organisation providing a presentation then the meeting was opened for questions.

During these meetings the delegation met with, at the Alliance Trust, Ian Goddard, Company Secretary, Shona Dobbie, Head of Economics and Mr Grant Lindsey, head of Equities, then also met Dundee City Council's Lord Provost John Letford, Joe Morrow, Convener of the Economic Development Department, Doug Grimmond, Director of the Economic Development Department and Stan Ure, Business Development Manager. At Scottish Enterprise Tayside, the delegation met Shona Cormack, Chief Executive, and David Anderson, Business Growth Team Manger, and from Aberdeen and Grampian Chambers of Commerce, Chief Executive Geoff Runcie and Reith Still, International Business Director. Others were Fiona Ann Ogilvie, and John Mitchell of Inward Investor Support, Karen Tolmie, Manger Competitive Business of Aberdeen and Grampian, Scottish Enterprise, and Mark Gordon, Business Development Manager of Aberdeen City Council's Business Development Department. In Glasgow, the delegation met Liz Cameron, Director of the Scottish Chambers of Commerce, Richard Cairns, head of Economic and Social Initiatives, Peter Russell, Principal for the International Office Glasgow City Council, Alan Wilson, Chief Executive and Iain McTaggart, General Manager.

Scottish Executive
The Scottish Executive continues to support the activities of the Institute through participation in symposiums, arranging for the Fourth Summer School to visit the Scottish Parliament, and taking an active interest in the activities of the Institute as a higher education institution in Scotland.

From 11 to 18 February 2005, the Scottish Executive Minister for Finance and Public Service Reform, Mr Tom McCabe MSP, made an unofficial visit to Dubai. Whilst he was there he was able, through the Institute, to have a meeting with HH Shaikh Hamdan Bin Rashid Al-Maktoum and with senior people of the Emirates, including the Chairman of the Institute Board. Following from this, Mr McCabe paid a visit to the Institute on 18 April, where I met with him to discuss how to develop strategically the relationship between Scotland and Dubai. We were also delighted that Mrs Margaret Curran MSP, Scottish Executive Minister for Parliamentary Affairs, visited Dubai in the summer of 2005 for a private visit.

Mrs Margaret Curran delivered the opening speech at the Symposium on Multiculturalism held at the Institute on 20 April 2006. Tom McCabe (MSP), Minister for Finance and Public Service Reform was invited to open Heriot Watt's University's campus in the Academic City in Dubai. During his visit to Dubai from 29 March to 1 April 2006, he met HH Shaikh Hamdan Bin Rashid Al-Maktoum when Mr McCabe highlighted directly to Shaikh Hamdan how much Scottish Ministers value the presence and the work of Al-Maktoum Institute in Scotland.

On 18 August 2006, I met Mr Dominic Munro, International Strategy Division, the Scottish Executive at the Institute to hear more about our mission, vision and New Agenda. I particularly highlighted the creation of a Scottish House in Dubai as being a fundamental element in the progress of the cultural and economic relationship between Scotland and the UAE.

Visit of Mr Edward Oakden – British Ambassador designate to the UAE

On 5 July 2006, I met HE Edward Oakden British Ambassador designate to the UAE prior to his taking up his post in Abu Dhabi at the British Embassy in September 2006.

The British Council

I was invited to a Connecting Futures reception organised by The British Council on 15 March 2002. Good contacts have been established with senior officers of The British Council, and these contacts and relationships have so far led to some developments for the benefit of the Institute. We also received a visit from the Professional Award candidates from the British Council on 17 June 2002. The Professional Award candidates are staff from British Council offices overseas who undertake a professional qualification in education counselling.

The Institute also received visits from Mr Francis King, Deputy Director of British Council's Connecting Future project, on 20 August 2002, and Mr Ian Simms, British Council Director for Middle East and North Africa, on 3 October 2002. All these contacts ensure that the Institute's potential as a key provider of higher education in the Study of Islam and Muslims is recognised by one of the main agencies promoting British educational establishments worldwide.

A group of four graduates who work within the British Council in Dubai came to the UK for a familiarisation visit. As part of this visit they came to the Institute in December 2005 where they were given a presentation and tour of the campus. The graduates were very interested in the courses on offer at the Institute. They took the opportunity to spend some time with a few of the current students, asking them questions pertaining to their studies here at Al-Maktoum Institute.

The Renfrewshire Chamber of Commerce
Two representatives from Renfrewshire Chamber of Commerce, Andrew McDuff and Liz Cameron, visited the Institute on 11 May 2004, to discuss possible opportunities to trade with Dubai following the introduction of direct flights between Glasgow and Dubai.

On 8 June 2004, I was invited to attend a meeting in Renfrewshire Chamber of Commerce to meet members, Warrick Malcolm, Deputy Director of the Scottish Chambers of Commerce, and other companies in the Glasgow area.

Dubai Municipality Delegation to Dundee Annual Flower Show
Dubai Municipality was invited to attend Dundee's Flower Show on 3-7 September 2004. During their visit to the City, they paid a visit to the Institute where I gave them a guided tour of the campus. In addition, I hosted a Business Dinner at the Hilton, which included discussion about development between Dubai and Scotland in general but in particular in the areas of agriculture and horticulture. The Business Dinner was attended by the Dubai delegation: Mr Abdulla Rafia, Mr Ahmed Abdul Karim, and Mr Mohammed Al-Fardhan; in addition to myself, Mr David Whitton, Mr Ernie Ross, Councillor Jill Shimi, Rev Erik Cramb, Mr Steve Cartwright, Councillor Bruce Mackie, Mr Stev Grimmond and Councillor Jim Barrie were also present.

Raising awareness of business opportunities with Dubai
As Dundee City Council wants to build on the developing relationship with Dubai, Al-Maktoum Institute hosted an event on 6 October 2004, jointly organised by Dundee City Council and Business Gateway International Tayside. Representatives of more than 60 companies from across Tayside attended the event aimed at raising awareness of trading opportunities with Dubai. Speaking at the event were our Chancellor, Lord Elder, and myself. The other speakers were Denise Holmes from Emirates Airline, David Smith, SDI, and Colin Saywood, Business

Gateway International. During the session, it became obvious to the audience that Al-Maktoum Institute is The Gateway to Dubai.

Dundee City Council Meeting

A meeting between Dundee City Council and the Institute was held at the Institute on 17 December 2004. It was attended by the Dundee City Council leader of Administration Councillor Jill Shimi, Chief Executive Alex Stephen, Joe Morrow Convener of Economic Development and Doug Grimmond, Director of Economic Development for Dundee City Council

During the meeting I briefed them on the Vision of HH Shaikh Hamdan Bin Rashid Al-Maktoum, and advised them how to develop the relationship between Dundee City Council and Dubai Municipality.

Dundee Youth Festival

Dundee Youth Festival was held in April, to which a delegation of high school students was sent from Dubai. The delegates were involved in various events during the Festival, which took place from 21 to 25 April 2005. A Cabaret Dinner was held on Friday 22 April. The Institute provided staff with the opportunity to attend this Cabaret Dinner, held at the Apex Hotel. Other events included the Youth Parade, the 'Music Around the World' social evening on Saturday 23 April, and the Dundee Schools Music Theatre Concert on Sunday 24 April.

Trade Mission to Dubai

On 16 February 2006, I met Stan Ure, Business Development Manager and Jennifer Casewell, Team Leader, of the Economic Development Department of Dundee City Council, who were acting for Business Gateway International to assist with a delegation of business people who wished to undertake a trade mission from Dundee and Angus to Dubai.

After initial discussion and advice, from the Principal, the Business Gateway International and the Economic Development Department organised an Awareness and Pre-recruitment session for the Dubai Trade Mission on Thursday 6 April at the Institute. The event was attended by almost 30 people and was very successful, with people signing up for the trade mission on the day of the event.

Prior to the delegation's going out to Dubai I met with Joe Morrow, Convener of the Economic Development Department, Stan Ure, Jennifer Casewell and two of the members delegation. When the delegation returned it was reported that the trip had been successful. The feedback from the businesses which took part was very positive and there were early indications of concrete business as a result.

A more focused Scottish textiles trade mission to UAE will be organised by the Scottish Development International, in connection with Business Gateway International Tayside, in June 2007. The Institute is pleased to host, another awareness and recruitment seminar on 8 March 2007.

Visit of Liz Cameron – Scottish Chambers of Commerce, to the Institute

Liz Cameron, the Director of the Scottish Chambers of Commerce, paid a visit to the Institute on Monday 20 February 2006. This took place after the meeting on 16 November 2005 with the Delegation of Dubai Economic Development Department at the Scottish Chambers of Commerce in Glasgow.

Discussion focused on ways in which the Scottish Chambers of Commerce can work with Al-Maktoum Institute to develop the relationships between Dubai and Scotland. Liz Cameron stated, 'Scottish Chambers of Commerce are committed to the establishment of a Scottish House in Dubai and will work with Al-Maktoum Institute on the practical steps necessary to achieve this. We warmly welcome the Scottish Executive's involvement in helping to create this house in Dubai.'

Two UAE Ministers Visit Dundee

During the Fourth Summer School in 2006r, the Economic Development Department assisted the Institute when two UAE Ministers, HE Dr Hanif Qassimi, UAE Minister for Education and HE Miriam Al-Roumi, Minister for Social Affairs flew into Dundee Airport on 17 July 2006. A welcoming party comprised of Councillor Jill Shimi, Baillie Helen Wright and myself along with a piper was arranged to meet them on the tarmac at Dundee Airport.

Adam Smith College, Fife

On 17 August 2006, HE Dr Hanif Qassimi, UAE Minister for Education, and Lord Elder and myself were invited to visit Adam Smith College in Kirkcaldy, Fife by the Principal of Adam Smith College, Craig Thomson. To follow up this meeting, Mr Thomson visited the Institute on 19 October 2006.

National Library of Scotland

On 25 September 2006, I met Giles Dove, the Director of Development for the National Library of Scotland. Mr Dove was seeking advice regarding a possible visit to Dubai and other parts of the Gulf relating to development and support for the National Library of Scotland's work.

Joint International Academic Symposium on Multiculturalism and Cultural Engagement

Zayed House for Islamic Culture in Al-Ain, UAE and Al-Maktoum Institute are organising a joint International Academic Symposium on the topic of 'Multiculturalism and Cultural Engagement: Mapping an Agenda for the Twenty-First Century' which will be hosted by Zayed House for Islamic Culture at Emirates Palace Abu Dhabi on 8 April 2007. The main aim of the symposium will be to look to develop a framework for practical models of multiculturalism and cultural engagement, looking at both the challenges and opportunities that such multiculturalism and cultural engagement brings us, at the local, national and international levels.

The symposium is inviting scholars to explore the issues of cultural diversity in today's world, and to provide a constructive model for cultural engagement that works to build bridges. Prominent speakers from the UK and the Gulf Region will address issues such as multiculturalism and cultural engagement in the twenty-first century, Islamicjerusalem as a model for peaceful co-existence, cultural engagement, and multiculturalism, the challenges of multiculturalism, multiculturalism and the challenges of globalisation, education in a multicultural society, and good practice of multiculturalism and cultural engagement.

Education is one of the most contested areas in multicultural societies as it brings diverse sometimes-conflicting cultural and religious values into an inevitable interaction. To explore the questions raised by the challenges of education in multicultural societies, the symposium will examine the role, relevance and task of education in responding to and combating the threat of religious extremism in culturally and religiously diverse societies.

11

ANNUAL SUMMER SCHOOLS

As part of the Institute's strategic plan to build bridges between Scotland and the UAE as well as providing international training for local UAE nationals, Al-Maktoum Institute organised four training programmes in multiculturalism and leadership for female students from the UAE (including students from Qatar University), and two training programmes on English language, multiculturalism and leadership for local UAE from Dubai Media Incorporated. The aim was to provide a more focused working model for cultural engagements.

The Training Programme in Multiculturalism and Leadership for Female Students from the UAE (including students from Qatar University)

In the past four years, the Institute organised and hosted in Dundee four summer schools for female' students from the UAE (including students from Qatar University) in 2003, 2004, 2005, and 2006.

The 2003 Summer School

The Institute received a group of 23 students from Zayed University on 21 June 2003. This was the first cultural exchange programme organised by the Institute and it was indeed a great success. The students were chosen by Zayed University based on their potential to become senior top administrators and decision makers in many key areas in the future. By hosting these future leaders, the Institute ensured that good connections have been established.

The students spent their mornings studying at the Institute. A range of activities were arranged for them including visits to various sites around Scotland. Among the places they visited were the Scottish Parliament where they attended the First Minister's Questions, DC Thomson, Grampian TV, Glamis Castle, Stirling Castle, St Andrews and Glasgow.

The feedback received from the students of Zayed University was very positive. Indeed it helped to build a strong relationship between the Al-Maktoum Institute and Zayed University.

The 2004 Summer School

From 24 June to 12 July 2004, Al-Maktoum Institute was again delighted to host the second three week Summer School for Students from the UAE. Building on the success of previous year's Summer School for students from Zayed University, this year's event was expanded to include students from three different institutions of higher education in the UAE: Zayed University, UAE University, and the Higher Colleges of Technology (Dubai Women's College). The Summer School was organised for 10 female students from each of these institutions, with each group accompanied by a member of staff as chaperone, so making up a total group of 33.

The programme followed a similar structure to the 2003 Summer School, but was marked by a number of significant developments and additions. Highlights were a visit to the Scottish Parliament in Edinburgh to view First Minister's Question Time on the Parliament's final day in their old premises, which also included a meeting with Wendy Alexander MSP talking on the role of women in Scottish politics. The students also visited the City Chambers of both Dundee and Glasgow city, meeting the Lord Provost of Dundee and the Deputy Lord Provost of Glasgow. A visit to Aberdeen included a tour of the University of Aberdeen Business and Medical Schools, and a tour of Grampian Television state-of-the art studios. The students had two visits to Dundee College to try their hands at web page and graphic design, digital photography, and traditional Scottish baking. They also visited the College of Duncan of Jordanstone, University of Dundee to hear of postgraduate opportunities for learning and research in art and design.

The Summer School programme also included a Public Lecture at the Al-Maktoum Institute, by Councillor Jill Shimi, the leader of Dundee City Council, on 'The leading role of women in Dubai in the 21st Century'. Drawing on her recent experiences in Dubai, when she led a delegation from Dundee that was taking part in a 'Sister Cities' Forum alongside 11 other cities from around the world, Jill Shimi highlighted the key role that women are performing in the success of contemporary Dubai, and the investment that the state is making in educating women as the next generation of leaders. Looking back at the past, she also made interesting comparisons on the similarities of women living in the United Arab Emirates in the early part of last century and the former

female jute workers of Dundee. Councillor Shimi's speech was then
followed by short presentations by UAE students on their own
experiences of the leading role of women in twenty first century Dubai.

The 2005 Summer School

From 24 June to 13 June 2005 Al-Maktoum Institute was again delighted
to host the third Summer School for Students from the UAE. Again
building on the success of the previous two years Summer Schools, the
2005 event was further expanded to include students from the University
of Qatar which brought the number of universities involved in the
Summer School to four: Zayed University, UAE University, Higher
Colleges of Technology (Dubai Women's College), and Qatar University.
The Summer School was organised for 50 female students (10 from each
of these institutions. Each group accompanied by a member of staff as
chaperone, so making up a total of 54.

The students met leading individuals from nearly all walks of life
including Tom McCabe MSP, Minister of Finance, Margaret Curran
MSP, Minister of Parliamentary Business, Jill Shimi, Head of
Administration, Dundee City Council; the Deputy Lord Provost of
Glasgow, Bridget McConnell, Head of Cultural and Leisure Services,
Glasgow City Council, Alan Harden, Chief Executive of the Alliance
Trusts; Wendy Alexander MSP, and Frances Guy, Head of the Engaging
with the Muslim World Department in the Foreign Office. In addition
to this, they met HSH Prince Philipp of Liechtenstein, and to watched a
video presentation by Dr Pia Beckmann, the Lord Mayor of Wurzburg
in Germany.

The students experienced Scotland and its people through visits to
many local and national attractions including Edinburgh Castle, the
Scottish Parliament, Scottish Executive, Dundee Contemporary Arts
Centre, Verdant Works and City Chambers. For example, on June 29 the
Summer School students visited the Scottish Parliament and Scottish
Executive as part of their studies on leadership and multiculturalism.
They were welcomed to the parliament by two Ministers from the
Scottish Executive, Mrs Margaret Curran MSP, Minister for
Parliamentary Business, and Mr Tom McCabe MSP, Minister for
Finance and Public Service Reform.

Speaking to the students, Margaret Curran spoke of her delight and
excitement at meeting such a large group of women who were sure to
become leaders of their countries and societies. In addition, she
explained the role of women in the Scottish Parliament and stressed its
importance. She later spoke about her experience and the difficulties that

women may face in their life and the challenges and opportunities for women to work at the highest level.

Tom McCabe said that the Scottish Executive are very proud that Scotland is the home of the Al-Maktoum Institute, not only for the very important link that it has established between Scotland and Dubai, but also because it is such an excellent example for the rest of the world, as a centre working for the pursuit of multiculturalism and religious tolerance. He stressed that 'we are so proud that we have the Al-Maktoum Institute promoting multiculturalism and religious tolerance… It shines so well with some of the things we believe that we have to change in society… Since the Institute is located here, we can speak to the whole world including Scotland of having the Al-Maktoum Institute… One of the exciting aspects of Scotland's future is the ability and willingness to engage with other cultures and look for mutual understanding which will be for the mutual benefit, and the girls' visit will hopefully encourage that…'

The visit to the Scottish Parliament also included a tour around the new state-of-the-art parliament building, including a visit to the debating chamber and the Scottish Parliament members' offices. When the Summer School visited the Scottish Executive building at Victoria Quay, they were met by the International Officer of the Executive, Mr Robert Dunn. Mr Dunn gave a presentation on the history and current role of the Parliament, and took questions from the students on a number of matters – including the workings and finances of the Executive and the leading role of the Executive and Parliament for the participation of women. Following the meeting he commented on how impressed he was by the quality of the students.

The 2006 Summer School

From 27 June to 18 July 2006, Al-Maktoum Institute was again delighted to host the fourth Summer School Training Programme in Multiculturalism and Leadership for three weeks for Students from the UAE (including students from Qatar University). Building on the success of the previous Summer Schools, 2006 event again included students from four different institutions of higher education in the UAE: 10 female students from Zayed University, 10 female students from UAE University, 10 female students from Higher Colleges of Technology (Dubai Women's College), and 5 female students from Qatar University. Each group was accompanied by a member of staff as chaperone, making a total of 39.

The 2006 programme focused more on the academic content of the training with the students mostly attending the Institute Monday to Friday, and the weekends set aside for the more social and cultural aspects of the programme. The New Agenda formed the basis of the training programme with classes based upon the contents of this very important document. Main highlight of the programme this year, was a visit to the Scottish Parliament in Edinburgh where the students were welcomed to Scotland by Mr Tom McCabe, Minister for Finance and Public Service Reform and Mrs Margaret Curran, Minister for Parliamentary Business. The students returned to the Scottish Executive for a discussion on devolution later in their programme. They heard talks and were involved in discussion with prominent people and leaders from various industries including Councillor Jill Shimi, the Head of Administration for Dundee City Council, Edward Oakden, Ambassador Designate to UAE, Dr Pia Beckmann, the Lord Mayor of Wurzburg, Alan Baird, the Director of Dundee City Council Social Work Department, Alan Harden, Chief Executive of Alliance Trusts, Stewart Murdoch, the Director of Dundee City Council's Leisure and Communities, and representatives of Glasgow Chambers of Commerce.

The students were very fortunate to take part in two specially prepared all-day events with the Dundee City Council's Social Work Department and the Leisure and Communities Department. The intention of the programme was for the students to grasp a basic understanding of each of the department's activities, including their aims and objectives. An opportunity was given to all students to visit some of the facilities of these departments. The day with the Social Work Department concluded in a joint evening dinner and lecture; which was delivered by Dr Fatima Al-Sayegh of the UAE University on the 'The Leading Role of UAE Women in the Twenty-First Century'

A day out to Edinburgh included a visit to Edinburgh Castle and the Royal Museum of Scotland accompanied by the Lord Mayor of Wurzburg, Dr Pia Beckmann.

The concluding ceremony of the Fourth Summer School was attended by the Chairman of the Board of the Institute, HE Mr Mirza Al-Sayegh, and two UAE Ministers, HE Dr Hanif Qassimi, Minister for Education and HE Miriam Al-Roumi, Minister for Social Affairs, and Lord Elder, Chancellor of the Institute. A special video message was conveyed to the students from HH Shaikh Nahyan Bin Mubarak Al-Nahyan, the UAE Minister for Higher Education.

The Training Programme on English Language, Multiculturalism and Leadership for Local UAE from Dubai Media Incorporated

As part of the Institute's strategic plan to build bridges between Scotland and the UAE as well as providing international training for local UAE nationals, Al-Maktoum Institute organised two training programmes for UAE nationals from Dubai Media Incorporated in summer 2005 and summer 2006.

The 2005 Summer School

In June Mohammad Obaid Bin Ghannam, Secretary General of Al-Maktoum Foundation, and I had a meeting in Dubai with Mr Ali Khalifa al-Rimiathi , Head of Dubai TV, where it was discussed how to go about strengthening the relationship between the Al-Maktoum Institute and Dubai TV. From this meeting emerged a proposal for the Institute to organise English language training for a group of seven employees from Dubai TV from 31 July to 11 September 2005.

The English language classes were: General English, English for Business, and English for the Media. As part of their training, the group attended training activities which included the presentation of Shaikh Hamdan Bin Rashid Al-Maktoum Awards for Multicultural Scotland 2005, in the Apex Hotel Dundee on 15 August 2005, a session with David Whitton at Al-Maktoum Institute on 1 September 2005, and a visit to BBC Scotland in Glasgow on 7 September 2005.

The seven staff from Dubai TV were also given a briefing about HH Shaikh Hamdan's Vision, The Agenda of Al-Maktoum Institute, Dundee Declaration for the Future Development of the Study of Islam and Muslims, Al-Maktoum Institute Programmes, and the links between Al-Maktoum Institute and Dubai TV.

The 2006 Summer School

Following the successful first training in 2005, Ali Khalifa al-Rimiathi, Head of Dubai TV, asked Mr Mirza Al-Sayegh, Chairman of Al-Maktoum Institute Board, (15 August 2005) if the Institute could organise a second training programme in summer 2006. Accordingly, on 27 February 2006, Mr Hussain Ali Lootah, Chief Executive Officer of Dubai Media Incorporated, sent me a letter egarding organising this second training. On 29 April 2006, Ali Khalifa al-Rimiathi informed me that they had advertised this training opportunity and had received around 60 applications from local UAE nationals who are working in Dubai Media Incorporated. They selected ten to receive this training.

On this basis, a group of 10 staff (5 males and 5 females) came to Dundee for a period of around 45 days (6 weeks of classes) from 29 July 2006 to 10 September 2006 for full time English language learning for 5 weeks (from 31 July to 1 September 2006); and a training programme on multiculturalism and leadership (from 4 to 8 September 2006).

The ten students attended English Language Classes at the University of St Andrews. The English language classes were: General English, English for Business, and English for the Media. They were also given sessions at the Institute on: Multiculturalism, Leadership, the New Agenda for the Future Development of the Study of Islam and Muslims, the new field of inquiry of Islamicjerusalem Studies, Al-Maktoum Institute postgraduate programmes, and the links between Al-Maktoum Institute and Dubai TV.

The students were awarded at the end of their six weeks study with certificates presented by the Institute Council members Councillor Jill Shimi and the Reverend Erik Cramb. The male staff received an Al-Maktoum tie and the female staff received a shawl.

Al-Maktoum Institute Summer School Alumnus Network

During the last four years, the total number who participated in the summer schools was 166 UAE nationals which included 12 female students from Qatar University. The Summer Schools for UAE females students (including students from Qatar University) had 149 students altogether (12 from Qatar University): 25 in 2003, 31 in 2004, 54 in 2005 (including 6 from Qatar University), and 39 in 2006 (including 6 from Qatar University). The Summer Schools for Local UAE from Dubai Media Incorporated totalled 17 staff: 7 in 2005 and 10 in 2006.

During the visit to Al-Maktoum Institute of Mr Edward Oakden, the British Ambassador Designate to the UAE, on 5 July 2006, Mr Oakden discussed with me his desire to see the future development of relations between the UK and the UAE as his primary aim. As a practical implementation of this, he was keen to see further consolidation of the important work already done by Al-Maktoum Institute through the four annual summer schools in Dundee, Scotland for UAE students. One proposal coming from this discussion was for the creation of an alumnus network that would bring together all the students who had benefited from the Institute's multicultural training programmes.

In support of this idea, Mr Oakden made the suggestion that the British Embassy in Abu Dhabi could host a reception for the alumnus students at some point in spring 2006-07, and in further discussion a date for such an event has now been established.

Aims of the Network

Following the success of the four Summer Schools and the two Dubai TV training programmes at Al-Maktoum Institute, the Alumnus Network was established by the Academic Council to:

i.   Facilitate and encourage the networking in the UAE between students and individuals from the different groups who have attended the Institute's multicultural training programmes
ii. Facilitate and encourage the ongoing contact between all these students and individuals and Al-Maktoum Institute in Dundee
iii. Continue their association with Scotland in particular and the UK in general
iv. To encourage these students and individuals to implement the training programmes' aims of global awareness and citizenship, and to develop their particular training in multiculturalism and leadership
v.   To also encourage the groups and individuals to continue to strive to implement the Vision for Education and Multiculturalism of HH Shaikh Hamdan Bin Rashid Al-Maktoum
vi. Through these contacts, to facilitate the development of the important international relationship between the UAE and Scotland and the UK

The Alumnus Network will be launched with a reception held at the British Embassy, Abu Dhabi, hosted by the British Ambassador to the UAE, HE Mr Edward Oakden. This will take place on 8 April 2007. The launch of this Alumnus Network will form part of the celebrations of the fifth anniversary of the foundation of Al-Maktoum Institute in Dundee, Scotland.

All students from the UAE and staff from Dubai TV and Dubai Media Inc who have participated in the training programmes will be invited to this reception, through their respective universities and institutions (or former universities). That is, students from Zayed University, UAE University, and Higher Colleges of Technology (Dubai Women's College), and staff from Dubai TV and Dubai Media Inc.

Membership of the Alumnus Network will be open to all participants in the Institute's summer/winter schools and multicultural training programmes. At the launch, a form will be distributed to all the students inviting them to provide contact details and to join the new Alumnus Network.

The Alumnus Network will then continue to hold regular activities in Dubai, Abu Dhabi, and elsewhere in the UAE to facilitate contacts between the members and the Institute. These will include both social gatherings and public lectures. The Institute will continue working with HE Mr Oakden and the British Embassy, who has kindly offered his support to the Institute for this Alumnus Network.

The relationship between the UAE and Scotland has been strengthened and developed through these educational Summer Schools, which invest in education and young people as future leaders through a long term vision. Indeed, education is clearly recognised as a fundamental element in the future relationship between the UAE and the UK, and the Alumnus Network will be an important means by which educational contact is maintained and developed between the two countries.

CONCLUSION

I have been studying, teaching and researching in the Study of Islam and Muslims at both Arab and British universities for 30 years (from 1977). In addition, I received training in Political Sciences, History, Middle Eastern Studies, and Islamic Studies; and taught for a number of years in History departments, Religious Studies department, Arabic and Islamic Studies department, and the Study of Islam and Muslims Department.

Accordingly, the Study of Islam and Muslims has always been the focal point of my work and a field which I have enjoyed immensely. I lived in both the Arab Muslim countries and the West, in particular the UK, and have a thorough knowledge of their history, politics, cultures, societies, and religions. I have not only studied Islam in depth, but have lived under conditions where different ideas and viewpoints were expressed and debated at length. I had the privilege of meeting leading figures from many Arab, Muslim and Western countries, representing the whole spectrum of Arabic, Muslim and Western thought and various schools. This experience enabled me to form a much broader approach to the field and compare the differing views of Arab, Muslim and Western schools. This is a very clear indication of an ability to build strong research links between the Study of Islam and Muslims in the widest sense.

For me, the Study of Islam and Muslims is a field which should include a number of disciplines and approaches, looking both at the religion of Islam and also Muslims in particular social and historical contexts within a number of different methodologies, e.g. political sciences, history, geography, anthropology, and Islamic Studies. The aim is to gain understanding of a broad range of issues relating to the study of Islam and Muslims, looking at the field in many different ways, and in many global contexts, spanning a variety of disciplines and methodologies; and distinct from traditional approaches where the focus has been to study Islam and Muslims from just one limited perspective. My philosophy is to offer interdisciplinary and multidisciplinary training in the Study of Islam and Muslims within a number of different methodologies, eg., history, political sciences, geography, as well as traditional areas in Islamic Studies.

In the last five years, my main focus has been to set the new agenda for cultural engagements to generate an atmosphere in which a constructive dialogue can take place rather than a clash. I firmly believe that through multicultural education as the key means to defeat religious and secular fundamentalism and extremism, we will contribute to achieve a common ground and space, mutual understanding and respect, and peaceful co-existence between and within people, nations, religions, and cultures. I recognise that not everyone will agree with this vision, and I do not pretend to have all the answers, but at least I am putting forward some ideas on how to improve understanding between people of different religions and cultures. For my part, I have been doing all I can to promote cultural engagements that will see people acknowledging and respecting their differences BUT willing to share a common ground and space, living and working together in a peaceful co-existence.

One of my central aims has been to promote a greater understanding of different religions, and cultures in a multicultural context, for the benefit of the wider community, and to build bridges between the Muslim and Western worlds of learning at this crucial time. In the last five years, the Institute witnessed a vast number of developments to promote such a vision. For example, to institutionalise the new agenda for cultural engagements and promotion of multiculturalism, I have taken several structural steps, including electing leaders of the local communities into the Institute Council and establishing Al-Maktoum Institute Students Society. The diversity of the Executive members' countries of origin is yet another reflection of the multicultural ethos we have developed at the Institute.

The issue of multiculturalism is also firmly at the heart of the Institute's academic work. This includes, for example, the creation of a professorial chair in multiculturalism. We were the first higher educational institution in the UK to create such a post, currently held by Professor Malory Nye. The chair was created in response to the dire need to engage in a more serious and structured way in research and teaching in multiculturalism. We also established 'The Centre for Research on Multiculturalism and Islam and Muslims in Scotland', which aims to contribute to the development of awareness of multicultural Scotland. Among other activities, it organised an international symposium in Spring 2006 on the Challenges of Multiculturalism. A special think-tank 'Multiculturalism Research Unit' was formed. The theme of the Institute Summer School for female' students from the UAE (including female' students from Qatar University) in the last four years (2003, 2004, 2005, 2006) was multiculturalism and leadership. The Multicultural Awards for Scotland we started with the support of the Scottish Executive (Government) and are designed to recognise and encourage individual and institutional contributions to multicultural Scotland in which religious diversity, cultural equality, social justice, and civilisational dialogue flourish. The awards are made up of a principal award combined with seven smaller awards, including multicultural education, multicultural healthcare, multicultural in the media, multicultural in sport, civilisational dialogue, Arab-British understanding, and Scottish-Emirates relations. The Honorary Fellowship of the Institute is given to individuals who have demonstrated their commitment to the multicultural vision. Sponsorship and support is given to local clubs and societies who have demonstrated their commitment to multiculturalism and for projects to further this aim. Last but not least, the Al-Maktoum Multicultural Garden was established for the Fun Factory Out-of-School Club at Park Place Primary School in Dundee, Scotland.

We have clearly also established a niche for ourselves as a unique institute with a timely new agenda. I am proud to be one of the key leading scholars behind the development, implementation, and dissemination of this new innovative agenda in the Study of Islam and Muslims, which defined the field as Post-Orientalist, Post-Traditionalist, Multicultural, and Interdisciplinary and Multidisciplinary in its methodology as well as its theoretical framework. The aim of this unique new agenda is to challenge and develop current teaching and scholarship, recognising that this is a time for change in Islamic Studies. There must be better education at university level on Islam and Muslims in today's world which reflects the needs of our contemporary multicultural society. The agenda has been developed to bring scholars together from all backgrounds, based on a principle of mutual respect, in order to develop a common intellectual goal in the field of the Study of Islam and Muslims.

Indeed, there is an urgent need for a new agenda to develop Islamic Studies into the Study of Islam and Muslims to challenge both the more traditional approaches that were often faith based and excluded non-Muslims and the orientalist approaches that often alienated Muslims. Indeed, the call for a new agenda is truly timely and necessary, particularly to prevent the misguided and narrow interpretation of Islam which is the source of so many problems in many societies. It is only through multicultural education that we can work to eliminate extremism and fundamentalism. We are promoting this agenda through our teaching of postgraduate programmes, which address the needs of local, national and international need in the twenty-first century.

The success of the Institute comes from its new agenda. To reflect this, the Institute, during the past few years, has seen significant developments, which address the exciting growth of the Institute and the wider network of relationships. The Institute, for example, started the process of disseminating and implementing this new agenda by working internally at the Institute and externally with our sixteen partner universities. I feel also very proud that we have established and are in the process of disseminating our New Agenda in the Study of Islam and Muslims. The success of our academic programmes has been clearly acknowledged by a number of indicators, not least the glowing reports and comments we have received from our external examiners.

In the last seven years (2000-2007), I have successfully established a leading distinctive national and international centre of academic excellence for developing teaching and research in the Study of Islam and Muslims of the highest standard. This is based on critical and analytical debate in which better understanding of Islam and Muslims can be developed – both for Muslims and non-Muslims – in an environment focused on a common sense of purpose and belonging. I feel proud that the Institute is playing a unique and key role in setting the new agenda in cultural engagement and shaping and developing teaching and research in the Study of Islam and Muslim at university level in the UK and internationally. Indeed, we are now a unique seat of learning and research-led institution of higher education, which offers postgraduate programmes of study (validated by the University of Aberdeen).

Through the Institute, I have also been actively involved in educating the next generation of scholars both nationally and internationally to enable them to face the challenges and opportunities of a diverse and multicultural world. Indeed, cultural engagement and multiculturalism are now at the centre of the Institute's vision and structure. Our multicultural ethos is visibly translated and implemented in our day-to-day operation. Our staff and students come from diverse national and cultural backgrounds including both Muslims and non-Muslims, and our research is taken forward by a team of internationally renowned scholars. For example, the plan is to balance our student profile by having 50% home students and 50% international students.

The Institute takes great pride in the continual growing success of our Master and PhD students. With the 14 graduates in 2006 (7 with PhDs), this brings the total of PhD and Masters Graduates to 54. Indeed, as the Founding Principal and Vice-Chancellor, I feel very proud that we have now a community of 54 graduates working across the globe at several levels. These students are to be highly commended for their hard work. They are truly one of the Institute's greatest assets. I am absolutely delighted that we are playing our part in educating the new generation of scholars who will take that message of cultural engagement and multiculturalism out into the wider world, and will go out into the world of work ready to challenge the old ways of thinking, teaching and learning.

As we are celebrating the excellent achievements of the foundation and first stages of the Institute's history in this very short period, there is much we can look back on with pride. Indeed, the Institute's success is not only impressive but also well deserved. I feel very proud of the progress and growth in the last five years. I am enormously privileged and honoured to be the Founding Principal and Vice-Chancellor of the Institute, which has been extremely successful in achieving its vision, mission, aims and objectives in the first five years of its existence and beyond. It has been a remarkable period for the Institute, demonstrating our uniqueness at both academic and communities levels.

If the first year was the phase where we worked hard to set up the foundations for a successful endeavour, the following years were spent more on building on the foundations and developing our core competence. Our hard work in these first five years was in order to ensure that we continue to foster excellence in everything we do, especially in teaching and research. Indeed, the Institute has generated and established a very strong foundation and framework for solid and continuous delivery of results, which will help the Institute to continue playing its leading role at both academic and communities levels.

The Institute's achievements demonstrate our continuous success in developing our academic activities, in particular the development and enhancement of our research culture, enhancing the learning environment and community, our quality assurance systems, our new agenda, and the widening and strengthening of our international academic network and collaboration. Our reputation as a centre of academic excellence is well established, acknowledged, and recognised. Our name is now becoming more and more recognised nationally and internationally, at the levels that we hope will bring benefits to the Institute and to the communities that we are part of.

Through the Al-Maktoum Institute, I have been actively setting the new agenda for cultural engagement and encouraging dialogue across cultures and people which has enhanced greater understanding and appreciation between the Arab and Muslim worlds and the west in general and between the UAE and Scotland in particular. Indeed, the Institute has played a fundamental role in building progressive links between the UAE and Scotland. We have been continually striving to implement the vision to further facilitate the creation of mutually beneficial relationships between the two people. Our strategic aim was to help promote a two way traffic for this developing relationship between the two nations.

At the personal and professional levels, the last five years of establishing and building the Institute have been challenging, demanding, hard and tiring work BUT an enjoyable experience. In each successful step, I have felt very strongly that we are making a positive change and making history. I believe that we have made a groundbreaking development both at the academic and communities levels. Indeed, the last five years have been inspiring years where we have set the new agenda for the Study of Islam and Muslims globally, and through the results of our major academic research we have begun a constructive dialogue and debate on how the future of the study of Islam and Muslims should be developed in the twenty first century.

Yet even while we celebrate our achievements, we know there is still much to do to promote our vision for cultural engagements, and to get our message across that we are playing a major part in trying to bring peace to the world. In the last five years, the Institute has been clearly focused upon the niche of Al-Maktoum Institute's Vision, Mission and New Agenda and should continue to maintain the passion and ambition demonstrated so far towards the strategic attainment of its collective goals at the local, national and international level. On these strong foundations and history, the Institute's future looks promising indeed. The Institute's eyes are now firmly fixed on the future so that we can see nothing else but a better and brighter life for all ahead.

To break down the barriers that separate and divide the contemporary world, there is an urgent need to establish and develop this new agenda for cultural engagement through education in both the west and the Arab and Muslim world. Although we were successful in setting the new agenda for cultural engagement in Scotland and the UK at both academic and communities levels through the establishment of Al-Maktoum Institute in Scotland, we urgently need to establish this new agenda in cultural engagement in the Muslim world. Through the

Institute in Scotland, we have done everything possible to encourage a two way traffic in developing cultural engagement, in particular through serving the local, national, and international communities, and by forging international academic links, scholarship and collaborations with sixteen of the world's leading Universities in Europe, Africa, Asia, the Gulf States, and South East Asia, BUT this is not enough.

At this stage of setting the new agenda in cultural engagements, it is time to establish a similar institute in the Muslim world which will hopefully complete the circle of laying the foundation for the new agenda for cultural engagement. Indeed, to ensure really successful cultural engagement, it should be well established and accepted by all the peoples in the world including China, Japan and Africa BUT at least at this stage by both the Western and Muslim worlds.

Setting this new agenda in the Muslim world will be at the top of my priorities in the coming years. I have devoted all of my professional and personal life to education. As a scholar and leader who established several academic projects nearly from scratch, I enjoy innovative, creative, and challenging big ideas. As a person and a professional, I am very passionate about progressive education, research and community welfare. One of my central arguments is that, to improve the quality of life in a country and to transfer that country into a knowledge-based society, the leaders of that country need to work with scholars to provide world-class educational opportunities for its citizens. In addition, I am a great supporter of higher education institutions in the Muslim countries who are trying to maintain their credibility as leading public institutions in their own country and be responsive to the local and international market needs. To address the needs of our local and international societies, and to prepare our graduates to take their place in developing their society, there must be better education at university level in the fields of humanities and social sciences, in particular Islamic Studies and the Study of Islam and Muslim.

I am looking forward to continue working with colleagues in both western and Muslim worlds to face the challenges and opportunities of the twenty first century.

APPENDICES

APPENDIX I

STATEMENTS

'I would like to register my special thanks for the hard work done by Professor Abd al-Fattah El-Awaisi, Principal and Vice-Chancellor of the Institute. I have all the trust in his leadership and his unique role in establishing and developing the Institute. He has, undeniably, shown excellent skills and commitment to establish and run the Institute very successfully.' **His Highness Shaikh Hamdan Bin Rashid Al-Maktoum (6 May 2002)**

'The pioneering and development of the discipline of Islamicjerusalem Studies took a major step through the establishment of Al-Maktoum Institute for Arabic and Islamic Studies in Scotland, for which I designated the leading scholar Professor Abd al-Fattah El-Awaisi as Principal and Vice-Chancellor. It is through Professor Abd al-Fattah's academic research that this role of Islamicjerusalem as a model of multiculturalism has now been understood and established.' **His Highness Shaikh Hamdan Bin Rashid Al-Maktoum (23 June 2004)**

'Working with the ethos of promoting a greater understanding and building bridges through academic partnerships the Institute has become an integral part of Scottish society particularly in Dundee. As well as building strength in academia, the Institute has been working hard to enhance the relationships between Scotland and Dubai' **The Rt Hon Jim Wallace (MSP), Scottish Deputy First Minister and Minister for Enterprise and Lifelong Learning (11 December 2003)**

'The Scottish Executive is very proud that Scotland is the home of the Al-Maktoum Institute, not only for the very important link that it has established between Scotland and Dubai, but also because it is such an excellent example for the rest of the world, as a centre working for the pursuit of multiculturalism and religious tolerance... we are so proud that we have the Al-Maktoum Institute promoting Multiculturalism and religious tolerance... It shines so well with some of the things we believe that we have to change in society... Since the Institute is located here, we can speak to the whole world including Scotland of having the Al-Maktoum Institute...' **Mr Tom McCabe (MSP), Scottish Minister for Finance and Public Service Reform (27 June 2005)**

'How proud Scotland are to have Al-Maktoum Institute, particularly for the work that the Institute is doing, as an example for the rest of the world, to promote multiculturalism and religious tolerance.' **Mr Tom McCabe (MSP), Scottish Minister for Finance and Public Service Reform (30 June 2005)**

'The Scottish Minister greatly value the presence and work of the Al-Maktoum Institute in Dundee. The Scottish Government, and the First Minister in particular, is committed to celebrating cultural diversity in Scotland, challenging the systems, behaviour and attitudes that cause discrimination or prejudice, and therefore the proposal for an Al-Maktoum Cultural Centre in Dundee to promote understanding and bring communities together are very encouraging. I would like to take this opportunity to reiterate the First Minister's invitation for you (HH Shaikh Hamdan Bin Rashid Al-Maktoum) to visit Scotland. I understand that you may come to Dundee for the ground breaking ceremony of the Al-Maktoum Cultural Centre – I am grateful to Professor El-Awaisi for keeping me informed of this possibility, and will work closely with him regarding possible meetings that might usefully form part of a programme for such a visit.' **Mr Tom McCabe (MSP), Scottish Minister for Finance and Public Service Reform (22 June 2006)**

'It is very important to us that Al-Maktoum Institute goes from strength to strength in Scotland. We have a high regard for the ethos behind the school. We very sincerely believe if we do that as a society we will be richer and stronger. We greatly value the work done and the strong links developing between Scotland and Dubai. Those links were strengthened earlier this year when I visited Dubai in March. I received a very warm welcome in Dubai and was delighted with the discussions that took place. I met His Highness Shaikh Hamdan and we talked about further relationships between Scotland and Dubai. It is important to recognise what lies behind the thinking and the creation of the Institute.' **Mr Tom McCabe (MSP), Scottish Minister for Finance and Public Service Reform (28 June 2006)**

'I have been involved with the Al-Maktoum Institute on a number of occasions. I was privy to the lectures given earlier this year when International Academics were debating multiculturalism. The breadth of that thinking will be a huge learning experience for you and us.' **Mrs Margaret Curran (MSP), Scottish Minister for Parliamentary Business (28 June 2006)**

'Working with the ethos of promoting a greater understanding and building bridges through academic excellence and serving the communities, the Institute has become an integral part of Dundee's City and society. In addition, this has promoted Dundee as home to a centre excellence in Arabic and Islamic Studies.' **Extract from the Sister Cities Agreement between Dubai, United Arab Emirates and Dundee, Scotland (6 April 2004)**

'How extremely proud the city of Dundee are to be the home of Al-Maktoum Institute.' **Councillor Jill Shimi, Dundee City Leader (30 June 2005)**

HH Prince Philipp spoke of how much he had enjoyed his visit to Al-Maktoum Institute and Dundee, and how he had found the Institute a very impressive institution. **(30 June 2005)**

'Your well respected Professor Abd al-Fattah El-Awaisi impressed me with his continued conversation about his beloved country, United Arab Emirates, as a model of a modern country which has established itself very successfully in the last thirty five years. Indeed, he is an excellent ambassador for his country.' **Dr Pia Beckmann, Lord Mayor of Würzburg (July 2005)**

'That this House congratulates Dundee's Al-Maktoum Institute on the publication of its report entitled Time for Change: Report on the Future of the Study of Islam and Muslims in Universities and Colleges in Multicultural Britain; [it] congratulates the authors, Professor Abd al-Fattah El-Ewaisi and Professor Malory Nye, on their hard work; [it] believes the report to be an important contribution to the debate surrounding the study of Islam and Muslims in UK universities; [it] shares with the authors a belief that better education will lead to better understanding of Islam and Muslims; [it] further shares their belief that education is one of the main ways to tackle extremism, and hopes that this report will provide the basis for an ongoing debate about these important issues.' **An Early Day Motion at the House of Commons (Number 2864, dated 25 October 2006)**

'That the Parliament notes the publication of Time for Change: Report on the Future of the Study of Islam and Muslims in Universities and

Colleges in Multicultural Britain by Dundee's Al-Maktoum Institute for Arabic and Islamic studies; [it] congratulates the authors, Professor Abd al-Fattah El-Ewaisi and Professor Malory Nye, on their work which represents an excellent contribution to this vital debate for Scotland and the United Kingdom; [it] believes that education has a crucial role to play in tackling extremism and promoting diversity and multiculturalism in Scotland; [it] recognises all the efforts being made throughout Scottish society to promote multiculturalism, and hopes that this report will provide the basis for further debate on this crucial issue.' **Motion at the Scottish Parliament (Number S2M-5037 dated 30 October 2006)**

APPENDIX II

OPENING SPEECH BY HIS HIGHNESS SHAIKH HAMDAN BIN RASHID AL-MAKTOUM AT THE OFFICIAL OPENING CEREMONY OF THE INSTITUTE 6 MAY 2002

Distinguished Guests, ladies and gentlemen,

I am very pleased to be part of this historic day – a day in which we are establishing a new stage in the academic discipline of Arabic and Islamic studies in the West. And I am very grateful to all of you for coming today, to be part of the ceremony to officially open Al-Maktoum Institute for Arabic and Islamic Studies, which is the first unique academic and cultural establishment of its kind in the West.

I am very proud to say that this Institute is the biggest Institute for Arabic and Islamic studies in Scotland, if not in the whole of United Kingdom. The Institute is a unique development in this academic field. Indeed, the setting up of this Institute marks an advanced step forward in encouraging dialogues to enhance the understanding between the Arab and Muslim worlds and the West.

Choosing Dundee as the location is undoubtedly the right choice because of the long-established link that has existed between the City and the Arab and Muslim worlds. I sincerely hope that the presence of the Institute will help to strengthen this link, and that the Institute will also further facilitate the creation of mutually beneficial relations between the United Arab Emirates and the United Kingdom in general, and between Dubai and Dundee in particular.

I am also impressed by the quality of the academic programmes and the facilities offered here at the Institute. I am very happy to note that within a relatively short period of time, the Institute has been successfully developed and established as an international centre of excellence.

In appreciation of the unique roles and the distinctive capabilities of the institute, I am pleased to announce the inauguration of a new scholarship scheme for young students to come and study here at this Institute. This new scheme will start with five scholarships for students from the United Arab Emirates and two more scholarships for students from Palestine to undertake full-time study at the Institute from September this year.

In this historic moment, I would like to register my special thanks for the hard work done by Professor Abd al-Fattah El-Awaisi, Principal and Vice-Chancellor of the Institute. I have every trust in his leadership and his unique role in establishing and developing the Institute. He has, undeniably, shown excellent skills and commitment to establish and run the Institute so successfully.

With these remarks, I now declare Al-Maktoum Institute for Arabic and Islamic Studies officially opened and I wish it every success.

APPENDIX III

HIS HIGHNESS SHAIKH HAMDAN BIN RASHID AL-MAKTOUM'S VISION FOR MULTICULTRALISM

Vision

My vision is based on 'Umar's Assurance of Safety and the central principle of Islamicjerusalem as a key model for multiculturalism, civilisational dialogue, and mutual understanding and respect. This vision encompasses my passion for the twin pillars of multiculturalism and education, which are both essential building blocks for global harmony and mutual understanding in the twenty-first century.

Islamicjerusalem gives us a model of a common space in which people from different backgrounds can live together. Islamicjerusalem is described in the Holy Qur'an as 'surrounded with *barakah*': a place which radiates goodness and blessings. This understanding of Islamicjerusalem, so central to Islam and Muslims, and for a place which is so important to three great faiths, has become clear as a region in which diversity and pluralism thrive. It has been through my passion for Islamicjerusalem that our understanding of this place of hope, safety, mutual respect and peaceful co-existence has been nurtured and developed.

My priority is to work to achieve the implementation of practical models, to build bridges between peoples, nations, cultures, and religions. Working through education, mutual engagement, and promoting better communication and understanding, my vision is to find ways of breaking down the barriers that separate and divide the contemporary world. My actions aim to establish strong foundations for the building and the realisation of this vision.

A first step in this process was the establishment of the new field of inquiry of Islamicjerusalem Studies, which I have supported and encouraged with great passion. The pioneering and development of the discipline of Islamicjerusalem Studies took a major step through the establishment of Al-Maktoum Institute for Arabic and Islamic Studies in Scotland, for which I designated the leading scholar Professor Abd al-Fattah El-Awaisi as Principal and Vice-Chancellor. It is through Professor Abd al-Fattah's academic research that this role of Islamicjerusalem as a model of multiculturalism has now been understood and established.

Implementation

Al-Maktoum Institute in Dundee is a unique academic and cultural establishment in the west, which is a new stage for understandings of Islam and Muslims in the west and a key bridge between the peoples of today's world. Al-Maktoum Institute is a practical step through which I am working to pursue better understanding and communication across the world and a living and tangible model of inclusiveness which reflects and demonstrates this vision of Islamicjerusalem.

Radiating from this is my model of co-operation that is bridging Scotland and Dubai, particularly through a series of further practical steps. The establishment of Al-Maktoum Institute for Arabic and Islamic Studies, which I have authorised to implement my vision, is the starting point for this. At the academic level, the Institute is a research-led centre of excellence in research and teaching, with its new agenda for the study of Islam and Muslims. The Institute is also forging an international academic network, and is working to educate the next generation of scholars in the study of Islam and Muslims, to enable them to face the challenges and opportunities of a diverse and multicultural world in the twenty-first century. The Institute is also actively working to serve the local, national, and international communities.

From this starting point, the Institute has led to a number of important achievements in a short space of time, including:

- the linking of Dundee and Dubai in a Sister Cities agreement
- the creation of Al-Maktoum Cultural Centre in Dundee – as a facility for all the communities of the City and of Scotland, and as a model for multiculturalism in Scotland
- a new model for the future study of Islam and Muslims, set out in the Dundee Declaration at the Al-Maktoum Institute in March 2004, establishing the new agenda for the discipline which is post-orientalist, post-traditionalist, multicultural, and both inter-disciplinary and multi-disciplinary
- the direct Emirates daily flight from Dubai to Scotland
- a number of higher education links between Scotland and Dubai, including the establishment of the British University in Dubai, the linking of University of Aberdeen with Zayed University, and Summer Schools at the Al-Maktoum Institute in Dundee for female students from the UAE
- my commitment to multiculturalism has been shown in particular by the launch of the Shaikh Hamdan Bin Rashid Al-Maktoum

Awards for Multicultural Scotland, which will be awarded for the first time in August 2005

- and Al-Maktoum Institute is continually striving to implement my vision to further facilitate the creation of mutually beneficial relationships by establishing practical models for global cross-cultural understanding, with co-operation between the UAE and UK in general, and between Dubai and Scotland in particular as an example

All these steps come directly from my vision to follow and implement the model of multicultural Islamicjerusalem. Through Al-Maktoum Institute – together with Al-Maktoum Foundation, in Scotland – I am actively working to encourage dialogue across cultures and peoples, which will enhance greater understanding and appreciation between communities and peoples at all levels across the world in general, and between the Arab and Muslim worlds and the west in particular.

My passion for Islamicjerusalem and vision for the implementation of this model into practical steps has created the foundations for co-operation and the encouragement of a multicultural ethos of mutual respect and common understanding for this globe.

Hamdan Bin Rashid Al-Maktoum
Dubai, 23 June 2004

APPENDIX IV

INSTITUTE MISSION STATEMENT

The mission of Al-Maktoum Institute for Arabic and Islamic Studies is to pursue excellence in teaching, research, and consultancy in the academic study of Islam and Muslims as an implementation of the vision for education and multiculturalism of HH Shaikh Hamdan Bin Rashid Al-Maktoum.

Al-Maktoum Institute is a research-led institution that works to achieve the following goals:

- To set the agenda for the future development of the study of Islam and Muslims and to take a leading role in the establishment and implementation of this agenda, for example by working in partnership with other academic institutions
- To educate the next generation of scholars, both nationally and internationally, in the Study of Islam and Muslims, to enable them to face the challenges and opportunities of a diverse and multicultural world in the twenty-first century
- To promote intelligent debate and understanding on Islam and the role of Muslims in the contemporary world
- To build bridges between communities and peoples at all levels across the world

As a unique academic post-orientalist institute that is working to serve the communities and to promote a greater understanding of different religions and cultures, multiculturalism is at the heart of Al-Maktoum Institute's vision and structure, and is to be practically implemented in all aspects of its work.

APPENDIX V

INSTITUTE AIMS AND OBJECTIVES

1) To foster excellence in teaching, research and consultancy in Arabic and Islamic Studies:

   a. To provide high quality flexible education which enables students from any religion, gender or cultural background to follow clearly defined pathways which lead to a range of exit awards at postgraduate level;
   b. To provide a postgraduate educational pathway relevant to the needs of potential students and employers both nationally and internationally and to maintain the relevance of programmes to market needs via a range of ongoing reviews;
   c. To support scholarship, research and consultancy activities in Arabic and Islamic Studies by ensuring that teaching is underpinned by relevant research and consultancy and to further develop the research and consultancy profile of the Institute.

2) To create an exciting academic environment for Arabic and Islamic studies;

   a. To encourage students and staff to achieve both Institutional and personal goals;
   b. To provide a strong focus for inter-disciplinary advanced teaching and research in Arabic and Islamic studies;
   c. To promote academic developments in Arabic and Islamic studies with the aim of recruiting highly qualified students for postgraduate study and research.

3) To provide a meeting point between the Western and Muslim worlds of learning and to encourage scholarship and academic co-operation:

   a. To act as a national resource in the Scottish and UK context for consultation by government bodies, public organisations, industry, business and the media;
   b. To develop international links in pursuit of collaboration and mutually beneficial academic and professional ties, such as

research projects; recruiting students, facilitating academic exchanges and achieving enhanced levels of library resources.

4) To serve the communities:

    a. To create, maintain and strengthen beneficial relationships and links with the local, national and international communities;
    b. To work with local bodies to serve the local communities in Scotland in general, and Dundee in particular.

APPENDIX VI

DUNDEE DECLARATION
For the Future Development of the Study of Islam and Muslims

First international symposium on Islamic Studies
Islamic Universities League and Al-Maktoum Institute for Arabic and
Islamic Studies

In a spirit of co-operation, the delegates of the first international symposium on the development of Islamic Studies organised by the Islamic Universities League and the Al-Maktoum Institute for Arabic and Islamic Studies in Dundee, under the patronage of HH Shaikh Hamdan Bin Rashid Al-Maktoum, Deputy Ruler of Dubai and Minister of Finance and Industry in the United Arab Emirates, have agreed to make the following declaration of our common ground, and shared interests and goals:

1. We recognise the need to develop the Study of Islam and Muslims as the development of a discipline with long established roots, but which must now face the challenges and opportunities of the twenty-first century.

2. We share a common aim to build bridges and to provide a meeting point between the Muslim and Western worlds of learning and to encourage scholarship and academic co-operation at this crucial time.

3. We acknowledge that the acceptance of the Al-Maktoum Institute into the Islamic Universities League is an important step towards achieving this goal. Co-operation between Islam and the West in the last century began with Muslim-British relations. The Al-Maktoum Institute in Dundee is a symbol of co-operation which bridges the gap between Islamic civilisation and the West.

4. The Islamic Universities League, which consists of more than one hundred universities, including Al-Azhar University, encourages all creative efforts in the domain of establishing Islamic universities and academic institutes. It supports all efforts to present the image of Islam as a religion which aims at liberating human kind, supporting human rights, and the good of all humanity.

5. The crisis in the contemporary Muslim world is the absence of co-operation between knowledge and power. We are in pressing need to adopt and lead academic, scientific, ethical studies, that are objective to work to change the image of Islam in the West.

6. We seek to work towards the encouragement of research and teaching in a focused field of the Study of Islam and Muslims.

7. This developing field of inquiry is highly indicated in historical, sociological, political, anthropological, gendered, and legal aspects of the Study of Islam and Muslims.

8. As a discipline, the Study of Islam and Muslims must seek to develop and define itself as post-orientalist and multicultural, in which it is recognised that there is no single methodology or approach, but is both inter-disciplinary and multi-disciplinary.

9. The Study of Islam and Muslims is based on a principle of respect by all involved in this field of academic study, in which both Muslims and non-Muslims can share together a common sense of purpose and belonging.

10. At the root of this discipline is a shared ethic of research, which the group and its networks will seek to define as a source of good academic practice for the field. This ethic is based on principles of multimethodology, multiculturalism, academic freedom, human rights, tolerance, etc., and these aspects are all deeply rooted in the teachings of Islam.

11. Scholars, researchers, and teachers within the Study of Islam and Muslims are expected to be trained to the highest possible standards in the field of their research.

12. Most importantly, the Study of Islam and Muslims is based on achieving the highest quality of research and teaching based on critical, analytic, and scientific standards.

13. In short, the Study of Islam and Muslims should be based on the principle of 'One Discipline, Many Approaches', which is pursued by a cross-cultural academic body which may include people of any faith. The differences between our cultural and religious backgrounds are what give strength and importance to this field of study, and the different cultural lenses that we each bring add to our pursuit of a common intellectual goal.

As practical steps to achieve after the conclusion of the symposium, we agree to work together to achieve the following goals:

1. To seek to develop in the UK a new professional academic network or association for the field of the study of Islam and Muslims, open to all scholars with an interest in the academic study of the field, which may be called, for example, the British Association for the Study of Islam and Muslims (BASIM). The Al-Maktoum Institute will offer its facilities to work to establish this group, in particular through the hosting of BASIM's first conference.

2. From this, to further develop a European and/or International network or association for the same.

3. For the Islamic Universities League to work as a central focus for the development of this post-orientalist field of studies.

4. To foster active co-operation and collaboration between institutions and organisations, particularly through establishing common research and teaching projects.

5. To actively promote the development of the new field of inquiry of Islamic Jerusalem Studies as a core part of the curricula of all Islamic Universities. As the pioneers of this new field of inquiry, the Al-Maktoum Institute will play and co-ordinate a major role in this development.

6. To establish a group with the remit to draw up and disseminate a shared statement on research ethics and good practice for the field of the study of Islam and Muslims.

7. To encourage the application of research methodologies of verification and amendment in the field of Islamic historical studies, particularly to aid the development of post-orientalist studies of Islam and Muslims.

8. We agree upon paying attention to the importance of the study of fiqh and usul-al-fiqh in the study of Islam and Muslims to better understand legal rules from original sources.

9. To encourage the development of high quality reference works, such as a dictionary of technical terminology or an encyclopaedia, to address the teaching and research needs of the future study of Islam and Muslims.

10. Universities in Muslim and Western countries should ensure that the teaching of Arabic and English and other European languages should go hand-in-hand for the development of the study of Islam and Muslims in the twenty-first century.

11. The Islamic Universities League will take the lead for Muslim universities to provide modules in English and other major contemporary languages.

12. In recognition that the historical division of the world into 'dar-al-harb' and 'dar-al-islam' is not based on any Islamic legal principles, we will work towards the holding of a symposium on this issue which includes both historians and fuqaha. However, as a term which is subject to considerable misuse in the contemporary world, we also urge all scholars in the field of the study of Islam and Muslims to work towards a better understanding of contemporary global, cultural, religious, and national differences.

In conclusion, we are most grateful to Shaikh Hamdan Bin Rashid Al-Maktoum for his support both for the Al-Maktoum Institute in Dundee and for the international symposium, which is being held for the first time in Scotland, and feel proud and honoured to be given the opportunity to work to pursue his efforts for developing this new stage for the establishment of the field of Islamic Studies as part of the pursuit of creating better understanding and communication across the world. We have achieved the bringing together of a network of distinguished international scholars for debate, and through our common dialogue we can now work towards the development of the field of the study of Islam and Muslims in a spirit of multiculturalism, and to enhance the understanding between the Arab and Muslim worlds and the West.

Dundee 18 March 2004

APPENDIX VII

THE FUTURE DEVELOPMENT OF THE NEW FIELD OF INQUIRY OF ISLAMICJERUSALEM STUDIES

With profound gratitude to HH Shaikh Hamdan Bin Rashid Al-Maktoum, Deputy Ruler of Dubai and Minister of Finance and Industry in the United Arab Emirates for his patronage and continued support of the Al-Maktoum Institute and the new field of inquiry of Islamicjerusalem Studies.

Where we have been

In accordance with the saying 'the facts of today are the dreams of yesterday, and the dreams of today are the facts of tomorrow', the Al-Maktoum Institute is seeking to implement Shaikh Hamdan Bin Rashid Al-Maktoum's vision for the future development of the new field of inquiry of Islamicjerusalem Studies.

Through the generous patronage of Shaikh Hamdan Bin Rashid Al-Maktoum, the Al-Maktoum Institute and ISRA have been successful in establishing this new field of inquiry, particularly through its now being offered at postgraduate level at British universities – as an MLitt and PhD programme at the University of Aberdeen. It is very clear that Shaikh Hamdan Bin Rashid Al-Maktoum's generosity in funding several postgraduate scholarships in Islamicjerusalem Studies in April 1999 was the major turning point for the establishment of the new field of inquiry. His passion and commitment to develop Islamicjerusalem Studies led to the establishment of the Al-Maktoum Institute for Arabic and Islamic Studies in Dundee.

On 21st April 2003, Mirza al-Sayegh, Chairman of the Institute Board, stated that 'The most recent and perhaps the clearest example of HH Shaikh Hamdan's commitment in ensuring the development of Islamicjerusalem Studies is the establishment of the Al-Maktoum Institute here in Dundee.' On 21st April 2003, Lord Elder, Chancellor of the Al-Maktoum Institute, stated in his introduction to the 2003 International Academic Conference on Islamicjerusalem, 'We feel proud that the new field of inquiry of Islamicjerusalem Studies was founded on the intellectual and academic hard work of our Principal, Professor El-Awaisi. From the initial efforts, determination and clear vision of one man, we are now seeing this new field of inquiry flourishing.'

In the 2004 International Academic Conference of Islamicjerusalem Studies, Professor El-Awaisi first provided the concise definition of

Islamicjerusalem Studies, which has now been further refined and developed as presented below. In January 2006, Professor Abd al-Fattah El-Awaisi published the ground breaking key reference work on the subject, *Introducing Islamicjerusalem* (Al-Maktoum Institute Academic Press, 2006).

Indeed, the unique relationship between HH Shaikh Hamdan Bin Rashid Al-Maktoum and Professor Abd al-Fattah El-Awaisi is a model of a relationship between a ruler and a scholar, based on trust, respect, and full co-operation, which has led to the successful translation of both visions and dreams into reality.

The next stage

On the basis of the success so far in establishing this new field of inquiry in the UK, the Centre for Islamicjerusalem Studies is now looking towards promoting and expanding the new field on an international basis. It is proposed to develop three regional centres – or hubs – from which the field can be promoted:

- The Al-Maktoum Institute for Arabic and Islamic Studies, in Dundee for Europe.
- To establish a basis in Malaysia for that country and for South East Asia.
- A centre within the Arab countries.

Teaching and research on Islamicjerusalem Studies should also be encouraged and supported on an international basis. However, any developments in teaching and research in this area should be linked closely to the Centre for Islamicjerusalem Studies at the Al-Maktoum Institute for Arabic and Islamic Studies, and should be firmly rooted in the following principles:

i.   In accordance with the recommendations of the Dundee Declaration on the future development of the study of Islam and Muslims, the teaching of Islamicjerusalem Studies should be both in English and Arabic

ii. The involvement of the Al-Maktoum Institute will be necessary to ensure that teaching in this important area focuses on academic research

Conclusion

In conclusion, Al-Maktoum Institute in Dundee are most grateful to Shaikh Hamdan Bin Rashid Al-Maktoum for his support for the continuing development of the field of Islamicjerusalem Studies. We are very proud and honoured to be given this opportunity to work to pursue his vision for developing this new field of inquiry.

Islamicjerusalem: A New Concept and Definitions (Abd al-Fattah El-Awaisi (2006), *Introducing Islamicjerusalem* (Al-Maktoum Institute Academic Press).

Islamicjerusalem is a new terminology for a new concept, which may be translated into the Arabic language as Bayt al-Maqdis. It can be fairly and eventually characterised and defined as a unique region laden with a rich historical background, religious significances, cultural attachments, competing political and religious claims, international interests and various aspects that affect the rest of the world in both historical and contemporary contexts. It has a central frame of reference and a vital nature with three principal intertwined elements: its geographical location (land and boundaries), its people (population), and its unique and creative inclusive vision, to administrate that land and its people, as a model for multiculturalism.

Islamicjerusalem Studies can be fairly eventually characterised and defined as a new branch of human knowledge based on interdisciplinary and multidisciplinary approaches. It aims to investigate all matters related to the Islamicjerusalem region, explore and examine its various aspects, and provide a critical analytic understanding of the new frame of reference, in order to identify the nature of Islamicjerusalem and to understand the uniqueness of this region and its effects on the rest of the world in both historical and contemporary contexts.

APPENDIX VIII

ISLAMICJERUSALEM: A NEW CONCEPT AND DEFINITIONS[1]

Abd al-Fattah Muhammad El-Awaisi

As an essential part of introducing Islamicjerusalem, it is important to be clear on what we mean by this new terminology; we at least need to establish a working definition. To help the reader appreciate how difficult it was to arrive at a definition, a number of questions need to be raised. Is Islamicjerusalem the same as Jerusalem the city? What sort of Jerusalem are we talking about? Is it simply the area of al-Aqsa Mosque? (This is only 1/5 of the Old Walled City.) Is it the Old Walled city of Jerusalem, East Jerusalem, West Jerusalem, Greater Jerusalem, the whole of Palestine or part of Palestine? All these questions address the question of a definition from a contemporary context. However, in order to produce a definition it is important to link this to a historical context.

In addition to introducing new definitions of Islamicjerusalem and Islamicjerusalem Studies, the aim of this chapter is to discuss the background of the new field of inquiry of Islamicjerusalem Studies. It will also highlight the latest research on Islamicjerusalem.

Background[2]

The establishment of the new field of inquiry of Islamicjerusalem was a journey that took nearly a decade, 1994-2003, adopting the principle of gradual development and travelling through several stages. It also went through a number of stages on the road to its establishment through an integrated programme which included a number of new academic initiatives.

As part of his vision for the new field, the founder paid particular attention to establishing the concept of Islamicjerusalem Studies in the

---

[1]   This is the first chapter in Abd al-Fattah El-Awaisi (2006) *Introducing Islamicjerusalem* (Al-Maktoum Institute Academic Press) with update on the latest research on Islamicjerusalem Studies.

[2]   This background of the new field of inquiry of Islamicjerusalem Studies was based on Aisha al-Ahlas (2004), Islamic Research Academy: 1994-2004, background, activities and achievements, with special reference to the new field of inquiry of Islamicjerusalem Studies (ISRA, Scotland).

building of its foundations. From the initial stages he was keen to provide practical steps to deliver the essential contributions of knowledge in the new field to the world of learning, and to encourage young researchers to specialise in this field. These have been delivered mainly through organising an annual international academic conference on Islamicjerusalem Studies (seven to date), the *Journal of Islamicjerusalem Studies*, and the securing of a good number of postgraduate research studentships in Islamicjerusalem Studies. These elements were very significant steps towards creating the new frame of reference for the study of Islamicjerusalem. Indeed, both the annual conference and the *Journal* have successfully 'highlighted the gap in the available literature' on Islamicjerusalem Studies, provided the 'necessary knowledge' to develop the field, and become an international discussion forum for scholars who are interested in the field[3].

Other serious practical steps were needed to institutionalise the development, integration and promotion of the field. These were initiated through his developing the first new unit entitled 'Islamicjerusalem', which he taught at undergraduate level at the University of Stirling. This unit has been developed into a taught Master's programme at Al-Maktoum Institute. Indeed, to pioneer the field, Al-Maktoum Institute embodied the founder's vision by inaugurating the first and unique taught Master's programme in Islamicjerusalem Studies worldwide. Following the establishment of Al-Maktoum Institute was the creation of its first academic post, the first chair in Islamicjerusalem Studies. The Centre for Islamicjerusalem Studies was founded to focus all its efforts, and to play a key role in developing the new field. This was a natural progressive development aimed at structuring the research and teaching of Islamicjerusalem Studies.

Shaikh Hamdan Bin Rashid Al-Maktoum's passion and commitment ensured the development of the new field. When the field was in its initial and crucial stage of development, Shaikh Hamdan played an essential part by providing scholarships for young scholars to pursue Islamicjerusalem Studies at postgraduate level. His second major involvement was to promote the development of the new field by establishing Al-Maktoum Institute. Aisha al-Ahlas argued that the 'main reason behind the success' of establishing the new field of inquiry of Islamicjerusalem Studies was related to the 'uniquely close relationship

---

3   Ibid., p. 35.

between the two elements, knowledge and power'[4]. This formal model of relationship between ruler and scholar is absent in Arab and Muslim countries. Indeed, as stated in the Dundee Declaration for the Future Development of the Study of Islam and Muslims on 18 March 2004, one of 'the crises in the contemporary Muslim world is the absence of co-operation between knowledge and power'.

Definitions
In the first few years of establishing the new field, a number of Arab and Muslim scholars were very concerned about this new terminology, especially the word 'Islamic'. Their main worry was that the use of this word could open up hostility and non-acceptance by some Western scholars. At that time, the author's main counter-argument was that, without the term Islamic, the whole terminology would lose its niche, meaning and definition. In addition, if it were to be only Jerusalem without the term Islamic, which Jerusalem would we be talking about? As well, there were already many research and teaching programmes in Jerusalem Studies which meant that our contribution to knowledge would be very limited. However, Islamicjerusalem opened up a new area of specialisation with a new frame of reference. Probably the term Islamic could be the right term to shock, cover new ground, promote serious dialogue and initiate debates that will shed light on new lines of explanation.

After the initial research on Umar's Assurance of Safety to the people of Aelia, the author started from 2000 to develop his new findings. In 2004 this helped to define both Islamicjerusalem and Islamicjerusalem Studies. Indeed, Umar's Assurance was the jewel of the first Muslim Fatih (i.e., introducing new stage and vision) of Aelia, and the beacon for developing Islamicjerusalem's unique and creative vision and nature.

I– Islamicjerusalem
Aisha al-Ahlas argued that the fifth international academic conference on Islamicjerusalem Studies held on 21 April 2003 was 'a turning point' in the history of the new field of inquiry of Islamicjerusalem Studies[5]. Although he was the one who in 1994 had invented this new terminology of Islamicjerusalem, the author was very confused when he was trying, especially in the last five years (2000 – 2005), to come to an understanding of what he specifically meant by Islamicjerusalem.

---

[4]   Ibid., p. 80.
[5]   Ibid., p. 32.

On 21 April 2003 in the fifth international academic conference on Islamicjerusalem 'Islamicjerusalem: Prophetic Temples and al-Aqsa Mosque Demystifying Realities and Exploring Identities', the author presented a keynote speech on 'Exploring the identity of Islamicjerusalem'. Here he publicly admitted this confusion and said, 'It took me nearly three years to come to the working definition which I would like to present to you today.' He added, 'We need to start with a working definition. So, what do we mean by Islamicjerusalem? ...'

Although the author did not at that time present his final definition of Islamicjerusalem, his presentation contained the key elements: 'There are three elements of this working definition. Its geographical location (land), its people (i.e.: who lives or used to live there) and its vision to control or to rule that land and its people. It is not possible to separate these three elements as they are interlinked. In addition, they are linked with their historical context.' (For the author, if geography is the theatre, history is the play.) For the first time, he argued that Islamicjerusalem is not a mere city or another urban settlement, but a region which includes several cities, towns and villages. One can thus see from this definition that Islamicjerusalem is to be described as a region with three key interlinked elements. Identifying the centre of the *Barakah* led him to develop a new significant innovative theory: 'the *Barakah* Circle Theory of Islamicjerusalem'. It is based on new interpretations of the core Muslim sources and history. He also made the same point when he presented his public lecture at the Academy of Islamic Studies at the University of Malaya on 24 September 2004. However, what is presented here is the revised definition which takes into consideration the discussions the author has had since then, and the new definition of Islamicjerusalem Studies.

Islamicjerusalem is a new terminology for a new concept, which may be translated into the Arabic language as Bayt al-Maqdis. It can be fairly and eventually characterised and defined as a unique region laden with a rich historical background, religious significances, cultural attachments, competing political and religious claims, international interests and various aspects that affect the rest of the world in both historical and contemporary contexts. It has a central frame of reference and a vital nature with three principal intertwined elements: its geographical location (land and boundaries), its people (population), and its unique and creative inclusive vision, to administrate that land and its people, as a model for multiculturalism[6].

The term Bayt al-Maqdis has been used in the past in both core and early Muslim narratives and sources to refer to the Aelia region.[7] It may be claimed that Prophet Muhammad was the first to use the term Bayt al-Maqdis to refer to the Aelia region. Indeed he used both terms, Aelia and Bayt al-Maqdis, in many of his traditions. However, one can argue that the Arabs before the advent of Islam may also have used the same term to refer to the same region. Although the Prophet did use Bayt al-Maqdis, the author cannot be certain who was the first to use 'the term'[8].

The word-for-word translation of the Arabic term Bayt al-Maqdis could be 'the Holy House'. This might be understood from a theological point of view, but it would definitely be difficult to understand from historical and geographical contexts. In addition, the use of the term Bayt al-Maqdis does not represent the definition which has been presented in this section. This is especially true after it became very obvious that Islamicjerusalem is a new concept which carries historical, geographical, religious, cultural, and political backgrounds. In addition, it is also not only al-Aqsa Mosque nor the Walled City of Jerusalem, as some out-dated arguments might suggest. Indeed, it is not a city nor yet another urban settlement, but a region which includes several villages, towns, and cities which have an inclusive multicultural vision. In short, the new terminology of Islamicjerusalem cannot be understood without placing it in historical, geographical and religious contexts.

However, the terminology Islamicjerusalem was a new concept which appeared and was used in its comprehensive sense for the first time originally in the English language by this author, as has been

---

[6]   According to the Oxford English Dictionary, terminology means a 'set of terms relating to a subject'; term (s) means 'a word or phrase used to describe a thing or to express an idea'; concept means 'an abstract idea'; abstract means 'having to do with ideas or qualities rather than physical or concrete things'; nature means 'the typical qualities or character of a person, animal, or thing'; and vital means 'absolutely necessary'. The author is very grateful to Sarah Hassan, an MLitt postgraduate student in Islamicjerusalem Studies, for collecting these definitions from the Oxford English Dictionary.

[7]   Othman Ismael Al-Tel (2003), *The first Islamic conquest of Aelia (Islamicjerusalem): A critical analytical study of the early Islamic historical narrations and sources* (Al-Maktoum Institute Academic Press, Scotland), p. 291.

[8]   The use of this terminology *Bayt al-Maqdis* needs further research.

documented, characterised and defined in this article. It should be noted that Islamicjerusalem is one word not two separate words, i.e. Islamic and Jerusalem. It should also be made clear that Islamicjerusalem is not the same as Jerusalem or Islamic Quds al-Quds al-Islamiyyah. It is also different from Muslim Jerusalem as in Jewish Jerusalem and Christian Jerusalem. The historical period when the Muslims ruled Islamicjerusalem for several centuries should be called Muslim Jerusalem and not Islamicjerusalem. Islamicjerusalem is a new concept, whereas Muslim Jerusalem refers to the periods when Muslims ruled Islamicjerusalem. To illustrate this point, Umar Ibn al-Khattab's Fatih of the region is the first Muslim Fatih of Islamicjerusalem. Indeed, this should also apply to the later Muslim period up to 1917 and to any Muslim rule of Islamicjerusalem in the future. In addition, contemporary Muslim Jerusalem is shaped in part by dialogue with the concept of Islamicjerusalem, the classical and modern history of Muslims, and in part by response to external interests and influences in the region. Accordingly, contemporary Muslims seek to relate their heritage in Muslim Jerusalem from the concept of Islamicjerusalem and the Muslim past to the radical situation of today.

It is worth mentioning that, since its launch in the winter of 1997, the *Journal of Islamicjerusalem Studies* has also carried the Arabic term Al-Quds al-Islamiyyah or Islamic Quds. However, the author's new findings on Umar's Assurance of Safety to the people of Aelia has led to a change in the use of that Arabic term. The change of the Arabic title of the *Journal of Islamicjerusalem Studies* from Al-Quds al-Islamiyyah to Bayt al-Maqdis occurred in the summer 2000 issue. This was the same issue of the *Journal* which published the author's article on Umar's Assurance in both the English and Arabic languages.

The last part of the definition has been partly borrowed from the political-science theory of the three elements of any state, but replaces the concept of sovereignty with the vision of inclusivity and plurality of Islamicjerusalem. Indeed, this unique creative vision of Islamicjerusalem is more important than the issue of sovereignty in the case of Islamicjerusalem. It could be argued that the final product is normally the issue of sovereignty. However, the agenda for Islamicjerusalem should not be the desire to achieve colonial goals of ruling lands and people which could be based either on economic ambitions or on racist nationalist and theological claims, or on any other interests and claims. If there is no vision or a vision of exclusivity in Islamicjerusalem, sovereignty would naturally lead internally to oppression, divisions in society and its communities, and externally to the involvement of external powers to try to resolve these internal troubles and problems, which would lead to instability and barriers to the steady progress and prosperity of the region. Indeed, the unique aspect of Islamicjerusalem is highlighted through its vision, which presents a model for peaceful co-existence and a way for people from different religious and cultural backgrounds to live together in an environment of multiculturalism and religious and cultural engagement, diversity and tolerance.

This understanding of Islamicjerusalem as a model for multiculturalism was presented by the author, for the first time, in his public lecture on 'Islamicjerusalem as a Model for Multiculturalism' at the Academy of Islamic Studies at the University of Malaya on 24 September 2004. It was based on the findings of his research on Umar's Assurance in 2000. However, in *Introducing Islamicjerusalem*'s book is the revised presentation, which takes into consideration the discussions he has had since then, especially his revised version of Umar's Assurance in that book, and the new definitions of Islamicjerusalem and Islamicjerusalem Studies.

II– Islamicjerusalem Studies

The sixth international academic conference on Islamicjerusalem Studies organised on 31 May 2004 celebrated the tenth anniversary of the foundation of the new field of inquiry of Islamicjerusalem Studies. This was another significant event in the history of the new field. Indeed, in his keynote speech, the founder presented for the first time his definition of Islamicjerusalem Studies. However, what is present here is the revised definition of Islamicjerusalem Studies, which has taken into consideration the discussions he has had since, and the new definition of Islamicjerusalem.

> **Islamicjerusalem Studies** can be fairly eventually characterised and defined as a new branch of human knowledge based on interdisciplinary and multidisciplinary approaches. It aims to investigate all matters related to the Islamicjerusalem region, explore and examine its various aspects, and provide a critical analytic understanding of the new frame of reference, in order to identify the nature of Islamicjerusalem and to understand the uniqueness of this region and its effects on the rest of the world in both historical and contemporary contexts.

Indeed, Islamicjerusalem Studies is a field of inquiry which covers several disciplines, such as the study of Islam and Muslims, history and archaeology, art and architecture, geography and geology, environment and politics, and other related disciplines. Accordingly, it has interdisciplinary and multidisciplinary approaches which include historical and theological, theoretical and conceptual, empirical and cultural approaches. The new field also adopts the policy of escaping the trap of reacting to others and trying to engage with them through creating a new agenda, dialogue and debate on the subject which will lead to more constructive dialogue between scholars in several disciplines.

The new field will not only provide an understanding of Islamicjerusalem but will examine the new frame of reference within which Muslims approach Islamicjerusalem. Several questions will be the key to addressing this point: What are the reasons for Muslims having close links to and concern with Islamicjerusalem? What is the significance of Islamicjerusalem to Islam and to Muslims? Does Islamicjerusalem have any special status compared with any other region?

In-depth discussion of the various aspects and dimensions of Islamicjerusalem will open up new horizons for those interested in understanding its vision, nature and the reasons for its distinctness from other regions. For example, the study of the inclusive vision of Islamicjerusalem should not only be restricted to its people's religions and cultures, but should include 'equal measures' of the role of its two genders, male and female. A young promising Egyptian scholar, Sarah Hassan, argues that:

Women as much as men left their marks in the beginning of the Muslim history of, and the physical attachment, to Islamicjerusalem, and both genders played a role in asserting its inclusiveness to religions and genders. [Only] when this crucial element of inclusiveness is sufficiently taken into account, can Islamicjerusalem become a model for 'multiculturalism' in practice.[9]

As 'gender' has become 'a useful category of historical analysing',[10] the author agrees with Sarah Hassan's argument that 'the usage of gender as a tool for analysing both its (Islamicjerusalem) past and present is a

---

[9] Sarah Mohamed Sherif Abdel-Aziz Hassan (2005), *Women: Active Agents in Islamising Islamicjerusalem from the Prophet's Time until the End of the Umayyed Period,* (Unpublished Master's dissertation, Al-Maktoum Institute for Arabic and Islamic Studies), p. 69.

[10] Joan Wallach Scott (1999), *Gender and the Politics of History,* (Columbia University Press, New York), pp. 28-50.

necessity for the completion and advancement of this new field of inquiry (of Islamicjerusalem Studies) '[11].

In order to demonstrate this inclusive vision, there is a need to use gender as a tool of analysis in approaching the study of Islamicjerusalem through examining the active role played by Muslim women and their vital contributions in underpinning and demonstrating the significance of Islamicjerusalem. This calls for a re-examination of the interpretation of the Qur'anic verses that were interpreted, the Ahadith that were narrated, and the Muslim juristically rulings that were made by Muslim women and compare them with the ones made by Muslim men regarding Islamicjerusalem. Also Muslim women's participation should be compared and their role reinstated in the making of Islamicjerusalem history in all its periods. For example, Sarah Hassan claims of the Mother of Believers, Safiyyah Bint Huyayyi Ibn Akhtab that her 'life story in general, and her visit to Islamicjerusalem in particular, illustrate vividly how the whole process of negotiating her Jewish background and her Muslim religion culminates in Islamicjerusalem.'[12]

In addition, this new field could be argued as consolidating the Qur'anic, Hadiths and Muslim historical disciplines by shedding light on new lines of explanation. Numerous verses revealed about Islamicjerusalem in the Qur'an, and about the frequency with which the Prophet spoke about Islamicjerusalem[13], leads one to argue that the new field has revealed greater insights into several disciplines such as the interpretation of the Qur'an and the Hadiths. In addition, it has clarified several contradicting historical events and resolved a number of problematic historical issues.

Finally, one could argue that a definition should be short, precise and to the point; yet these definitions of Islamicjerusalem are very long. However, what has been provided for the first time is a scholarly

---

[11]   Sarah Mohamed Sherif Abdel-Aziz Hassan (2005), *Women: Active Agents in Islamising Islamicjerusalem from the Prophet's Time until the End of the Umayyed Period*, pp 2-3.

[12]   Ibid., p. 54. In the conclusion, Sarah Hassan presented her dissertation as 'merely the cornerstone for a whole range of possible further gender studies on Islamicjerusalem. The interdisciplinary and multidisciplinary approaches that characterise Islamicjerusalem Studies must be utilised in further discussions and examinations of gender in Islamicjerusalem.' p. 69.

[13]   Abd al-Fattah El-Awaisi (1998), 'The significance of Jerusalem in Islam: an Islamic reference', *Journal of Islamicjerusalem Studies*, vol. 1, no. 2 (Summer 1998), p. 49.

presentation of what can be fairly eventually characterised and defined of Islamicjerusalem and its field. So the definition is not only the definition of Islamicjerusalem and its field but also the characteristics of these definitions. Moreover, these definitions which appear for the first time in this format try to shock, confuse, and throw doubt on some of that which has been taken for granted in the past by a variety of scholars representing various schools of thought, trends, and approaches. Such definitions also aim to raise questions and provide researchers and scholars in the field with the key aspects of Islamicjerusalem.

Although these definitions are the author's most important contributions to the field, they should be considered as working definitions to set the scene for the field's future development. These by no means claim to be theological or divinity Ilahiyyat definitions which cannot be changed or developed, as some Muslim traditionalist theologians would claim. They are, as in the case of Islamicjerusalem Studies, characterised and defined as a new 'branch of human knowledge'. Indeed, there are human explanations and interpretations of new concepts and terminology which are subject to change and development based on the latest scholarly research in the field.

Latest Research on Islamicjerusalem Studies
Al-Maktoum Institute has developed unique teaching programmes, based on current and progressive research, which take into consideration the needs and preferences of our local, national and international students, so that they can appreciate and understand the various schools of thought within a specific line of study. This has produced waves of postgraduate students with a first Master's degree in Islamicjerusalem Studies[14], students who hopefully now have a thorough grounding in the new field.

In addition, the Institute has trained qualified students and created a team of young scholars in a variety of disciplines in Islamicjerusalem Studies and has conducted high-quality research either at taught Master or PhD levels. For example, the following list contains some of the latest research on Islamicjerusalem Studies:

---

[14] The total number to date is twenty-two. Among them, five have registered for their PhD degree in Islamicjerusalem Studies. During this coming academic year, 2005/2006, four more postgraduate students will begin the taught Master's in Islamicjerusalem Studies.

1. Othman Ismael al-Tel wrote his PhD thesis (2002) on The first Islamic conquest of Aelia (Islamicjerusalem): A critical analytical study of the early Islamic historical narrations and sources. (July 2003)

2. Haithem Fathi Al-Ratrout wrote his PhD thesis (2002) on The Architectural development of Al-Aqsa Mosque in Islamicjerusalem in the early Islamic period: Sacred architecture in the shape of the 'Holy'.

3. Maher Younes Abu- Munshar wrote his PhD thesis (2003) on A Historical Study of Muslim Treatment of Christians in Islamicjerusalem at the Time of Umar Ibn al-Khattab and Salah al-Din with Special Reference to the Islamic Values of Justice. (Nov 2003)

4. Mohammad Roslan Mohammad Nor wrote his PhD thesis on The Significance of Islamicjerusalem in Islam: Quranic and Hadith Perspectives. (Dec 2005)

5. Aminurraasyid Yatiban wrote his Master's dissertation (2003) on The Islamic Concept of Sovereignty: Islamicjerusalem during the First Islamic Conquest as a Case Study. He also wrote his PhD thesis on Muslim understandings of the concept of Al-Siyada (sovereignty): an analytical study of Islamicjerusalem from the first Muslim conquest until the end of the first Abasid period (16-264AH/637-877CE) (April 2006).

6. Khalid Abd al-Fattah El-Awaisi wrote his Master's dissertation (2003) on Geographical Boundaries of Islamicjerusalem. He also wrote his PhD thesis on The geographical extent of the land of Bayt al-Maqdis, the Holy Land and the Land of Barakah (Aug 2006)

7. Ra'ed Jabaren wrote his PhD thesis on Muslim Juristic Rulings of Islamicjerusalem with special reference to Ibadat in Al-Aqsa Mosque: A Critical Comparative Study (April 2006).

8. Fatimatuzzahra' Abd Rahman wrote her Master's dissertation (2004) on Political, Social and Religious Changes in Islamicjerusalem from the First Islamic Conquest until the end of Umayyad period (637 to 750CE): An Analytical Study. She is now writing her PhD thesis on The Muslim Concept of Change: An Analytical Study of the Political, Social and Economic Changes in Islamicjerusalem from the First Muslim Conquest till the End of the Fatimid Period (637-1099 CE).

9. Abdallah Ma'rouf Omar wrote his Master's dissertation (2005) on Towards the Conquest of Islamicjerusalem: the Three Main

Practical Steps Taken by Prophet Muhammad – Analytical Study. He is now writing his PhD thesis on The Prophet Plan towards Islamicjerusalem

10. Mahmoud Mataz Kazmouz wrote his Master's dissertation (2006) on The Ottoman implementation of the vision of Islamicjerusalem as a model for multiculturalism with a special reference to Sultan Suleiman I, the magnificent (1520 – 1566). He is now writing his PhD thesis on Islamicjerusalem as a Model for Multiculturalism.

11. Aisha Muhammad Ibrahim Al-Ahlas wrote her Master's dissertation (2003) on Islamic Research Academy (ISRA) 1994-2003: Background, Activities and Achievements with Special Reference to the New Field of Inquiry of Islamic Jerusalem Studies.

12. Sarah Mohamed Sherif Abdel-Aziz Hassan wrote her Master's dissertation (2005) on Women: Active Agents in Islamising[15] Islamicjerusalem from the Prophet's Time until the End of the Umayyed Period.

13. Ramona Ahmed Ibrahim wrote her Master's dissertation (2005) on Islamicjerusalem as a Model of Conflict Resolution: a Case Study of the Negotiations between Salah al-Din and Richard the Lionheart (1191 – 1192 CE).

In short, with determination and clear vision the new field of inquiry of Islamicjerusalem Studies was founded, together with interdisciplinary and multidisciplinary approaches. It established a new frame of reference on Islamicjerusalem. Through the establishment of the Academy, the founder planned that research and scholarship take place in building the

---

[15] The author strongly disagrees with the usage of this terminology, 'Islamising Islamicjerusalem', in the context of Sarah's dissertation. Indeed, it goes against the recent historical findings, the historical nature of Islamicjerusalem, and its vision at the time under dissection in her dissertation. After she submitted her dissertation, the author felt bound to discuss this issue with Sarah at length. He also raised the point that, on examination of the dissertation, it was revealed that she did not mean 'Islamising Islamicjerusalem'. In addition, he pointed out that she used phrases such as 'underpinning the significance of Islamicjerusalem', 'demonstrating the significance of Islamicjerusalem', 'making the significance of Islamicjerusalem', and 'developing the significance of Islamicjerusalem'. Sarah agrees with the author's argument that this is not the appropriate terminology to use in this context.

foundation stones of his vision for the field. In addition, through taking practical steps, he institutionalised the development, integration and promotion of the new field within academia, especially within the British higher education establishments.

APPENDIX IX

PRESS RELEASE
NEW INTERPRETATION BY LEADING ACADEMIC
WILL HELP TO BEAT MUSLIM TERRORISTS

- Muslim fundamentalists waging war against non-Muslims are going directly against the core Muslim teachings of the Qur'an and Prophet Muhammad.
- New interpretations of the Qur'an should mean peace and not war between religions.
- Academics should take their work away from religious or political activist agendas.
- A model for 'global common space' and 'peaceful co-existence and mutual respect' which leads to security, stability, and prosperity.
- Islamicjerusalem should be an 'open' region and a 21st century model for multiculturalism.

Those are among the challenging conclusions in a new book written by one of the UK's leading academics in the Study of Islam and Muslims, Professor Abd al-Fattah El-Awaisi. Professor El-Awaisi, who is Principal and Vice Chancellor of the Al-Maktoum Institute in Dundee, introduced the new field of Islamicjerusalem studies five years ago.

In his book *Introducing Islamicjerusalem*, published by Al-Maktoum Institute Academic Press, he is trying to address some of the sensitive key issues and promote intellectual and academic debate with new lines of explanation. One of the most interesting and challenging aspects of the book is how Professor El-Awaisi supports his central arguments by referring to the core Muslim sources but with new interpretations.

The book presents his explanation of what is meant by this new term and concept by looking at three key elements: Its geographical location, its people, and its inclusive vision for the area to be a model of multiculturalism

In his book Professor El-Awaisi says the area that covers Islamicjeruslaem is not a city but a region with many cities, towns and villages ranging over an area more than 250 square miles. Within its boundaries lie the cities of Jerusalem, Nablus, Ramallah, Jericho and Hebron.

Over the years Muslims, Christians and Jews have fought over and made claims to the land but the author maintains that Islamicjerusalem should be regarded as a 'land for everyone'. The basis for this conclusion is a new study of 'Umar's Assurance of Safety to the People of Aelia,' a more detailed re-examination of text from the Qu'ran to gain an improved literal and inside translation from Arabic into English and a conclusion by the author that one established translation of Umar's Assurance is in fact a fake. Umar Ibn al-Khattab was the second Caliph after Muhammad, and his conquest of the region Aelia in the 7th century, now known as Islamicjerusalem, and his Assurance of Safety to the people of all religions and none who lived in the area at the time is presented by Professor El-Awaisi as the foundation of multiculturalism and a model for conflict resolution today.

He goes on to argue, using text from the Qu'ran, that Adl (the concept of justice) means Muslims must deal with non-Muslims justly. (Qur'an 5:8) He uses the words of the Prophet Muhammad to denounce Muslim fundamentalists by quoting Muhammad who said: 'He who hurts a non Muslim hurts me, and he who hurts me hurts Allah.'

Professor El-Awaisi also presents an interesting account about the Najran Christian delegation that came and visited Prophet Muhammad in Medina. Muhammad not only welcomed them in his Mosque but also allowed them to say their prayers there. 'During their visit, they used to pray in one part of the Prophet's Mosque while the Muslims performed their prayers in another part.'

Professor El-Awaisi argues that closer study of the history of Islamicjerusalem and better translation of the Qu'ran shows Muslims should believe that all humans are from the one family and despite different races and cultures should treat everyone, especially non-Muslims, in the same way they'd treat their parents, with Birr (love and passion Qur'an 60:8-9). He argues that the Qur'an also requests followers of Islam to solve conflict through argument in the 'most beautiful and polite' manner and not through violence. (Qur'an 16:125)

He also takes issue with some academics who present their works as part of a political or religious agenda and calls for a separation between political and religious activism and scholarship. He goes on to argue that Umar's historical Assurance is a lesson from the past that should be adopted in the 21st century. 'Our understanding of Islamicjerusalem as a model for multiculturalism could be seen as the twenty-first century's contribution to establishing a new agenda and new frame of reference for safety, peace, stability, security, progress, development and prosperity in the region.'

'Umar was trying to resolve a local conflict with an international approach-in other words he was 'thinking globally' and 'acting locally.'

Umar's Assurance of Safety not only rejected the notion of the supremacy of one people or race over others but also presented Islamicjerusalem as a model both for multiculturalism and for conflict resolution.

'It presents a model for peaceful co-existence and mutual respect and offers a way for people from different religious and cultural backgrounds to live together in an environment of multiculturalism and religious and cultural diversity and tolerance. This is a lesson which is vital for us to learn in today's world, especially after the 7th of July London bombings.'

Professor El-Awaisi concludes that Islamicjerusalem should now be regarded as a 'global common space' where the human family could live together in peaceful co-existence.

The book will be launched on January 30 at the Scottish Parliament in Edinburgh. Its conclusions will also be discussed at an international academic conference being held at the Al-Maktoum Institute in Dundee later this year.

APPENDIX X

PRESS RELEASE
'ISLAMIC STUDIES FAIL 21ST CENTURY TEST'

Islamic studies in Britain's higher education establishments are failing to meet the needs of a 21st century multicultural society. That is one of the major findings of a two-year research Report published today (Wed, 25 October) and written by two of the UK's leading experts in the study of Islam and Muslims.

Called 'Time for Change: Report on the Future of the Study of Islam and Muslims in Universities and Colleges in Multicultural Britain' the report has examined 55 higher education departments and centres currently offering courses in the study of Islam and Muslims looking to see if they are 'relevant to contemporary multicultural British society.'

The authors, Professor Abd al-Fattah El-Awaisi and Professor Malory Nye, have some controversial things to say about the relevance of courses presently on offer in many of the British higher education establishments, and the international political links of Muslim institutions in Britain.

With a population of over 1.5 million British Muslims now living in multicultural UK they are the largest non-Christian grouping; and yet the last report related to Islamic Studies was commissioned by the Government over 40 years ago. According to Professor El-Awaisi: 'The call for a new agenda is timely and necessary to prevent the misguided and narrow interpretation of Islam which is the source of so many problems in our multicultural society. It is only through multicultural education we can work to eliminate extremism and fundamentalism. I want to stress that our report only looks at one aspect – the role of education, particularly higher education, to address issues surrounding the study of Islam and Muslims by people of all backgrounds in multicultural Britain.'

The report states that 'there are some deeply embedded issues within our society regarding Islam and Muslims, of stereotyping, hostility, Islamophobia and misunderstanding... there needs to be appreciation that Muslims are no longer 'others', they are part of the fabric of British society'. It goes on to say, 'It is also clear most British non Muslims do not 'get' Islam, and they do not understand what makes Muslims 'tick'. Many British communities, including British Muslims, have failed to understand one another and have failed to engage effectively in multicultural Britain. There is mutual incomprehension and this can only be addressed by education.'

The 'Time for Change' Report claims that current education structures are 'letting down' Muslims who were born and brought up in Britain and it goes on to say – 'The most favoured option so far of Muslim schools and colleges set up and run by Muslims for Muslims for educating Islamically is NOT the answer to these difficult questions. The agenda needs to be much more challenging than that for all involved. 'The authors of the Report argue that 'Multiculturalism is not about separatism, ghettoisation or balkanisation, it is instead recognition of diversity, the need for common ground, mutual respect and cultural engagement.'

The authors also state that they recognise not everyone will agree with their recommendations but they hope it will act as a catalyst for debate. The main focus of their document is to examine the study of Islam and Muslims in Britain and map out how this field needs to be developed. To widen the debate, they are organising a national symposium to discuss issues raised in the report to be held in Dundee early next year.

Turning to the performance of current departments and centres in the UK providing programmes in Arabic and Islamic Studies, Middle Eastern Studies and Religious studies, the report argues that the current crisis is not caused by lack of funding; instead it says there are a number of clear problems including:

- Departments not focusing on the needs of 21st century multicultural Britain, concentrating instead on out of date and irrelevant issues
- Some departments choosing local Imams and religious leaders as lecturers for 'political correctness'
- Evidence of some departments failing to replace experts in Islamic studies
- Lack of clarity on where and how the subject should be taught
- Many Muslim institutions focusing on their own political links and agendas to serve their own needs and not those of multicultural Britain

A number of these Muslim institutions are singled out for comment including The Muslim College in London, founded by the late Professor Zaki Badawi and largely funded by Libya, The Markfield Institute of Higher Education in Leicester with links to Jamaat-e-Islami in Pakistan and the Muslim Brothers, The European Institute of Human Sciences in

Wales, also linked to the Muslim Brothers, London Open College, based on Al-Muntada Al-Islami in London with links to the Salafi movement in Saudi Arabia, and The International Colleges of Islamic Sciences and the Islamic college for Advanced Studies which are Shi'ite institutions with links to movements in Iran, Iraq and Lebanon.

Here the authors pose two questions – Is it right to say that Islamic Studies can only be pursued by Muslims? And does Islamic Studies require a Muslim institution? The report's answer to these is a very definite NO.

The Report says there is an urgent need for a new agenda to develop Islamic Studies into the Study of Islam and Muslims to challenge both the more traditional approaches that were often faith based and excluded non-Muslims and the orientalist approaches that often alienated Muslims.

The authors argue that in today's multicultural Britain, the field of study must be open to bring together people of all backgrounds, something they have been doing for the past five years at Al-Maktoum Institute in Dundee.

The Report also identifies the key issues of multiculturalism, globalisation, post colonialism and Muslims in the west and how these must set the agenda for the field to meet these new challenges in the 21st century. Accordingly, it argues that Britain needs to set a new agenda for the study of Islam and Muslims among its higher educational establishments.

'Time for Change' Report concludes with a series of recommendations for action, including:

- Priority should be given to producing the next generation of young British nationals (of all backgrounds) as scholars in the study of Islam and Muslims
- Muslim institutions should focus on training British Muslim Imams and Muslim religious leaders who understand how to live in multicultural Britain
- Some Muslim institutions should be encouraged to integrate more actively into the British higher education system, particularly on issues of quality assurance and multicultural engagement with the wider society
- As a matter of urgency the Government should commission a study on Muslim institutions i.e. schools, colleges, and institutions, and their place in the development of Islam and Muslims as an integral part of multicultural British society.

Professor Nye concluded: 'All those who participate in the development of this area of higher education have the responsibility to respond to the new realities of contemporary multicultural Britain. We must ensure the integration of all aspects of society within these debates and also recognise the need to make the understanding of Islam and Muslims a mainstream part of the curriculum.'

A news conference to launch the 'Time for Change' Report will be held in the Dinsdale Young Room of Central Hall Westminster, Storey's Gate, Westminster on Wednesday October 25, 2006 at 10 a.m. A full copy of the report will be available at the news conference.

NOTES TO EDITORS

1. Arabic and Islamic studies were established in the UK 250 years ago. The earliest Chairs in Arabic were Oxford in 1640 and Cambridge in 1660.
2. The three major reports commissioned in the past were -- The Reay Committee in 1909, The Scarborough Committee in 1947 and The Hayter Committee in 1961.

APPENDIX XI

THE FIRST 'RECOGNTION OF ACHIEVEMENT CEREMONY'

The Principal and Vice-Chancellor address
28 November 2003

It gives me great pleasure to welcome you all on behalf of Al-Maktoum Institute for Arabic and Islamic Studies. The success, last summer, of the Concluding Ceremony to mark the end of the academic year led the Academic Council to decide to organise an annual 'Recognition of Achievement Ceremony'. This first ceremony today is to recognise and congratulate the excellent achievements of our students who graduated in November 2003.

As you know, the Institute is now well into the third year of academic operation. Last year demanded some serious commitment from the Institute's family to build a strong base for the Institute to grow. Our success so far is not only impressive but also well-deserved. Indeed, we feel proud of the progress and growth of the Institute as a whole. I would like to take this opportunity to thank HH Skaikh Hamdan Bin Rashid Al-Maktoum for his vision to establish the Institute and his continued support.

Success
The institute is continuing to build strength in its core activity – academia. With the decline of student numbers in the field of Arabic, Middle Eastern, and Islamic Studies in the Country, we feel very pleased with the steady increase of student intake since the Institute's conception in 2001. Starting with one student in October 2001 and 12 students during the whole academic year 2001/2002, the current number of enrolled students is 38 students, 16 attending the taught Masters courses and another 22 conducting research in various specialisations within Arabic and Islamic studies. It is truly inspiring to see the steady significant increase of students walking the halls of the Al-Maktoum Institute and we hope that this will set the pace for future advancement.

We are also very pleased with the progress made by our students at the Institute. We feel very proud that two of our PhD students completed their studies at the Institute and that twelve graduated with an MLitt award, seven gaining awards with Distinction; and one student has completed a postgraduate Certificate. The course Assessment Board, in its meetings in June and September 2003, were impressed with the performance of our students in the taught Masters course. If you examine our student enrolment and completion figures, you will realise that the Institute's completion rate is nearly 100%. Indeed, this is an excellent achievement in a very short period of time. This is due, in part, to both the high quality assurance procedures adopted at the Institute to select our students, the teaching quality criteria in delivering all aspects of teaching at the Institute, and the support services provided by the Institute. Our graduate students and our team of internationally renowned scholars are to be highly commended for their hard work and commitment. They are truly an asset to the Institute and indeed echo the motto of Al-Maktoum Institute of 'Fostering Excellence in Teaching and Research'. I would like to congratulate all our students for their success.

Let me elaborate further on the reasons for this success. The Institute is a distinctive and unique development at the academic and communities levels.

Academic Approaches
In the past, the focus has been to study Islam and Muslims from just one limited perspective. Here at the Institute we look at Islam and Muslims in many different ways, and not only in the Middle Eastern but also in British and Scottish, as well as many other contexts. The success of the Institute comes from the fact that it is one of the key post-orientalism institutions in the world. In addition to the quality, the main features and distinctiveness of its programmes are i) that it is contemporary, and ii) that it reflects diversity. The programmes are based on current and progressive research, and take into consideration the needs and preferences of our local, national, and international students.

The Institute does not seek to offer Islamic Studies training within a single methodology. Rather, an inter-disciplinary approach has been used so that our students can appreciate and understand the various schools of thought within a specific line of study. Indeed, it reflects a diversity of teaching and research interest, spanning a variety of subject areas and methodological approaches in the field of Arabic and Islamic Studies. It is committed to the interdisciplinary and cross-cultural study of a variety of fields in Arabic and Islamic Studies.

Research and Research Culture
Research is the underpinning activity at the Institute; and is at the top of the Institute's agenda. The Institute is indeed very committed to research and to further enhance its research culture. Our research is taken

forward by a team of internationally renowned scholars. The establishment of the three unique research centres at the Institute as part of the Institute's development strategy signifies our commitment to the fields. They are also unique developments in academia and they undeniably provide the Institute with very distinctive capabilities and expertise in this niche.

Enhancing the research culture at the Institute, last year's international conference was highly successful and unique as it presented new and innovative theories on Islamic Jerusalem Studies.

We also continue to organise regular Research Seminars and Postgraduate Research Seminars in the effort to further cultivate the thirst for knowledge and strengthen the scholarly culture with the Institute.

A three-day successful Annual Postgraduate Summer Workshops was organised in June this year to ensure that both our staff and students are up-to-date with recent and important development in our fields.

The academic council has decided to establish a Research Development Fund to assist our scholars in their research and to further strengthen our research culture.

The Al-Maktoum Institute Academic Press was established to foster intellectual discourse in related fields by encouraging the publication of scholarly works and making them available to both the academic community and the general public,

His Highness Shaikh Hamdan Bin Rashid Al-Maktoum has generously funded many scholarships which have given great benefits to young scholars from around the world. Currently, scholars from the Arab world, Far East as well as Scotland are studying under the scheme.

The Institute has continuously invested in the Library with the aim of making it a well-equipped recourse centre. All these are to help the Institute achieve its aim of fostering excellence in teaching and research.

Creation of a Learning Environment and Community

We are very proud that within less than two years the Institute created a learning environment and community with a friendly atmosphere and which addresses the diverse needs of Al-Maktoum Institute family. This includes providing facilities to our students and staff, Annual Lunch, and the three day Postgraduate Taught and Research Students Induction workshop.

The Institute campus also has been developed to allow closer interaction between staff and students. We feel that this close bond will help to foster a better environment in which academia and proper understanding can flourish.

Students

We view our students as partners in the process of producing future scholars in the fields of Arabic and Islamic Studies. In addition to having their own student body, they are involved at most levels at the Institute. We feel proud that the Interim Al-Maktoum Students Society Executive put together a constitution that was adopted last summer by the Students Society' AGM.

External examiners

The serious efforts of the institute to foster excellence in teaching and research are well received and acknowledged by many. The institute's external examiners, appointed by the University, have written particularly glowing reports and comments. A letter from one of the external examiners indicates a high level of satisfaction with our procedures and quality, and indeed has outlined a ringing endorsement of the Institute. 'I strongly believe that the Institute is credited for the variety of courses offered which cover a unique combination of both traditional and modern approaches to Islamic studies. I believe it is a unique approach which has made your institute distinguished among other British and international academic institutions. This is what students need in the 21st century.'

Fundamentalism, extremism, and ignorance

I am much aware that there are forces of fundamentalism, extremism, ignorance and jealousy from different sides who resent success and innovation and the challenge that a 21st century education presents.

Extremism, often portrayed as a one-sided enemy of the West, is in fact, a global issue and as a term cannot be restricted or confined to one religion or creed. In reality, one finds extremists in all societies. It often comes from an extreme interpretation of religious Holy Scriptures without considering the time, location or social, political and economic climate within which one is based. There is an interesting verse in the Holy Qur'an which warns 'Do not go to extremes in your religion.' (5:77)

However it is not always a religious extremism; a non-religious extremist will base his/her actions on an extreme interpretation of a society's values and customs or on individual desires or ideologies.

The other major problem, ignorance, and in particular, ignorance of 'the Other' leads to the development of hatred towards them and this is clearly evident from both sides. Muslims in Muslim countries have painted a particular picture of Western culture often very ignorantly about the reality of Western society. Vice versa, we see that Western societies have coloured their understanding of Muslim countries with a blind ignorance. In such a way, ignorance, like extremism, will lead to hatred.

And thus, we should recognise that our real greatest enemies are extremism and ignorance. Therefore, all effort should be made, from both sides, to tackle them. These are global issues and are not likely to go away by themselves so to say the least, we have to do something about them.

Democracy would solve some problems in the Muslim countries but will the imposition of a system establish a truly democratic society? Will democracy tackle what I feel are the two most fundamental problems in both Muslim and Western countries: extremism and ignorance?

A major force that must be employed to deal with the rise of extremism and ignorance is education. Any successful democracy whether in Scotland, the UK, Europe or anywhere else needs an excellent system of education. The alternative and solution to these two pertinent enemies is education: an equally important education for both Muslims and non-Muslims. I strongly believe that education is the solution that will help people to break free from the chains of ignorance and rise above limited or extreme interpretations of scriptures.

It is only through education that greater understanding between different religious and social groups will be developed. Such an understanding will build bridges between countries and communities. The mutual co-existence of people of different creeds, colours and backgrounds celebrating their diversity at local, national and global levels is not a far-off fantasy, but one that can be achieved through education. It is imperative, therefore, that this matter should not be left in the hands of extremists or ignorant individuals.

As a unique Institute that prides itself with a multicultural vision, we encourage integration and co-operation. What we do here at the Institute within both the academic and community spheres is to use education to overcome that ignorance of different cultures and beliefs and build bridges with different communities at local, national and global levels. Building is hard and tiring work and we have a long way to go in that process. It is my opinion that the Institute has made groundbreaking developments in this process of elevation through education.

We must make a relentless effort to work for and serve the communities and the wider society at the academic, cultural and artistic, economic, scientific and technological and sport levels, to try to make a positive change, and we see this as a very vital role for the Institute to fulfil.

Multiculturalism

Instead of being a religious organisation, the Institute is an academic institution examining the fields of Arabic and Islamic Studies. As an academic institute that promotes a greater understanding of different religions and cultures in a multicultural context, for the benefit of the wider community, and to build bridges between the Muslim and Western worlds at this crucial time, multiculturalism remains the centre of our vision and structure. Our multicultural ethos is visibly translated and implemented in our day-to-day operation. Our staff and students come from diverse national and cultural background including both Muslims and non-Muslims. The Institute also works with a number of partners in the local community, including the Dundee City Council, churches, health authorities, education department, schools, clubs, local theatre, sports and businesses.

The Al-Maktoum Institute Students Society is another indicator of the multicultural ethos which exists within the Institute. The diversity of the current elected Committee members' countries of origin is yet another reflection of the multicultural ethos fostered by the Institute. Bringing together the best of all worlds, they are sure to bring to the Institute new dimensions of multicultural interaction and add to the exciting environment that has been created at the Institute.

Links and serving the Communities

On 3 June 2003, the Institute became a member of the Islamic Universities League. We are the first British Higher Education institutions to be part of this international league. This membership will indeed help the Institute to achieve its aim of building bridges and providing a meeting point between the Western and Muslim worlds of learning and to encourage scholarship and academic co-operation at this crucial time.

Indeed, the Institute believes that academic excellence can be achieved by working in partnership with other institutions. We also believe that we can contribute to the development of Arabic and Islamic Studies worldwide. To this end, we have created links and entered into partnerships with several institutions locally, nationally and internationally. We have good working relationships with various universities including the University of Abertay Dundee, Zayed

University in Dubai, the British University of Dubai, UAE University in Al-Ain, Qatar University, and Al-Azhar University in Cairo, which is the world's biggest and oldest Muslim university.

All these links will certainly help to enhance our teaching and research capabilities and ultimately will benefit our students. The Institute sees our links with institutions, whether locally, nationally or internationally, as part and parcel of our efforts to serve the communities. The benefits from all the relationships that we form will ultimately be channelled back to the community in one way or another. It will also help to promote Dundee and Scotland as a home to a centre of excellence in Arabic and Islamic Studies.

Last summer, the Institute received a group of 23 students from Zayed University. This was the first cultural exchange programme organised by the Institute and it was a great success. The students were chosen by Zayed University based on their potential to become senior top administrators and decision makers in many key areas in the future. By hosting these future leaders, the Institute has ensured that good connection has been established. Plans are in place to organise a similar programme next summer.

Local Communities
Working with this ethos of building bridges through academic excellence and serving the communities, the Institute is fast becoming an integral part of Dundee's society. Several activities and exciting new developments have been taken to solidify our connections with the communities.

The Institute has adopted a policy of giving priority to local businesses. Almost all works are contracted out to local companies. This includes the major works which were undertaken to renovate this campus. In addition to the creation of new jobs in Dundee, and what our staff, students, and visitors have spent in Dundee, the Institute, proudly, has made a significant investment in the local economy of more than 1.5 million pounds in the last two years.

The Institute actively seeks to work with organisations that share our aspiration to serve the local communities. Thus, we have provided funding and sponsorship to several institutions and organisations in Dundee over the year. For example, to help the University of Abertay Dundee enhance its research capacity, the Institute donated a sum of £100,000 to fund a research project. In addition, the Institute, proudly, sponsored the Rep Theatre Production of Shakespearean comedy *Twelfth Night*, Lochee Freestyle Karate Club, Fun Factory Out-of-School Club in

Park Place Primary School and provision of Iftar for around 150 Muslim students in Dundee during the month of Ramadan.

In the effort to further serve the local communities, the Academic Council has also decided to expand on the success of the Arabic Language Evening Class by setting up a Community Education Unit. The aim is to respond to the high demand from the local communities to provide better understanding of Islam and Muslims.

During the Kirking of the Parliament in May this year, a student from the Institute recited from the Holy Qur'an, making it the first time in history that the Holy Qur'an had been read in a Kirking Ceremony.

Further away from home, the Institute is involved with the 'Books for Baghdad' Project in which three Universities in Iraq are to be provided with $300,000 worth of books to help reconstruct the higher education system there.

Scotland – Dubai

In addition to being a centre of academic excellence, the Institute has been working hard to enhance the relationship between Dubai, Dundee and Scotland. Having His Highness Shaikh Hamdan Bin Rashid Al-Maktoum as Patron of the Institute certainly helps to strengthen our ability to do this, and the Institute's presence in Dundee, has certainly helped as well.

It is with great pleasure that the Institute can report that 'Emirates, the award-winning international airline', announced last week 'a major boost for Scottish air travel by unveiling plans for a new daily service to Dubai... The world's fast growing major airline will launch non-stop daily flights from Glasgow Airport to Dubai on 10 April 2004.

'It will provide Scottish air travellers and cargo shippers with direct (and convenient) access to Dubai, one of the world's most dynamic and fast emerging centres for tourism and commerce. Likewise, the Scottish economy will reap the benefit of inward trade, from increases in both inbound tourism and imported goods.'

This new major development follows on from the historic and successful visit of His Highness Shaikh Hamdan Bin Rashid Al-Maktoum to officially open the Al-Maktoum Institute in Dundee on 6 May 2002, when His Highness Shaikh Hamdan invited a senior delegation to visit Dubai. The Institute played a key role in catalysing and organising the delegation's visit to Dubai on 20 – 25 October 2002. The delegation was led by Dundee Lord Provost John Letford and brought back potential projects between Dundee, Scotland and Dubai at different levels.

During the audience with His Highness Shaikh Hamdan on 21 October 2002, the delegation proposed to HH Shaikh Hamdan that Emirates Airline should fly to Scotland. Indeed this proposal brought the issue back into discussion and under active consideration.

This is another major development to further solidify the links between Scotland and Dubai already created by His Highness Shaikh Hamdan's visit to Dundee.

This is great news for Scotland and the Al-Maktoum Institute for Arabic and Islamic Studies. The Institute is particularly pleased that our presence in Scotland further enhanced the relationship between Scotland and Dubai and helped, by proposing the revitalisation of the idea, to bring about this prestigious new service to Scotland.

HH Shaikh Hamdan has expressed his pleasure with the progress and achievements of the Institute, and with the way the relationship between Dubai, Dundee, and Scotland is developing. Indeed, HH Shaikh Hamdan sees that there are many more opportunities yet to be explored in the relationship between Dubai, Dundee and Scotland.

With all these achievements, and yet many more planned for the future, it is evident that the Al-Maktoum Institute for Arabic and Islamic Studies is generating an atmosphere on which a dialogue of civilisations can take place rather than a clash. Combating ignorance with the light of true understanding and knowledge, our work will sow the seeds of a better understanding between Muslims and other nations of the world.

Thanks

I would like to take this opportunity to thank everyone who has contributed to our achievements. Special thanks are due to HH Shaikh Hamdan Bin Rashid Al-Maktoum for his continuous advice, support, and encouragement. The Institute comes from his vision and a sign of his commitment to developing further relations. Our name is now becoming more and more recognised nationally and internationally, at the levels that we hope will bring benefits to the Institute and to the communities that we serve.

Although it has been challenging and demanding, our staff continues to work hard. I would like to thank my colleagues at the Institute for their support in making possible all that we have achieved in the last two years.

Huge thanks to all the members of Al-Maktoum Institute family, all staff and students. Thanks also to everyone in the City and in the communities who continuously support us and what we do. You are the ones who have made all the achievements possible and you are the ones who have worked so hard to ensure we continuously excel in all that we do.

Conclusion

The Institute can play an important role in enhancing the understanding of multi-cultural Scotland. We are proud to be putting Dundee at the head of that debate. We are looking forward to working closely with institutions, in particular with the Scottish Executive, and Scottish Parliament, to enhance that debate. We will continue to play our unique role in serving the communities in Dundee, Scotland and internationally.

I feel proud to be the Principal of the Institute which has so far been very successful in achieving its aims and objectives. We has generated the framework for solid and continuous delivery of results and several significant successes have already been achieved. The recent developments of our Institute have been remarkable and the future looks promising indeed. Potential projects are in the pipeline which will promote Dundee at national and international levels and present it as a model for the rest of the country. Our eyes are firmly fixed on the future and we can see nothing else but a better and brighter future.

Professor Abd al-Fattah El-Awaisi
Principal and Vice-Chancellor

APPENDIX XII

THE 2004 'RECOGNTION OF ACHIEVEMENTS CEREMONY'

The Principal and Vice-Chancellor address
26 November 2004

It gives me great pleasure to welcome you all on behalf of Al-Maktoum Institute. This ceremony today is to recognise, celebrate and congratulate the excellent achievements of the Al-Maktoum Institute family, especially our students who graduated this year. Indeed, this recognition of achievements ceremony has now become an annual fixture in our academic calendar.

Last year, the main theme of my speech was that education is the key to tackling fundamentalism, extremism and ignorance. It is a theme that is even truer today than before. As we witness daily events from world trouble spots on our TV screens I believe, more than ever, that a dialogue has to be encouraged between the Muslim and non-Muslim countries and between academics and others who inhabit those countries. There must be more serious civilisational dialogue.

For our part, here in the Al- Maktoum Institute, we are doing all we can to encourage such a dialogue. We are working to generate an atmosphere in which a dialogue of civilisations can take place rather than a clash.

Shaikh Hamdan Bin Rashid Al-Maktoum's Vision for Multiculturalism

At the heart of the work of the Institute is the vision and passion of HH Shaikh Hamdan Bin Rashid Al-Maktoum for the twin pillars of education and multiculturalism. In June 2004 all our work came together in a single document entitled Shaikh Hamdan Bin Rashid Al-Maktoum's Vision for Multiculturalism. This major document sets out the importance of the vision of Islamic Jerusalem as a model of a common space in which people from different backgrounds can live together. Shaikh Hamdan is passionate in his desire to actively encourage dialogue across cultures and peoples that will enhance greater understanding and appreciation between the Arab and Muslim worlds and the West in general and between Dubai and Scotland in particular.

This is a major development for us as it is influencing and will continue to influence the direction of the Institute and the whole of our work revolves around the implementation of this innovative vision.

I would like to reflect briefly on our recent developments and activities which have been initiated by the Institute in the last year to implement this vision.

Shaikh Hamdan Bin Rashid Al-Maktoum Awards for Multicultural Scotland

HH Shaikh Hamdan's commitment to multiculturalism will be demonstrated next year with a ceremony to present the first Awards for Multicultural Scotland. The award ceremony will be held in May/June of next year and it is hoped that the Shaikh will be present for the occasion.

Launched in Edinburgh earlier this year, the awards are designed to recognise and encourage individual and institutional contributions to multicultural Scotland in which religious diversity, cultural equality, social justice, and civilisational dialogue flourish.

Through the Awards, the Institute aims to promote further work and to reward achievements in the development of good multicultural practice at all levels of Scottish society including education, healthcare, sport, the media, civilisational dialogue, Scottish-Emirates relations, and Arab British understanding. The Awards seek to identify and encourage the efforts of many people in Scotland who share the Al-Maktoum Institute's vision for greater tolerance and understanding and engagement between people of different cultures, religions, and nations.

These new awards are a key element of the work of the Al-Maktoum Institute, not only to promote and encourage international research and teaching in the field of multiculturalism, but also to implement multiculturalism in practical ways.

Al-Maktoum Multicultural Garden for Dundee Out-of-School Club

Again, to promote multiculturalism at all levels, the Institute sponsorship scheme, from the current year, will only be provided to organisations and institutions that have demonstrated their commitment to multiculturalism and for projects to further this aim.

To this end, the Al-Maktoum Institute sponsored the creation of a new multicultural garden for the Fun Factory Out-of-School Club, Park Place, Dundee. The garden will be a new centre of activity for children attending the club and the school. The Institute is delighted to continue its support for the Fun Factory Out-of-School Club; and we look forward to the official opening of the Garden in 2005.

The success and the niche of the Institute

As you know, the aim of the Institute is to pursue excellence in teaching, research and consultancy in the academic study of Islam and Muslims, in the contemporary world, and to be a place of knowledge and reflection on the issues facing a diverse and multicultural world in the 21st century.

The success of the Institute comes from the fact that it is one of the key post orientalist, and now post traditionalist, institutions in the world. We recognise the need to develop the study of Islam and Muslims as a discipline with long established roots but which must now face the challenges and opportunities of the 21st century. To this end, we are actively working to educate the next generation of scholars both nationally and internationally to enable them to face the challenges and opportunities of a diverse and multicultural world. The Institute has developed teaching programmes based on current and progressive research and which take into consideration the needs and preferences of our local, national and international students.

Strategic Development: Dundee Declaration

This agenda is fully mapped out in a document we produced in March this year titled the Dundee Declaration for the future Development of the study of Islam and Muslims. This Dundee Declaration came out of a major International Symposium which was hosted by the Institute and organised together with the Islamic Universities League. The League has over a hundred members and Al-Maktoum Institute is the only one in the UK. It was a tremendous honour for us, as the newest member of the League, to host this gathering of international scholars, which helped us pursue one of our aims to provide a meeting point between the Western and Muslim worlds of learning and to encourage scholarship and academic co-operation at this crucial time. Here, in this very Conference hall, there was a real civilisational dialogue.

The major theme of the Conference was the establishment of a new agenda for the future development of teaching and research in the Study of Islam and Muslims. The Dundee Declaration emerged as the conclusion of the two days of intense discussion on the future development of the field. This innovative and very important document sets out in detail key issues for the field, stressing the importance for scholars engaged in this area to look to face the challenge of the future.

The Declaration makes it clear that the current crisis in the contemporary Muslim world is the absence of co-operation between knowledge and power, and academic research and teaching in the study of Islam and Muslims is based on a principle of mutual respect in which people of any faith can share together a common intellectual goal. (The full text of the Dundee Declaration is in Appendix 6).

Through this major development in teaching and research in the study of Islam and Muslims, the Institute has established its strategic objectives agenda as post orientalist, post traditionalist and multicultural.

The Future Development of the New Field of Inquiry of Islamic Jerusalem Studies

This was followed by another development in June, at the end of the 2004 International Academic Conference on Islamic Jerusalem Studies, when another important document was issued entitled 'The future development of the New Field of Inquiry of Islamic Jerusalem Studies'. Indeed, the conference felt that teaching and research in the field should be encouraged and supported on an international basis. To this end, it is proposed to develop three regional centres/hubs from which the field can be promoted: the Al-Maktoum Institute as a base for Europe; to establish a base in Malaysia for that country and for South East Asia; and a base within an Arab country, which is progressing to achieve these goals at a future date.

The Implementation of the Dundee Declaration

Since the drafting of the Dundee Declaration the Institute has now begun the process of strategic planning for disseminating and implementing this new agenda.

Externally

To that end, the Al-Maktoum institute will be working with our partner universities across the world during this coming year to find practical ways in which the new agenda of the Dundee Declaration may be developed and implemented worldwide. A truly global dialogue.

International Academic Links and Collaborations

In addition to the Institute's collaboration with the University of Aberdeen, we have to date signed Memoranda of Understanding with eleven of the world's leading universities across the world. During the past twelve months alone I am delighted to mentioned that we have signed a further six Memoranda of Understanding with leading universities: Johann Wolfgang Goethe University in Frankfurt, Germany; Al-Bayt University, Jordan; University of Jordan; University of Cairo, Al-

Azhar University (which is the oldest university in the world); and University of Malaya, Malaysia.

We are actively working to expand each of these relationships to help further the strategic objectives of the Institute around the world.

Internally: New Initiative

Major Research Project on Study of Islam and Muslims in the UK

In line with the Institute's strategic objective to develop the agenda of the Dundee Declaration and in order to find the intellectual ingredients for that debate, we at the Institute have also allocated funds for a significant research project which has been investigating the teaching and research in the study of Islam and Muslims in the UK.

We are close to finishing the first stage of the project which will lead towards the production of a report for dissemination in the wider academic community. This project will make a very important contribution to our understanding of the study of Islam and Muslims at this critical stage, and will of course hopefully provide useful research findings to indicate the key issues that the discipline must face over the next few decades.

University of Aberdeen Validation Agreement

During the course of last year, the Institute changed our partner university for the validation of our programmes, moving from Abertay to the University of Aberdeen. I would like to place on record our thanks to Abertay for validating our programmes during our early stage of growth, and of course today we recognise and celebrate the graduation of students under the University of Abertay programme.

Our new link with Aberdeen is a significant and exciting step for the Institute, which is very much in line with our aim to foster excellence in teaching and research in the study of Islam and Muslims. As you know, the University of Aberdeen is one of the oldest Scottish universities, having recently marked its 500th anniversary, and it has an international reputation for its teaching and research. In the 2001 Research Assessment Exercise (RAE) Divinity and Religious Studies were awarded the high rating of 5.

The Institute looks forward to working with the University of Aberdeen in a number of areas of collaboration in the fields of research and teaching.

Programme Review and Development

The new validation agreement with the University of Aberdeen has given the opportunity to review and develop the two MLitt programmes that we offer in Islamic Studies and Islamic Jerusalem Studies. These two programmes were first constructed in 2001, and taught for the first time in February 2002, and so the new validation has given us a timely opportunity for such a review. A key issue for the Institute has been to ensure that the programmes reflect the development of the discipline of the study of Islam and Muslims, and in particular issues raised by the Dundee Declaration and how this can be reflected in the teaching that takes place at the Institute.

Therefore, a fundamental review took place in autumn 2004, and the Academic Council of the Institute has now approved the new structure for both MLitt programmes. Together both programmes will establish the Institute as providing taught postgraduate courses that are unique and innovative, indeed unlike any other programmes offered in the UK. It is likely that the programmes will raise a lot of interest from potential students looking to engage in the post-orientalist, multicultural, and interdisciplinary agenda in the study of Islam and Muslims that is set out in the Dundee Declaration.

Restructuring

To reflect this vision of post orientalism, post traditionalist, and multicultural approaches, the Institute, during the past year, has seen significant developments through a process of restructuring. These developments are to address the exciting growth of the Institute and the wider network of relationships which have been developed in the last year.

The main focus of these developments was to incorporate Shaikh Hamdan's Vision for Multiculturalism and the Dundee Declaration into the Institute's teaching and research activities. Indeed, this Vision and Declaration laid the foundation for the strategic development of the Institute as a post-orientalist and multicultural institution.

Creation of the post of Depute Principal for Academic Affairs.

Professor Malory Nye, who holds the chair of Multiculturalism, Islam and Muslims at the Institute, was appointed in March 2004 to the new post of Depute Principal for Academic Affairs. As a leading expert in the field of multiculturalism and the study of religious diversity in the UK, Professor Nye in his new role will be of great assistance in building the reputation of the Institute, both nationally and internationally, as a leading institution for the academic study of Islam and Muslims.

Research Centres

In spring 2004 the Academic Council approved two important developments for one of the Institute's leading research centres. The Centre for the Study of Islam and Muslims has now been renamed as the: Centre for Research on Multiculturalism and Islam and Muslims in Scotland.

Further to this, the Academic Council also established within the Centre a special think-tank titled the Multiculturalism Research Unit (MRU).

Achievements

Recruitment and Graduates in 2004

Our roll of honour for students passing through the Institute is growing steadily. With all the major restructuring work of the Institute and change of awarding university, which happened just before the summer 2004, the Institute has succeeded in recruiting the same number of postgraduate students as last year. However, we continue to develop our recruitment and marketing strategies and look for further expansion in future years of highly qualified national and international students.

We are very pleased at the continuing success of our MLitt students. We recognise this through the achievements of the 13 students who completed their MLitt programmes this year and who graduate today, which brings the total of our PhD and Masters Graduates to 28. These students are to be highly commended for their hard work. They are truly an asset to the Institute. To recognise their successes, the Institute introduced this year two new prizes for distinction for our taught Master students. I would like in particular to commend one student, Fatimatuzzahra Abd al-Rahman, who in her research dissertation in September achieved a grade of 1, which is the highest possible grade. In addition, the Institute is pleased that among our graduates today are the Imams of the two main mosques in Dundee. We consider that all our staff and students are major resources in the implementation of the Dundee Declaration and should consider themselves as ambassadors for the promotion of this new agenda.

The Institute's sponsorship scheme which benefited a number of our graduates allows students who may not otherwise have had the opportunity to come and live and study in the West to further their education. This is a vital process in opening up dialogue and leading to greater understanding of different cultures.

Develop the Relationships between Dubai and Scotland

The Institute is actively continuing working to serve the local, national, and international communities. As a man of vision, Shaikh Hamdan works to achieve the implementation of practical models to develop the relationship between Dubai and Scotland.

As our busy year continued a second and then a third Scottish delegation from Al-Maktoum Institute visited Dubai in December 2003 and April 2004. The aims of the visits were to widen and strengthen the initial contact which had been established and to strengthen the business and economical connections between the two nations. Indeed, during the second delegation, the project to build Al-Maktoum Cultural Centre was announced, and Zayed University and Aberdeen University signed a Memorandum of Understanding. The Cultural Centre has been developed significantly as we are now in the final stage of the design of this landmark project for the city. I am delighted to mention that we have already been holding discussions with neighbouring residents and local groups who are looking forward to the new Centre opening and to using its facilities.

The Inaugural Emirates Flight to Glasgow

The third delegation returned to Scotland on the inaugural flight of Emirates Airline flying direct to Glasgow from Dubai. Indeed, the Al-Maktoum Institute is particularly pleased that our presence in Scotland helped the revitalisation of the idea to bring about this prestigious new service to Scotland. The idea was first discussed during the first delegation to Dubai in December 2002. We are proud that the Institute played a part in Emirates Airline's making that decision: another clear example of how dialogue can lead to a positive outcome.

Sister Cities Agreement between Dubai and Dundee

Another significant achievement of the third delegation was the signing of the Sister Cities Agreement between Dundee City and Dubai. The Institute played a major role to achieve this important agreement for Dundee and to facilitate Dundee City Council with the opportunity to promote Dundee at the national and international levels. Indeed, the presence of the Institute in Dundee certainly led to Dundee's being invited to become a sister city. Dundee is the only one in the UK.

Dubai Sister City Forum

This led Dundee City Council also to be invited to participate in Dubai's First Sister City Forum held in May this year alongside delegations from the other eleven cities from China, Japan, Australia, the United States, Switzerland and across the Arab and Muslim countries.

Raising awareness of business opportunities with Dubai

To assist Dundee to build on the developing relationship with Dubai, Al-Maktoum Institute recently hosted an event jointly organised by the City Council and Business Gateway International Tayside. Representatives of more than 60 companies from across Tayside attended the event, which was aimed at raising awareness of trading opportunities with Dubai.

2004 Summer School for Students from the UAE

Our ties with the higher education sector in the UAE continue to grow, in particular with the hosting by the Institute of the second three week Summer School for female students from the UAE. This year's event was expanded to include students from three different institutions - Zayed University, UAE University and the Higher Colleges of Technology (Dubai Women's College).

Again a full training programme for future leaders in the multicultural 21st century was arranged for them and I would like publicly to thank all those who played a part in making the visit such an enjoyable and successful one.

Word of these summer schools has spread with those fortunate enough to have taken part returning home and talking of their experience. Now the male students from the UAE are asking when it will be their turn to visit Scotland.

The Summer School programme also included a Public Lecture at the Al-Maktoum Institute by Councillor Jill Shimi, the leader of Dundee City Council, on 'The leading role of women in Dubai in the 21st Century'. Councillor Jill Shimi highlighted the key role that women are playing in the success of contemporary Dubai, and the investment that the state is making in educating women as the next generation of leaders.

This was further highlighted on 1 November 2004, when the late Shaikh Zayed appointed the first female government minister, Shaikha Lubna al-Qasimi, to the key job of economics and planning minister. As you know, there are other women ministers in the Gulf countries, in Bahrain, Oman and Qatar, but Shaikha Lubna's role is the most senior to date.

Next Year's Plan

As I said earlier, the award ceremony for Multicultural Scotland will be held in May/June of next year and it is hoped that Shaikh Hamdan will be present for the occasion. During the visit he will also lay the foundation stone for the Al-Maktoum Cultural Centre which is being built further up Blackness Road. The visit will also coincide with a major trade delegation coming from Dubai to Scotland next year, to explore business links here.

Honorary Fellowship of Al-Maktoum Institute

Finally, I would like also to announce today two new awards to recognise the efforts of individuals who have made a significant contribution both to the development of the Institute and to the aims and objectives of the Institute.

The recipients, the Bishop of Brechin, the Rt Revd Neville Chamberlain; and Mr Ernie Ross, MP for Dundee West, have both demonstrated their personal commitment to the multicultural vision that is at the heart of Al-Maktoum Institute and as a result in a moment we will be awarding them Honorary Fellowship of the Institute.

Conclusion

In conclusion I would like to thank Shaikh Hamdan Bin Rashid Al-Maktoum for his continued support. He is a man with a vision of a better world, a world where peoples of all faiths, colours and creeds can live together in peace. He is setting an example for others world leaders to follow:

- Through the creation of the Al-Maktoum Institute in Dundee
- Through the Dundee Declaration for the future Development of the study of Islam and Muslims
- Through our teaching programmes in Islamic Jerusalem Studies and the Study of Islam and Muslims
- Through the plan for the future development of the new field of inquiry
- Through our implementation and investigation of the central concept of multiculturalism
- Through the creation of the new Awards scheme for Multicultural Scotland
- And through our continuing efforts to serve the communities

We feel proud and honoured to be given the opportunity to work to pursue Shaikh Hamdan's vision for education and multiculturalism which has helped the Institute to play a key role in building progressive links between Scotland and Dubai but he sees that there are many more opportunities yet to be explored.

Indeed, Al-Maktoum Institute is continually striving to implement Shaikh Hamdan Bin Rashid Al-Maktoum's vision for further facilitating the creation of mutually beneficial relationships between Dubai and Scotland. Our strategic aim is to help promote a two way traffic for this developing relationship between the two nations and Shaikh Hamdan indicates very clearly that Al-Maktoum Institute is The Gateway to Dubai.

We have made a lot of progress in the last three years. The developments and achievements over the past twelve months demonstrate our uniqueness at both academic and community levels. Our reputation as a centre of academic excellence continues to grow, as do our links with the wider community in both Dundee and the rest of Scotland. Crucially, we have got the dialogue started on how the study of Islam and Muslims should be developed in the 21st century and through the results of our academic research we will continue this serious dialogue. That is the civilised way forward.

Thank you

Professor Abd al-Fattah El-Awaisi
Principal and Vice-Chancellor

APPENDIX XIII

THE 2005 GRADUATION CEREMONY
A Day of Celebration

The Principal and Vice-Chancellor address
1 December 2005

On behalf of the Institute, I am delighted to welcome you today to our first Graduation Ceremony to recognise, celebrate and congratulate the excellent achievements of the Al-Maktoum Institute family especially our students who graduated this year.

For those graduating it marks the successful completion of a full year's study. Today's graduands are about to join the growing number of graduates from this Institute. They are however, the first group of our students to graduate with a Master's degree from the University of Aberdeen.

This is a day of celebration, not just for the graduands but equally for those who have supported them: parents, family and friends. I hope that those of you graduating today will reflect on your time at Al-Maktoum Institute in Dundee as being a very happy and fruitfully challenging time in your life. The Institute is proud of you and you should be proud of yourselves. I offer you my sincere congratulations and wish you all every success in the years to come.

In the last two years, the main theme of my speech was the need to promote multicultural education as the means to defeat fundamentalism, extremism and terrorism. That message still holds good today. People in the UK were shocked to learn that the suicide bombers in London last July were not from some foreign land but had all been born and brought up here in Britain.

This was a clear signal that the doctrine of fundamentalism is not just concentrated in a few refugee camps situated somewhere in some foreign countries. After the 7 July bombings, I still firmly believe that multiculturalism is the means to achieve peaceful co-existence and mutual respect between people, nations, religions, and cultures.

For our part, here in the Al- Maktoum Institute, we are doing all we can to encourage such vision. The Institute was established here in Scotland to promote a multicultural future that will see people acknowledging and respecting their differences BUT willing to share a common ground, live and work together in a peaceful co-existence.

I would like to reflect briefly on the recent developments and activities which have been initiated by the Institute in the last year to implement our vision.

New Agenda for the Study of Islam and Muslims

The success of the Institute comes from its new agenda which places it as one of the leading post orientalist, post traditionalist, multicultural institutions in the world. We recognise the need to develop the study of Islam and Muslims as a discipline with long established roots BUT which must now face the challenges and opportunities of the 21st century. To this end, we are actively working to educate the next generation of scholars both nationally and internationally to enable them to face the challenges and opportunities of a diverse and multicultural world.

This innovative agenda sets out in detail key issues for the field, stressing the importance for scholars engaged in this area to look to face the challenge of the future and this world we live in today.

The new agenda makes it clear that the current crisis in the contemporary Muslim world is caused in part by the absence of co-operation between knowledge and power. And academic research and teaching in the study of Islam and Muslims is based on a principle of mutual respect in which people of any faith can share together a common intellectual goal.

To reflect this vision of post orientalist, post traditionalist, and multicultural approaches, the Institute, during the past two years, has seen significant developments. These developments are to address the exciting growth of the Institute and the wider network of relationships which have been developed in the last year.

For example, the Institute started the process of disseminating and implementing this new agenda by working internally at the Institute and externally with our 15 partner universities.

One of our key strategic partners is the University of Aberdeen. Our new link with Aberdeen is a significant and exciting step for the Institute, which is very much in line with our aim to foster excellence in teaching and research in the study of Islam and Muslims. As you know, the University of Aberdeen is one of the oldest Scottish universities, and it has an international reputation for its teaching and research. In the 2001 Research Assessment Exercise (RAE) Divinity and Religious Studies were awarded the high rating of 5.

Our validation agreement with the University of Aberdeen has given us the opportunity to review and develop the two Master programmes that we offer in Islamic Studies and Islamic Jerusalem Studies. A key issue for the Institute has been to ensure that the programmes reflect the development of the discipline of the study of Islam and Muslims, and in particular issues raised by our new agenda and how this can be reflected in the teaching that takes place at the Institute.

Together both programmes establish the Institute as providing taught postgraduate courses that are unique and innovative, indeed unlike any other programmes offered in the UK. This is urgently needed after the July bombings in London.

With our Scottish partner, the University of Aberdeen, the Institute has developed, and will continue to develop, teaching programmes based on current and progressive research and which take into consideration the needs and preferences of our local, national and international students.

The Institute looks forward to working with the University of Aberdeen in a number of areas of collaboration in the fields of research and teaching.

Here, I am please to announce the launch of our new prospectus for 2006/2007.

We consider that all our staff and students are major resources in the implementation of our new agenda and should consider themselves as ambassadors for its promotion. To achieve this, a number of initiatives have been developed which include a series of research workshops which have already organised for both academic staff and students to discuss and debate the Institute's new agenda on the study of Islam and Muslims.

The Institute's achievements in the last year demonstrate our continuous success in developing our academic activities, in particular the development and enhancement of our research culture, enhancing the learning environment and community, our quality assurance systems, our new agenda, and the widening and strengthening of our international academic network and collaboration.

The development and enhancement of research culture focused last year on Student Training and Development such as organising conferences, and research seminars attended by leading visiting scholars (from University of St Andrews, University of Edinburgh, University of Dundee, University of Wurzburg, International Academy of Philosophy, Liechtenstein).

Graduates in 2005

The continual growing success of our Master students brings great pride to the Institute. With the 12 graduates this year, this will bring the total of PhD and Masters graduates to 40. These students are to be highly commended for their hard work. They are truly an asset to the Institute. I would like in particular to commend two students, Sarah Hassan, and Abdullah Omar, who both achieved a distinction grade for their dissertations. To recognise their achievement, the Institute will present to them the Shaikh Hamdan Bin Rashid Al-Maktoum prizes for academic distinction.

Honorary Fellowship of Al-Maktoum Institute
In addition, today, we will be conferring honorary fellowships on two leading individuals in recognition of their efforts and significant contribution both to the development of the Institute and to the vision, mission, and aims and objectives of the Institute.

The recipients, Reverend Erik Cramb; and Councillor Jill Shimi, have both demonstrated their personal commitment to the multicultural vision that is at the heart of Al-Maktoum Institute.

Develop the Relationships between Dubai and Scotland
Al-Maktoum Institute is continually striving to implement Shaikh Hamdan Bin Rashid Al-Maktoum's vision for further facilitating the creation of mutually beneficial relationships between Dubai and Scotland. Our strategic aim is to help promote a two way traffic for this developing relationship between the two nations and Shaikh Hamdan indicates very clearly that Al-Maktoum Institute is The Gateway to Dubai. To strengthen this relationship, the Institute initiated last year several projects, including: the Third Summer Training School for female Students from the UAE in multiculturalism and leadership, the training of Dubai TV staff in Scotland, Shaikh Hamdan Bin Rashid Al-Maktoum Awards for Multicultural Scotland, Al-Maktoum Multicultural Garden for Dundee Fun Factory after School Club, UAE University Medical School visits to Aberdeen and Dundee, the participation of seven students from Scotland at the Women as Global Leaders conference at Zayed University led by Wendy Alexander (MSP), and the Institute association with the successful story of Emirates Airline for Scotland.

The relationship between Dubai and Scotland continues to flourish. This growth and expansion between the two countries highlights the hard work of the Institute to develop the relationship between Dubai and Scotland as an implementation of Shaikh Hamdan's vision.

Next Year's Plan

To conclude my message, let me take you back to the Institute's work which is to generate an atmosphere in which a dialogue of civilisations can take place rather than a clash. Here at Al-Maktoum Institute we are educating the next generation of scholars who will take that message of multiculturalism out into the wider world. We are also establishing a niche for ourselves as a place where debate on these key issues can take place.

Next month will see the publication of a major monograph, Introducing Islamicjerusalem, which I hope will stimulate further debate during 2006 about the interpretation of the core teachings of the Qu'ran and challenge academics, religious leaders and politicians to think in a different way.

During the year we will also be hosting an International Academic Network Forum in Dubai, an International Network Students Forum in Dundee and two International Conferences, one on the Challenges of Multiculturalism, and one on the Challenges of Islamicjerusalem.

There will be a lot of debate and discussion about this subject and my earnest hope is that from these discussions will come ideas for action and a greater understanding that Islamicjeruslam can be the way forward for conflict resolution by providing its model for multiculturalism.

We do not pretend to have all the answers but at least we are putting forward some ideas on how to improve understanding between people of different religions and cultures.

As I said earlier, we are also educating the new generation of academics who can carry these ideas forward. Some of them you see before you today.

For the relationship between Scotland and Dubai, the second round of Shaikh Hamdan Bin Rashid Al-Maktoum Awards for Multicultural Scotland will be launched sometime in the new year.

Our plan is to see, hopefully, the start of the building of Al-Maktoum Culture Centre in Dundee (we are currently waiting for the planning permission from Dundee City Council), and the major trade delegation coming from Dubai to Scotland to explore and investigate the possibility of trade business links here.

My hope is that our increased profile, along with the activities and the links we are building internationally will encourage more students to come here to Dundee.

We are also working to increase the recruitment of students from Scotland and elsewhere in the UK.

Conclusion

In conclusion we extend our gratitude to HH Shaikh Hamdan Bin Rashid Al-Maktoum for his continuous support for Al-Maktoum Institute. The Institute's staff and students feel a real sense of pride and honour to pursue his vision for education and multiculturalism.

Once again, I offer my sincere congratulations to all members of the Al-Maktoum Institute family especially our students who graduated today. I would like to congratulate the hardworking members of Al-Maktoum Institute family who have been responsible for putting this graduation ceremony together. I would like in particular to thank Anne Simpson, our academic administrator, for coordinating the hard work that was involved in organising this ceremony.

We feel proud of the progress and growth of the Institute in the last four years. The last year's developments and achievements demonstrate once again our uniqueness. We are also proud that we are now disseminating our New Agenda in the Study of Islam and Muslims. The success of our academic programmes has been clearly acknowledged by a number of indicators, not least the glowing report and comments we have received from our external examiner. The Institute's success is not only impressive but also well deserved and the future looks promising indeed. The Institute's eyes are firmly on the future and we can see nothing else but a better and brighter multicultural future for all of us.

Thank you

Professor Abd al-Fattah El-Awaisi
Principal and Vice-Chancellor

APPENDIX XIV

THE 2006 GRADUATION CEREMONY
A Day of Celebration

The Principal and Vice-Chancellor address
1 December 2006

On behalf of the Institute, I am delighted to welcome you today to our Second Graduation Ceremony with the University of Aberdeen. This graduation ceremony today is to recognise, celebrate and congratulate the excellent achievements of the Al-Maktoum Institute family especially our students who graduated this year.

For those graduating it marks the successful completion of a full year's study. Today's graduands are about to join the growing number of graduates from this Institute. They are the second group of our students to graduate with Master's or PhD degrees from the University of Aberdeen. I am glad that we have with us today Professor Steven Logan, Senior Vice-Principal of the University of Aberdeen, to award the degrees to our students.

This is a day of celebration, not just for the graduands but equally for those who have supported them: parents, families and friends. I hope that those of you graduating today will reflect on your time at Al-Maktoum Institute in Dundee as being a very happy and fruitfully challenging time in your life. The Institute is proud of you and you should be proud of yourselves. I offer you my sincere congratulations and wish you all every success in the years to come.

In the last three years, the main theme of my speech was the need to promote multicultural education as the means to defeat fundamentalism, extremism and terrorism. That message still holds good today. I still firmly believe that multiculturalism is the means to achieve peaceful co-existence and mutual respect between people, nations, religions, and cultures.

For our part, here in the Al- Maktoum Institute, we are doing all we can to promote a multicultural future that will see people acknowledging and respecting their differences BUT willing to share a common ground and space, live and work together in a peaceful co-existence.

In the last five years, the Institute witnessed a vast number of developments to promote such a vision. I would like to reflect briefly on our recent academic activities in the last year to implement our vision.

Disseminating the New Agenda for the Study of Islam and Muslims

The Institute's achievements in the last year demonstrate our continuous success in developing our academic activities, in particular the development and enhancement of our research culture, enhancing the learning environment and community, our quality assurance systems, our new agenda, and the widening and strengthening of our international academic network and collaboration.

The success of the Institute comes from its new agenda. We are actively working to educate the next generation of scholars both nationally and internationally to enable them to face the challenges and opportunities of a diverse and multicultural world.

To reflect this new agenda, the Institute, during the past three years, has seen significant developments. These developments are to address the exciting growth of the Institute and the wider network of relationships.

The Institute, for example, started the process of disseminating and implementing this new agenda by working internally at the Institute and externally with our 16 partner universities.

One of our key strategic partners is the University of Aberdeen. Last year was a period of important growth and development of the relationship between the two institutions, marked by a number of significant developments. Indeed, there has been real development with the University of Aberdeen, through a succession of productive meetings with Professor Duncan Rice, and Professor Steven Logan. Both institutions are proud of this strategic relationship. For the Institute, our link with Aberdeen is a significant and exciting step, which is very much in line with the Institute's aim to foster excellence in teaching and research in the study of Islam and Muslims.

Groundbreaking Monograph and Major Report

The development and enhancement of research culture has focused last year on student training and development such as organising conferences, and research seminars attended by leading visiting academics and scholars; and research training workshops in the winter and the summer. We have also seen the launch of a groundbreaking Monograph and a Major Report.

Introducing Islamicjerusalem

Introducing Islamicjerusalem was launched in three countries: UAE at Zayed University on 25 December 2005, Scotland at the Scottish

Parliament in Edinburgh on 30 January 2006, and Qatar at Qatar University on 9 March 2006. It is also in the process of being translated and published in three languages: Arabic, French, and Malay. It stimulated further debate during 2006 about the interpretation of the core teachings of the Qu'ran and challenged academics, religious leaders and politicians to think in a different way.

Time for Change: Report on the Future of the Study of Islam and Muslims in Universities and Colleges in Multicultural Britain
From 2004 to 2006, Al-Maktoum Institute commissioned a major research project on teaching and research in the Study of Islam and Muslims in UK higher education. This research has examined 55 higher education departments and centres where Islam and Muslims is taught, including Islamic Studies, Religious Studies, Middle Eastern and Arabic Studies, as well as departments of Politics and International Relations. The research led to a new major report entitled 'Time for Change: Report on the Future of the Study of Islam and Muslims in Universities and Colleges in Multicultural Britain' which was launched in the House of Lords on 25 October 2006.

The Report is not only providing a very important overview of the current situation, it also examines some of the key issues and challenges facing the field. It also makes recommendations on how the field must be reshaped and developed to face the challenges and opportunities of the twenty-first century. It concludes that Islamic studies in Britain's higher education establishments are failing to meet the needs of today: 'There must be better education at university level...which reflects the needs of our contemporary multicultural society.'

Teaching on Islam and Muslims has been an important part of university curricula in the UK for well over 250 years. BUT now is the time for change. The last report related to Islamic Studies was commissioned by the Government over 40 years ago (1909, 1948, and 1961). The Government should set up an immediate inquiry into the future of Islamic Studies at the UK higher educational institutions to determine a new agenda for the study of Islam and Muslims in the UK.

There is an urgent need for a complete re-examination of what is being taught about Islam and Muslims throughout the UK and a review of the relevance of the courses offered by these institutions. Some departments are not focusing on the need of 21st century life in multicultural Britain. This includes choosing local Imams and religious leaders as lecturers for 'political correctness'.

Too many courses on offer within the British higher education establishment lack relevance to the needs of contemporary multicultural British society on the one hand and at the same time Muslim institutions in the UK are following international political ideologies, which are not even relevant to the needs of the British Muslim communities.

The Report says that there is an urgent need for a new agenda to develop Islamic Studies into the Study of Islam and Muslims to challenge both the more traditional approaches that were often faith based and excluded non-Muslims and the orientalist approaches that often alienated Muslims. Indeed, the call for a new agenda is timely and necessary to prevent the misguided and narrow interpretations of Islam, which are the source of so many problems in our multicultural society. As I said earlier, it is only through multicultural education we can work to eliminate extremism and fundamentalism.

Indeed, there is a clear and very obvious need for the Study of Islam and Muslims to be developed as a significant field of study across all levels of education in Britain. This is not only for the education of British youth as global citizens with a good knowledge and understanding of the contemporary world, it is also essential as a means of understanding our own multicultural society.

We need to develop this field of study for today's world and, in particular, to rethink many of the loosely understood ideas that frame so much of the public debate surrounding this.

As a Scottish research-led higher education institution, Al-Maktoum Institute is very keen to develop the discussion and widen the debate on the issues raised by the Report on a scholarly level. For this purpose, the Institute is organising a national symposium on 'Time for Change: the Future of the Study of Islam and Muslims in Universities and Colleges in Multicultural Britain' to be held at the Institute here in Dundee on Friday 19 January 2007. The Institute is inviting academics, policy-makers and individuals with an interest in the field to attend and participate in the discussion.

To address one of the recommendations of Time for Change Report, the Institute formally established its first department named the Department of the Study of Islam and Muslims. We consider all our staff and students are major resources in the implementation of our new agenda and they should consider themselves as ambassadors for the promotion of this new agenda.

A Community of Graduates

The continual growing success of our Master and PhD students brings great pride to the Institute. With the 14 graduates this year (7 with PhDs), this will bring the total of PhD and Masters Graduates to 54. Indeed, as the founding Principal and Vice-Chancellor, I feel very proud that we have now a community of 54 graduates working across the globe at several levels. These students are to be highly commended for their hard work. They are truly one of the Institute's greatest asset.

I am absolutely delighted that we are playing our part in educating the new generation of scholars who will go out into the world of work ready to challenge the old ways of thinking, teaching and learning.

Al-Maktoum Institute Alumnus Network (Amian)

We hope that your gradation today will not be the end of your personal and professional relationship with the Institute. As we see our graduates as very important ambassadors for the Institute New Agenda, the Al-Maktoum Institute Alumnus Network (AMIAN) was established to enable former students to keep in touch with the Institute and with one another, and to provide opportunities for graduates to support the Institute, celebrate the Institute's ongoing success, and promote and facilitate lifelong links and partnership between the Institute and its graduates.

Honorary Fellowship of Al-Maktoum Institute

In addition, today, we will be conferring honorary fellowships on two leading individuals in recognition of their efforts and significant contribution both to the development of the Institute and to the vision, mission, and aims and objectives of the Institute.

The recipients, Baillie Helen Wright and Mr Alan Harden, have both demonstrated their personal commitment to the multicultural vision that is at the heart of Al-Maktoum Institute.

Next Year's Plan

To conclude my reflection, let me take you back to the Institute's work which is to generate an atmosphere in which a dialogue of civilisations can take place rather than a clash. Here at Al-Maktoum Institute we are educating the next generation of scholars who will take that message of cultural engagement and multiculturalism out into the wider world. We are also establishing a niche for ourselves as a unique institute with a timely new agenda.

In May 2007, the Institute will be celebrating the fifth anniversary of its formal opening. To celebrate the last five years of excellence, a series of events and celebrations have been planned, including:

Al-Maktoum Institute Summer School Alumnus Network

Following the success of the four Summer Schools and the two Dubai TV training programmes at Al-Maktoum Institute, the Alumnus Network was established.

Education is clearly recognised as a fundamental element in the future relationship between the UAE and the UK, and the Alumnus Network will be an important means by which educational contact is maintained and developed between the two countries.

The Alumnus Network will be launched with a reception held at the British Embassy, Abu Dhabi, hosted by the British Ambassador to the UAE, HE Mr Edward Oakden on 19 December 2006.

New initiatives with the University of Aberdeen

The Institute looks forward to continuing working with the University of Aberdeen in a number of areas of collaboration in the fields of research and teaching.

Indeed, with the University of Aberdeen, the Institute has developed, and will continue to develop, teaching programmes based on current and progressive research which take into consideration the needs and preferences of our local, national and international students.

A key issue for the Institute has been to ensure that our postgraduate programmes reflect the development of the discipline of the study of Islam and Muslims, and address in particular issues raised by our New Agenda and Time for Change Report and how this can be reflected in the teaching that takes place at the Institute. Accordingly, the Institute is currently in discussion with the University of Aberdeen to develop three new Taught Masters in: Multiculturalism; Muslims, Globalisation and the West; and Islamic Education, to be offered from September 2007.

Together these 5 postgraduate programmes will continue to establish the Institute as providing taught postgraduate courses that are unique and innovative. Indeed unlike any other programmes offered in the UK.

As part of disseminating and implementing the Institute's New Agenda to reach wider potential student communities, further expansion of our student recruitment base is also being proposed, for the delivery of our programmes through distant learning mode, along with the existing campus based mode. This will benefit two important recruitment markets: potential home students resident elsewhere in the UK with a strong interest in our programmes, but who are unable to move to study at the Institute in Dundee; and potential international students in particular in the UAE and the Gulf region, who are increasingly taking the opportunities of distance learning postgraduate study being offered by other Scottish and UK universities.

With the successful track-record of implementation of the validation agreement and the well established and matured relationship between the two institutions in the last two years, the two institutions are in agreement that this relationship should be developed from validation to accreditation which hopefully will come into effect in August 2007.

National and International Symposiums and Conferences
In additional to the National Symposium in January 2007, we will also be organising a joint international academic symposium on 'Multiculturalism and Cultural Engagement: Mapping an Agenda for the Twenty-First Century' with Zayed House for Islamic Culture in Abu Dhabi (8 April 2007), and two international academic conferences here in Dundee: one on Islamicjerusalem Studies and one on Multiculturalism.

We do not pretend to have all the answers but at least we are putting forward some ideas on how to improve understanding between people of different religions and cultures.

As I said earlier, we are also educating the new generation of academics who can carry these ideas forward. Some of them you see before you today.

Thanks
I would like to take this opportunity to thank everyone who has contributed to our successes and achievements. Special thanks to HH Shaikh Hamdan Bin Rashid Al-Maktoum for his continuous support for Al-Maktoum Institute. The Institute's staff and students feel a real sense of pride and honour to pursue his vision for education and multiculturalism.

I would like to thank all my colleagues at the Institute for their support in the last five years. Huge thanks to all the members of Al-Maktoum Institute family, all staff and students. Thanks also to everyone in the City and in the communities who continuously support the work of the Institute. You are the ones who made all the achievements possible.

Once again, I offer my sincere congratulations to all our students who graduated today. I would like to congratulate the hardworking members of Al-Maktoum Institute family who have been responsible for putting this graduation ceremony together. I would like in particular to thank

Abu Baker and Therese for co-ordinating the hard work that was involved in organising this ceremony.

Conclusion

The last year's developments and achievements demonstrate once again our uniqueness at both academic and communities levels. We are proud that we are now disseminating our New Agenda in the Study of Islam and Muslims.

We feel also proud of the progress and growth of the Institute in the last five years. I feel proud to be the founding Principal and Vice-Chancellor of the Institute, which has so far been very successful in achieving its vision, mission, aims and objectives. Our reputation as a centre of academic excellence is well established, acknowledged, and recognised. Indeed, the Institute has established a very strong foundation and framework for solid and continuous delivery of results, which will help it to continue playing its leading role at both academic and communities levels.

As we are celebrating the excellent achievements of the foundation and first stages of the Institute's history in this very short period, there is much we can look back on with pride. Indeed, the Institute's success is not only impressive but also well deserved.

I would like to share with you some of my personal experience. The last five years of establishing and building the Institute were challenging, demanding, hard and tiring work BUT enjoyable experience. In each successful step, I felt very strongly that we are making a positive change and making history. It is my opinion that we have made a groundbreaking development both at academic and communities levels. Indeed, the last five years were inspiring ones where we have set the new agenda for the Study of Islam and Muslims globally; and through the results of our major academic research we started the constructive dialogue and debate on how the future of the study of Islam and Muslims should be developed in the 21st century.

Yet while we celebrate our achievements, we know there is still much to do to promote our vision of a multicultural Britain, and to get our message across that from here in Dundee we are playing a major part in trying to bring peace to the world.

Thank you

Professor Abd al-Fattah El-Awaisi
Principal and Vice-Chancellor

APPENDIX XV

AL-MAKTOUM INSTITUTE: PRACTICAL MODELS FOR GLOBAL CROSS-CULTURAL UNDERSTANDING AND COOPERATION

Professor Abd al-Fattah El-Awaisi
Principal and Vice-Chancellor
Al-Maktoum Institute, Dundee

The 34th Scottish Council International Forum
The World We're In
17-18 March 2005
St Andrews Bay Hotel and Conference Centre

It is an honour to be invited to address this important and prestigious international forum. HH Shaikh Hamdan Bin Rashid Al-Maktoum, Deputy Ruler of Dubai, the UAE Minister of Finance and Industry, and Patron of the Al-Maktoum Institute, has asked me to convey his warmest greetings to all the Scottish delegates attending this Conference and he sends our meeting today his best wishes.

Introduction
In the last five years the world has witnessed a lot of debate on new forms of the global phenomena of fundamentalism and extremism. People are more aware of the intense political climate, clashes that have come to be known as 'fundamentalism' or 'extremism'. What these terms mean exactly has yet to be defined, but it is my view that at the root of such behaviour lies the disease of ignorance.

It is clear that many view Muslims as 'the Other' and vice-versa; an attitude of 'us and them' and the concept of a 'clash of civilisations' has become part of our everyday vocabulary. However, at the base of any such clash is either sheer ignorance or an extreme interpretation of the scriptures on which people found their beliefs and actions. Whichever way one looks at it, I believe strongly that education is the solution that will facilitate humankind to break free from the chains of ignorance and rise above extremism. A dialogue has to be encouraged between peoples and countries. This kind of civilisational and constructive dialogue must be taken more seriously.

Shaikh Hamdan Bin Rashid Al-Maktoum's Vision

His Highness Shaikh Hamdan Bin Rashid Al-Maktoum is passionate in his desire to actively encourage productive and effective civilisational dialogue across cultures and to build bridges between communities and people based on common ground, mutual respect, and shared goals and interest. Indeed, this is the civilised way forward to enhance greater understanding and appreciation between the Arab and Muslim worlds and the West. In this regard, His Highness is setting an example for other world leaders to follow.

As a man of vision, with a better world as a focus, HH Shaikh Hamdan works to achieve the implementation of practical models. Since 2001, one of his main focuses has been the creation of mutually beneficial relationships between Dubai and Scotland. The first step to facilitate the implementation of HH Shaikh Hamdan's vision and passion was the creation of Al-Maktoum Institute in 2001 in Dundee, which was officially opened by HH Shaikh Hamdan on 6 May 2002.

Al-Maktoum Institute has been established to implement HH Shaikh Hamdan's Vision for the twin pillars of education and multiculturalism; and to act as the Gateway to Dubai for Scotland. This has helped the Institute to play a key role in building progressive links between Scotland and Dubai. Its strategic aim is to help promote a two way traffic for this developing relationship between the two nations. HH Shaikh Hamdan indicates very clearly that Al-Maktoum Institute is The Gateway to Dubai.

Al-Maktoum Institute also works to generate an atmosphere in which a dialogue of civilisation can take place, rather than a clash. It works to build bridges between communities at all levels, in particular between people across the world at this crucial time by providing a unique and innovative academic environment and community for learning, teaching and research in the study of Islam and Muslims. This vision helps the Institute to establish its strategic agenda in the study of Islam and Muslims: as post orientalist, post traditionalist and multicultural.

As a unique development at the academic level and as a post-orientalist institution that is working to serve the communities and to promote a greater understanding of different religions and cultures, HH Shaikh Hamdan's vision is at the heart of Al-Maktoum Institute's mission, aims and objectives, and structure. Indeed, the whole of the Institute's work revolves around the implementation of HH Shaikh Hamdan's innovative and creative vision.

New Agenda for the Study of Islam and Muslims

Al-Maktoum Institute is a new and exciting development in teaching and research in the study of Islam and Muslims. It is a research-led institution of higher education which offers postgraduate programmes of study in these areas. It is an independent institution, with its degree programmes validated by our Scottish partner, the University of Aberdeen. The aim of the Institute is to be a centre of excellence in the Study of Islam and Muslims, in particular to promote intelligent debate and understanding of Islam and the role of Muslims in the contemporary world, and to be a place of knowledge and reflection on the issues facing a diverse and multicultural world in the twenty-first century. In pursuit of this aim the Institute is actively working to educate the next generation of scholars and leaders – both nationally and internationally – in the study of Islam and Muslims to enable them to face the challenges and opportunities of a diverse and multicultural world.

Accordingly, the Institute has developed unique teaching programmes based on current and progressive research which take into consideration the needs and preferences of our local, national and international students, so that they can appreciate and understand the various schools of thought within a specific line of study.

The academic niche of the Institute places it as one of the key post-orientalist, post-traditionalist, and multicultural institutions in the world. It recognises the need to develop the study of Islam and Muslims as a discipline with long established roots but which must face the challenges and opportunities of the twenty-first century.

The Institute's approach is distinctly different from traditional approaches, where the focus has been to study Islam and Muslims from just one limited perspective. Research and teaching at the Institute looks at Islam and Muslims in many different ways, and in many global contexts. This reflects a diversity of teaching and research interests spanning a variety of subject areas and methodological approaches in the study of Islam and Muslims. Indeed, the Institute does not seek to offer Islamic Studies within a single methodology. We offer interdisciplinary and multidisciplinary training in the study of Islam and Muslims within a number of different methodologies, e.g. history, political science, anthropology, sociology, geography, and area studies as well as traditional areas in Islamic Studies.

This new agenda for the study of Islam and Muslims globally is fully mapped out in the Dundee Declaration for the future Development of the study of Islam and Muslims.

The Dundee Declaration is an innovative and very important document which sets out in detail key issues for the field, stressing the importance for scholars engaged in this area to look to face the challenges of the future. It makes it clear that the study of Islam and Muslims must seek to develop and define itself as post-orientalist, post-traditional, multicultural, and interdisciplinary and multidisciplinary.

One feature of the Dundee Declaration is that it makes clear that the current crisis in the contemporary Muslim world is the absence of co-operation between knowledge and power; and academic research and teaching in the study of Islam and Muslims should be based on a principle of mutual respect in which people of any faith can share together a common intellectual goal.

In line with the Institute's strategic goals we aim to act as a national resource in the Scottish and UK context for consultation by government bodies, public organisations, industry, business and the media. Thus Al-Maktoum Institute has established a centre for research on multiculturalism and Islam and Muslims in Scotland, as well as a think-tank called the Multiculturalism Research Unit under the directorship of Professor Malory Nye.

One of the Institute's aims is to provide a meeting point between the Western and Muslim worlds of learning. Al-Maktoum Institute also believes that academic excellence can be achieved by forging international links and scholarship, particularly through working in partnership with other higher education establishments throughout the world, including not only Scotland but also leading universities in the Gulf, the Middle East, Europe and South East Asia.

Dubai – Scotland relations

Al-Maktoum Institute is also actively working to serve the local, national, and international communities. The Institute is in particular playing a key role in building strong links between Dubai and Scotland.

Our aim is to help promote a two way traffic for educational, cultural and business links between Dubai and Scotland, as a practical model of co-operation which is beneficial to both parties.

In the last three years, Dubai has provided a number of initial practical steps for co-operation that is bridging Scotland with Dubai. In a short space of time this has achieved the following:

- the development of Al-Maktoum Cultural Centre in Dundee – as a facility for all the communities of the City and of Scotland.
- the Sister City agreement between Dubai and Dundee (6 April 2004): Dubai has built a worldwide network of sister cities – eleven

in all – in countries such as China, Japan, Australia, the United States, Switzerland and across the Arab and Muslim countries. Due to the presence of the Institute, Dundee was invited to become a sister city of Dubai; it is the only one in the UK, and is alone among those sister cities in having an Al-Maktoum Institute. This is a tremendous advantage for Scotland. In May 2004, Dundee City Council leader, Jill Shimi, led Dundee City Council's delegation to Dubai First Sister Cities Forum.

- the establishment of Emirates Airline's daily direct flight between Dubai and Glasgow. This flight has been so successful that Emirates recently announced that it plans to boost the number of seats on this route by more than 50% (from 1 October 2005, from 278 to 427 seats), less than a year after the introduction of the daily direct service, which is, according to Mr Sheppard, Emirates Vice-President for the UK, a 'direct response to increasing demand from Scottish travellers'. This is a great achievement which represents, according to Stephen Baxter, Managing Director of Glasgow Airport, a 'real success story… Not just in terms of passenger numbers, but in an economic sense too. This expansion of Emirates represents a major economic boost for Scottish exporters'. This direct link with the major global economic centre of Dubai is a tremendous advantage for Scottish business development with the UAE and of course beyond, to other potential partners such as India and China. It is worth noting that Scotland doesn't have direct air links with many of these countries, but we do have direct links with Dubai. Where we have direct links with countries this gives us a strong foundation for business.

- HH Shaikh Hamdan's commitment to multiculturalism has been shown in particular by the launch of the HH Shaikh Hamdan Bin Rashid Al-Maktoum Awards for Multicultural Scotland, which will be awarded for the first time in 2005.

- a number of higher education links between Scotland and Dubai, including the establishment of the British University in Dubai, the linking of the University of Aberdeen with Zayed University, two summer training schools at Al-Maktoum Institute in Dundee for female students from the UAE, and the first student delegation from Scotland to an international conference in Dubai this week on 'Women as Global Leaders' organised by Zayed University. This delegation was led by Wendy Alexander who delivered a keynote speech.

- three Scottish delegations to Dubai (in October 2002, December 2003, and April 2004). The aim was to establish business and economic foundations between the two nations. One avenue now being explored is to bring a large delegation from Dubai to Scotland in 2005 before another Scottish delegation goes to Dubai. This Dubai delegation will accompany HH Shaikh Hamdan's second visit to Scotland in 2005, to lay the foundation stone of the new Dundee City's Al-Maktoum Cultural Centre and to present the first of the Awards for Multicultural Scotland that bear His Highness' name.
- Al-Maktoum Institute is continually striving to implement HH Shaikh Hamdan's vision to further facilitate the creation of mutually beneficial relationships between Dubai and Scotland. There is much to be gained for both Scotland and Dubai by the development of academic, business and economic links, and links in the worlds of culture and art, science and technology, medicine and sport.

Indeed, HH Shaikh Hamdan's vision is to promote multiculturalism (I would like to draw your attention to a very important document available at the exhibition stand on HH Shaikh Hamdan's Vision for Multiculturalism). That is not, in itself, surprising: Dubai, in the United Arab Emirates, has a population of just over one million people; Emirates nationals make up only 20% of that population. There is much for us in Scotland to learn from the Dubai experience of a multicultural workforce, using Fresh Talent as one of the key factors for the success and growth of Dubai's booming economy.

I would now like to take this opportunity to explore some of the suggestions that the Chairman of SCDI made this morning. I wholeheartedly agree that it is time that Scotland's horizons be set well beyond our own back yard, and we need to actively take our place in the new global economic and social environment. Anyone who has visited Dubai will recognise a similar small country that has benefited enormously from forging positive relationships across the world. We see there today a booming and stable economy.

Unlike other potential partners, here, today the door is open – we don't have to knock. The opportunity is here to invite Scotland's business leaders, politicians and academics to grasp this unique and golden opportunity being made available with booming Dubai. We at Al-Maktoum Institute stand ready to help develop this relationship in any way we can.

I confess that we are not yet sure of the best way to actively develop this relationship. We will be talking further with the Scottish Executive on the subject.

The key to doing business in Dubai is to be aware of and to respect the local culture – and to be prepared to be patient. A suggestion made to me by Dubai Chamber of Commerce and Industry, which I passed last year to key business people in Scotland, is that the best way for Scotland to do business in Dubai, is to establish a Scotland House in Dubai, where multiple agencies would work together to promote Scottish business and industry. Dubai and Al-Maktoum Institute would welcome any proposal to take forward this initiative as soon as possible. The most successful countries and companies trading in Dubai are those who have followed this advice.

The fact that Al-Maktoum Institute has been established here in Scotland sends a clear message to those living and working in Dubai that Scotland is a good place to visit and do business. The fact that HH Shaikh Hamdan is lending his name, his vision, and his full support to the Institute is a clear sign that Dubai is keen to work to develop this relationship with Scotland but with two way traffic for the benefit of both countries.

Dubai has made no secret that they want companies based in Scotland to take more advantage of the opportunities provided by Dubai's booming economic growth. HH Shaikh Hamdan has expressed his pleasure with the Institute's progress and achievements. However, he sees that there are many more opportunities yet to be explored in the relationship between Dubai and Scotland. HH Shaikh Hamdan has shown his commitment to this relationship through the many projects he has established. I hope that Scotland feels ready to respond to these positive signs from Dubai. To borrow the SCDI Chairman's phrase in her concluding remark, this could be a once-in-a-lifetime opportunity.

Conclusion

In many ways, Scotland's journey to Dubai starts at Al-Maktoum Institute in Dundee. Indeed, Dubai believes – and here I am speaking on behalf of HH Shaikh Hamdan, Deputy Ruler of Dubai and the UAE Minister of Finance and Industry – that the Institute is THE GATEWAY TO DUBAI.

Through Al-Maktoum Institute HH Shaikh Hamdan is actively achieving a forward looking step in encouraging dialogues across cultures and peoples, which will enhance greater understanding and appreciation between the Arab and Muslim worlds and the West in general, and between Dubai and Scotland in particular. Indeed, HH Shaikh Hamdan is providing practical models for global cross-cultural understanding and co-operation.

APPENDIX XVI

THE VISION OF HH SHAIKH HAMDAN BIN RASHID AL-MAKTOUM FOR MULTICULTRALISM

Professor Abd al-Fattah El-Awaisi
Principal and Vice-Chancellor

The First International Academic Symposium

The Challenges of Multiculturalism: Practical Issues and Comparative Perspectives

Shaikh Rashid Conference Hall – Al-Maktoum Institute
Dundee, Scotland
20 April 2006

His Highness Shaikh Hamdan Bin Rashid Al-Maktoum, Deputy Ruler of Dubai, the UAE Minister of Finance and Industry, and Patron of the Al-Maktoum Institute, has asked me to convey his warmest greetings to all the delegates attending this symposium and he sends to our meeting today his best wishes.

On behalf of His Highness Shaikh Hamdan Bin Rashid Al-Maktoum, I am delighted to welcome you all to our first international academic symposium on the Challenges of Multiculturalism. In particular, His Highness is very pleased to welcome here Mrs Margaret Curran MSP, Minister for Parliamentary Business, to open the proceedings of this symposium today.

The theme of this first symposium is 'Practical issues and comparative perspectives'. I am pleased to announce that we are in discussion with some of our international partners to organise similar symposiums jointly with them but with different themes on the challenges of multiculturalism.

Introduction
Following the July bombings in London last year, the debate about the viability and future of multicultural societies in western Europe has gained yet further significance. Participants in the public and private discussions in the media, in parliaments, and in academic circles have expressed a variety of opinions. These opinions range from the declarations of the 'death' of multiculturalism at one extreme to fierce

affirmations of multicultural ideals and practices at the other. Concepts such as integration, assimilation, segregation, alienation, and secularisation have become buzzwords for defining this debate. These concepts largely obscure the seemingly gentler (and more 'liberal') terms such as tolerance, respect, diversity, and pluralism that defined the debate in the 1990s.

What is largely missing in such public discussions are two fundamental building blocks of any theory and practice of multicultural society: Firstly that multiculturalism is a process, not an end product – this process is most often a challenging one, and sometimes may be unsuccessful. Secondly, these processes of multicultural practice need to be contextualised to particular circumstances, the ideals of multiculturalism (either for or against) require an understanding of the diverse practical contexts of particular societies.

Shaikh Hamdan Bin Rashid Al-Maktoum's Vision for Multiculturalism

His Highness Shaikh Hamdan Bin Rashid Al-Maktoum is passionate in his desire to actively encourage productive and constructive civilisational dialogue across cultures and to build bridges between communities and people based on common grounds, mutual respect, and shared goals and interests. Indeed, this is the civilised way forward to manage diversity and to enhance greater understanding and appreciation between the Arab and Muslim worlds and the West by providing a working example between Dubai and Scotland. As a man of vision, with a better world as a focus, HH Shaikh Hamdan works to achieve the implementation of practical models. Since 2001, one of his main focuses has been the creation of mutually beneficial relationships between Dubai and Scotland as an example of constructive civilisational dialogue.

The first step to facilitate the implementation of Shaikh Hamdan's model was the creation of Al-Maktoum Institute in 2001 here in Dundee, which was officially opened by His Highness on 6 May 2002.

At the heart of the work of the Al-Maktoum Institute is the vision and passion of HH Shaikh Hamdan Bin Rashid Al-Maktoum for the twin pillars of education and multiculturalism. On 23 June 2004 all our work came together in a single document from Shaikh Hamdan, entitled Shaikh Hamdan Bin Rashid Al-Maktoum's Vision for Multiculturalism.

In this document Shaikh Hamdan sets out the importance of the vision of Islamicjerusalem as a model of a common space of openness in which people from different backgrounds can live together. Islamicjerusalem is not an exclusive but inclusive region and a centre in which diversity and pluralism thrive in a spirit of mutual respect and co-existence. Through the creation of the Al-Maktoum Institute in Dundee, our teaching programmes in Islamicjerusalem Studies and the Study of Islam and Muslims, the Dundee Declaration for the future study of Islam and Muslims, our implementation and investigation of the central concept of multiculturalism, and our continuing efforts to serve the communities, Shaikh Hamdan is implementing practical steps to achieve this vision. Through all these Shaikh Hamdan is actively achieving a forward looking step in encouraging dialogue across cultures and peoples.

Shaikh Hamdan's passion for Islamicjerusalem and his vision for the implementation of this model into practical steps have created the foundations for co-operation and the encouragement of a multicultural ethos of mutual respect and common understanding for this globe. In this regard, His Highness is setting an excellent example to other world leaders to follow.

Promoting Multiculturalism

To implement this vision, we are, at Al-Maktoum Institute, doing all we can to promote multiculturalism. As we are a unique academic institution that promotes intelligent debate and a greater understanding on Islam and the role of Muslims in the contemporary world in a multicultural context, and to build bridges between communities, peoples, religions, and cultures across the world at all levels, multiculturalism is at the heart of the Al-Maktoum Institute's vision, mission, aims and objectives, and structure, and is practically implemented in all aspects of its work. The whole of the Institute's work revolves around the implementation of Shaikh Hamdan's innovative and creative vision. Our multicultural vision is visibly translated and implemented in our day-to-day operation. Our staff and students come from diverse national and cultural backgrounds and include both Muslims and non-Muslims.

To enhance the academic debate on multiculturalism, the Institute has established the first academic chair in the UK in Multiculturalism, along with a Centre for Research on Multiculturalism, and Islam and Muslims in Scotland and a think-tank called the Multiculturalism Research Unit under the directorship of Professor Malory Nye. Multiculturalism is also one of the key principles of the Institute's new agenda and one of the Institute's research priorities. A very important element of the Institute's teaching is a commitment to pursuing a better understanding of multiculturalism and the issues that cultural and religious diversity provide in the twenty-first century globalised context. One of the courses we provide to our taught Master students is called 'Islam and the West: globalisation, multiculturalism, and Muslims'.

To contribute to the development of Multiculturalism in Scotland at the communities' levels, the Institute in partnership with the Scottish Executive presented in August 2005 the first Shaikh Hamdan Bin Rashid Al-Maktoum Awards for Multicultural Scotland. These awards aim to recognise and encourage the contributions of various individuals and organisations working to promote multiculturalism in Scotland. We are now in a discussion with Dundee City Council's Leisure and Communities Department to launch a new award to promote multiculturalism at the local level here in Dundee and Tayside. The Summer Training Schools for female students from the UAE for the last three years were focused on training in Multiculturalism and Leadership.

To promote multiculturalism at all levels, the Institute sponsorship scheme, from 2004, was only provided to organisation and institutions that had demonstrated their commitment to promote multiculturalism and for projects to further this aim. In the last year, for example, we sponsored the creation of the Al-Maktoum Multicultural Garden for the use of the children of Park Place Primary School Fun Factory Out-of-School Club here in Dundee. To take this further, Al-Maktoum Institute is working in partnership with local agencies here in Dundee, in particular several departments within the local authority, to provide advice and training on multiculturalism. We are also working to develop a community facility for all the communities in Dundee and Scotland, to be known as Al-Maktoum Cultural Centre here in Dundee and run by the Al-Maktoum Foundation, a new registered charity in Scotland to promote multiculturalism.

Mutual Respect

So, what is the end product of all of these activities? In two words 'mutual respect'. We all have our own identities and beliefs but instead of there being a clash of cultures, East v West, Muslim v Christian, the Institute was established here in Scotland to promote a multicultural future that will see people acknowledging and respecting their differences BUT willing to share a common ground, live and work together in a peaceful co-existence.

Some may say that is a pipe dream but I do not believe that. Let me take you back to the Institute's work which is to generate an atmosphere in which a dialogue of civilisations can take place rather than a clash. We work to build bridges between communities at all levels, in particular between people across the world at this crucial time by providing a unique and innovative academic environment and community for learning, teaching and research in the study of Islam and Muslims. Here at Al-Maktoum Institute we are educating the next generation of scholars who will take that message of multiculturalism out into the wider world. We are also establishing a niche for ourselves as a place where debate on these key issues can take place. This vision helps the Institute to establish its strategic new agenda in the study of Islam and Muslims as post orientalist, post traditionalist and multicultural.

Multicultural Education
For the last three years, the main theme of my graduation speeches was the need to promote multicultural education as the means to defeat fundamentalism, extremism and terrorism. That message still holds good today. People in the UK were shocked to learn that the suicide bombers in London last July were not from some foreign land but had all been born and brought up here in Britain.

This was a clear signal that the doctrine of fundamentalism is not just concentrated in a few refugee camps situated somewhere in some foreign countries. After the 7 July bombings, I still firmly believe that multiculturalism is the most essential way to beat extremists and to achieve mutual respect and peaceful co-existence between people, nations, religions, and cultures.

What the Institute does both within the academic and community spheres is to use education to overcome ignorance of different cultures and beliefs and build bridges with different communities at the local, national and global levels. Building is hard and tiring work and we have a long way to go in that process. It is our opinion that the Institute has made groundbreaking developments in this process of elevation through providing practical models for global cross-cultural understanding and cooperation.

Such a pursuit of multiculturalism and education is not an easy option – it is a challenge to all communities who must be able to respect one another's differences AND ALSO to accept the common ground in the society which we all share and are part of. In multicultural Scotland we are discovering how to accept and learn from the many ways in which cultures, religions, communities, and peoples may differ, and how these differences enrich us all. But in multicultural Scotland this must not be seen as 'them and us' – 'their community' and 'our community' – but rather we all have a common and shared purpose to make our country flourish in the twenty first century. This is expressed very well by the concept of 'One Scotland, Many Cultures'. We are proud to be promoting Scotland, and to be at the centre of building bridges between Scotland and the Muslim world.

Conclusion

There is an urgent need to find ways of addressing all elements of our multicultural society, both through the seminar room and conference hall and through the questions we ask in our research. We do not pretend to have all the answers but at least we are putting forward some ideas on how to improve understanding between people of different religions and cultures.

I am pleased that this first symposium will today inspect the questions raised by the challenges of multicultural societies in a comparative perspective. I am looking forward to listening and participating on the debates and discussions of this symposium with a hope that we could learn from one another's experience and models to enhance our understanding of multiculturalism to face the challenges and opportunities of a diverse and multicultural world in the twenty-first century.

APPENDIX XVII

TIME FOR CHANGE
THE FUTURE OF THE STUDY OF ISLAM AND MUSLIMS IN UNIVERSITIES AND COLLEGES IN MULTICULTURAL BRITAIN

National Academic Symposium

Al-Maktoum Institute, Dundee, Scotland

Friday 19 January 2007

Keynote Speech

Time for Change: Making the Study of Islam and Muslims Relevant to the Needs of Contemporary British Society

Professor Abd al-Fattah El-Awaisi

Abstract

This keynote speech will outline the background of the El-Awaisi/Nye Report, *Time for Change: Report on the Future of the Study of Islam and Muslims in Universities and Colleges in Multicultural Britain*. The paper will summarise the main themes of the report, as outlined in chapters 1-3 of the report. It will stress in particular the need for a re-evaluation of the teaching of Islamic Studies in British higher education, to face the challenges of developing the field of study as relevant to the needs of contemporary multicultural British society.

Historical Background

Arabic and Islamic Studies has been taught in the UK for over 250 years and has a history that can be located in specific university Chairs and departments. The earliest established Chairs were in Arabic: firstly at the University of Oxford in 1640 and subsequently at the University of Cambridge in 1660. A number of specialist centres and positions in Orientalism, Arabic, and Islamic Studies developed at universities including Durham, Edinburgh, Leeds and Manchester in the nineteenth century. It is also significant to note the establishment of the School of

Oriental and African Studies, University of London in 1917 as a result of the Reay Committee Report of 1909.

Colonial Context

The development of these centres significantly coincided with the period of British colonial rule and it is clear that the growth of this discipline emerged from that context. That is, the development of the discipline of Arabic and Islamic Studies and its agenda was a response to the needs and the challenges of the time (the late nineteenth and early twentieth centuries). During this colonial era, the two main purposes of the development of the discipline of Arabic and Islamic Studies were:

1. The political and administrative needs of British foreign policy within the context of colonialism.
2. The religious need, with a substantial part of scholarship in Islamic Studies being pursued by theologians and thinkers for missionary purposes.

Of course, much of the scholarship in this era was also motivated by genuine intellectual and academic curiosity. Alongside this, however, the rationale for funding and development of the discipline was firmly rooted in what the Reay Committee Report portrayed as a balance between 'pure' scholarship and 'applied' practical training for 'future Indian and colonial officials' which was a task 'of vital importance to the Empire'.

Post-Colonial Context

During the time of decolonisation in the mid-twentieth century, new needs were identified and the UK government commissioned two landmark reports which were to have a significant impact on the field throughout the second half of the century. The Scarborough Committee Report in 1948 recommended expansion of Oriental Studies in British universities and selected five universities in which special facilities were to be made available. As a consequence, for example, a School of Oriental Studies was established in Durham, with special responsibilities for Middle Eastern and Islamic Studies.

The Hayter Committee Report on Area Studies in 1961 recommended extensive development in Middle Eastern and Islamic Studies in the UK with particular emphasis on contemporary affairs. This report recommended special support for centres at the Universities of Durham,

London and Oxford. Durham's Centre for Middle Eastern and Islamic Studies was set up in 1962.

Development in the 1960s and 1970s

- The establishment of a number of national centres was a result of the two reports.
- The development of the debate and critique of the concept of orientalism which reached its peak with the publication of Edward Said's *Orientalism* in 1978.
- This led to large-scale redesignation of Oriental Studies into Middle Eastern Studies but not any major structural or institutional changes.
- A number of significant international events including the 1967 Arab-Israeli War and the independence of a number of Gulf states in the late 1960s/early 1970s, for example, the United Arab Emirates.
- The development of the field of Religious Studies largely from the late 1960s onwards which broadly developed along two related strands. One of these was the growth of Religious Studies sections and programmes in Theology and Divinity departments and the creation of new departments of Religious Studies particularly associated with the model established by the University of Lancaster.
- The teaching of Islamic Studies became established as one of the core 'world religions' for these new Religious Studies programmes. This led to the appointment of scholars in the departments of Religious Studies and Theology and Religious Studies to contribute to teaching on Islam.

The Current Crisis

Following these developments in the late twentieth century, Islamic Studies and Middle Eastern Studies was no longer required to meet the needs of colonial foreign policy. This has left the field in something of a vacuum and it has so far failed to develop a significant rationale or purpose.

In addition to this, Islamic Studies has found itself in an uneasy position in balance between centres of Religious Studies and Area Studies (i.e. Middle Eastern Studies and African Studies).

The institutional allocation of Islamic Studies either within Religious Studies or within Middle Eastern Studies has prevented the field developing in an effective way and has left it in many cases marginal and vulnerable to both institutional restructuring and staffing changes.

Time for Change

As I said earlier, teaching on Islam and Muslims has been an important part of university curricula in the UK for well over 250 years. But now is the time for change. We need to develop this field of study for today's world and, in particular, to rethink many of the loosely understood ideas that frame so much of the public debate surrounding this.

There is a clear and very obvious need for the Study of Islam and Muslims to be developed as a significant field of study across all levels of education in Britain. This is not only for the education of British youth as global citizens with a good knowledge and understanding of the contemporary world. It is also essential as a means of understanding our own multicultural society.

We cannot avoid the real challenges of living in a diverse, multicultural and multi-religious British society. The London bombings in July 2005 and the August 2006 alleged bomb plots, and ongoing media coverage of what some call a 'clash of civilisations' all shout out to us to respond to these very real challenges. There is an urgent need to look for better ways of understanding religious and cultural diversity, in particular the role of Islam and Muslims in this dynamic, globalised context.

There is of course huge public interest in so many issues relating to Islam and Muslims in contemporary Britain, reflecting many concerns and perceived threats. The report does not intend to provide solutions to such issues. Our aim is to look at one particular aspect of this very broad set of debates -- that is, to highlight the role of education (and in particular higher education) as the key to address these issues. A re-evaluation of the teaching of Islamic Studies in British higher education will play some part in contributing to the wider issues and problems.

The Developing Debate on the Study of Islam and Muslims

This report is based on a two year research project, commissioned by Al-Maktoum Institute, Dundee, Scotland and jointly authored by Professor Abd al-Fattah El-Awaisi and Professor Malory Nye. Al-Maktoum Institute is an independent research-led institution of higher education, providing programmes in the study of Islam and Muslims at postgraduate level.

The report was prompted by the perceived changes and needs in the field of Islamic Studies, particularly in the wake of major contemporary issues such as globalisation and multiculturalism, but also within the national and international context of teaching and research in the field.

These issues have been at the forefront of the agenda for Al-Maktoum Institute. Indeed, the Institute jointly hosted an international symposium in March 2004 on the future development of Islamic Studies, from which emerged a framework titled the 'Dundee Declaration', intended to start the process of mapping out the development of the field. An obvious question for the Institute has come from this, of how do the Institute's concerns relate to other higher education institutions in Britain.

The issue of multiculturalism is also firmly at the heart of the Institute's academic work, and so it established in 2002 a Centre for Research on Multiculturalism and Islam and Muslims in Scotland, which amongst other activities organised an international symposium in Spring 2006 on the 'Challenges of Multiculturalism'. The Institute was also the first higher education institution in Britain to create a professorial chair in multiculturalism (currently held by one of the authors of this report, Professor Malory Nye).

As a corollary of this, the authors of this report have consistently argued for a number of years that education is one of the main ways to tackle extremism. The way in which higher education in the study of Islam and Muslim is structured and delivered must therefore be recognised as a key area for public debate and scrutiny.

The Study of Islam and Muslims in Multicultural Britain

In multicultural Britain today there are -- according to the most recent 2001 census -- approximately 1.5 million people who identify themselves as Muslims. Together these make up the largest non-Christian religious minority group in Britain, followed by Hindus, Sikhs, Jews, and people of many other faiths and none, along with people of many different Christian groups.

The majority of the British population face the considerable challenge that there are some deeply embedded issues within our society regarding Islam and Muslims, of stereotyping, hostility, Islamophobia and misunderstanding, and the legacy of orientalist thinking and attitudes is still very evident today. There needs to be appreciation that Muslims are no longer the 'others', they are part of the fabric of British society.

It is also clear that most British non-Muslims do not 'get' Islam; they do not understand what makes Muslims 'tick'. One point that comes up again and again in public debates on Islam and Muslims is the special place for Muslims of the Qur'an (the Muslim Holy Book) and Prophet

Muhammad, the Prophet of Islam. The wider society needs to recognise that there is a very deep sensitivity and volatility among Muslims to all issues related to these two aspects of Muslim faith. A clear illustration of this is that the major concerns and public demonstrations by Muslims in recent years have emerged from one or both of these issues, either the Qur'an or the Prophet Muhammad (for example, the Danish cartoons controversy in February 2006 and the remarks made by Pope Benedict XVI in September 2006).

At the same time, however, we need to recognise that many British communities, including British Muslims, have failed to understand each other, and have failed to engage effectively in multicultural Britain. Indeed, there is a mutual incomprehension between communities at the heart of this, and this mutual incomprehension can only be addressed by education.

As part of this, therefore, there is a strong need to improve education among minority communities, particularly British Muslims. There is clear evidence that the current educational structures are letting down Muslims who were born and brought-up in Britain. The most favoured option so far -- of Muslim schools and colleges, set up and run by Muslims, for Muslims, for educating 'Islamically' -- is not the answer to these difficult questions. The agenda needs to be much more challenging than that for all involved.

These points strike at some of the problems and issues of multiculturalism, which is itself a well debated term in some areas of contemporary British public debate. We acknowledge that there are various debates and understandings of the concept of multiculturalism, and that there have been considerable misplaced criticisms of the term. Multiculturalism is not about separatism, ghettoisation or balkanisation, it is instead a recognition of both diversity and the need for common ground, mutual respect, and cultural engagement. The demographics of cultural diversity and pluralism in today's Britain present us with many challenges and opportunities, and the onus of public debate should be to find effective ways of managing such diversity at all levels for the benefit of the whole society. As this report argues, separatism and tokenism are not appropriate responses to such challenges.

Main Themes of the Report

This report will be setting the scene for the development of the study of Islam and Muslims, by mapping out current provision of teaching in the broad areas of Islamic Studies -- that is, in Middle East Studies and Theology/Religious Studies departments and centres. In particular we will be showing the diversity and range of specialisms covered. In doing so, we will identify the structural gaps and weaknesses of the field, in particular the problem of dividing the study of Islam and Muslims into two separate subject areas, and the current lack of cohesion in the field.

In this report we pick up the considerable discussion, particularly among academics, of what is often referred to as a 'crisis' in the teaching of Islamic Studies. It is worth noting that the authors of this report are by no means the first to identify such a sense of crisis in the field, as is evident in reports and newspaper articles dating back to 2002 and 2003. This sense of crisis is also evident in the comments collected within the research for this report from heads of departments and centres, which are included in appendix 4 of the full report.

The report also identifies the key issues of multiculturalism, globalisation, post-colonialism, and Muslims in the west, and how these set the agenda for where the field needs to be developed to meet these new challenges in the twenty-first century. The final part of the report focuses on mapping the future for the field, with nine recommendations for government, policy makers and educationalists.

All those who participate in the development of this area of higher education have the responsibility to respond to the new realities of contemporary multicultural Britain. We must ensure the integration of all aspects of society within these debates, and also recognise the need to make the issues of the field a mainstream part of our curricular.

The Aims of the Report
The aims of this report are:

i.   to map out the current situation in the field of the Study of Islam and Muslims in British higher education institutions.
ii. to identify key contemporary trends and difficulties within the field.
iii. to present a framework for the development of the field which responds to the needs of a diverse and multicultural twenty-first century.

There are of course many aspects of the debates about Muslims in Britain, ranging across diverse areas of concern. We argue, though, that very little discussion has been focused on higher education, and in particular on how knowledge and understanding of Islam and Muslims is provided at this level. Therefore, the report aims to put what is being taught and researched in UK higher education institutions in the study of Islam and Muslims at the centre of public debates in Britain.

In addition, this report is intended to be a positive contribution to our understanding of current educational issues, to assist academic colleagues and policy makers working in this area. Indeed it is not by any way a criticism of any particular policy or institution. One of our main intentions is to get a debate started. We recognise that not everyone will agree with the recommendations of this report, but we sincerely hope that the report will act as a catalyst to spark a necessary debate about the role of education.

Furthermore, the aim of this report is not to examine the interpretations of Islam nor espouse any agendas concerning the 'reformation' of Islam. Additionally, the report is focused on teaching of Islamic Studies in higher education, and does not address wider issues in higher education such as the participation of Muslim students in all fields of study, or indeed their attitudes concerning higher education in the UK, or the wider Muslim community.

This report recognises that there is important work to be done on developing the curricula for teaching the Study of Islam and Muslims, both in terns of structure and content. Although some of these issues are referenced and explored in this report, it is beyond the scope of this report to address directly particular recommendations for curriculum development and delivery.

In short, the main focus of this report is to examine the study of Islam and Muslims in British higher education, and to map out how this field needs to be developed.

Brief Overview of the Methodology

The primary sources for the research in this report are the activities and documentation of the many departments and centres in the UK providing higher education programmes and courses in Arabic and Islamic Studies, Middle Eastern Studies, and Islamic Studies with Religious Studies and Theology, along with related areas such as Politics and International Relations. This section outlines the methodology followed to gather data for the project.

The development of the project followed three main stages between 2004 and 2006:

- Stage 1: the appointment of two postdoctoral Research Fellows from different disciplinary areas to make a wide-ranging survey of the departments and centres.

- Stage 2: the collation of data collected by the Research Fellows and other gathered material into a single framework by the two Project Directors.
- Stage 3: the writing of the report in summer 2006.

At the initial stage of the project in summer 2004, the two Research Fellows were given the following remit for the objectives of the research:

- To provide a review of the historical development of the study of Islam and Muslims in the UK, particularly with regard to institutional contexts for teaching and research in this area.
- To bring together information on current institutional activities in this field, particularly with reference to higher education departments and centres of Islamic Studies, Middle Eastern Studies, and Arabic Studies.
- To produce an interim report on the data and findings of the research, detailing a comparison of methods, approaches, and experiences of departments and centres in the field, along with an overview of the present standing and development of Islamic Studies in the UK.

Conclusion

Since the publication of the report in October 2006, we've been pleased to see that the debate has developed and there has been significant discussion of its findings and recommendations on the public level. In particular I would like to thank Mr. Jim McGovern, the MP for Dundee West, for putting down an Early Day Motion in the House of Commons in support of the Report, which by the end of December 2006 had received the backing of 22 MPs. I would also like to thank Richard Baker MSP, for putting forward a Motion in the Scottish Parliament in support of the Report. I think that both of these Motions demonstrate in a tangible way the considerable awareness and interest by politicians in this issue and its importance to the continuing debates on multiculturalism and education and particularly the development of the study of Islam and Muslims to meet the needs of today's society.

A number of Universities are sending scholars to the symposium but I am very disappointed that those we highlighted in our report for particular criticism have failed to take up the challenge to engage in the debate on the development of the Study of Islam and Muslims in higher education in Britain. It seems that they are deliberately ignoring the chance to argue their case or perhaps they have decided not to listen to our criticism just because we are based in Dundee.

I have been saying for a long time now that education is the way to defeat extremism and fundamentalism. We must engage in the battle for hearts and minds but using our brains and not bullets.

It has been over 40 years since the Government commissioned a report related to Islamic Studies. The Government should set up an immediate inquiry into the future of Islamic Studies at the UK higher educational institutions. There is an urgent need for a complete re-examination of what is being taught about Islam and Muslims throughout the UK and a review of the relevance of the courses offered by these institutions. We called for a Commission to be established and when you hear Gordon Brown echoing our call for the need to win hearts and minds through education then clearly the time is right for Government action on this matter. I hope our Symposium will help to persuade the politicians that it is time to act.

I hope that in the course of today we have some real discussion and debate and look forward to practical outcomes for this crucially relevant area of study.

APPENDIX XVIII

AL-MAKTOUM INSTITUTE SUMMER SCHOOL FOR UAE STUDENTS
(including students from Qatar University)

Programme in Multiculturalism and Leadership
23rd June – 13th July, 2005

Thursday 23rd June

Arrival: Welcome at Glasgow Airport and travel by coach to Dundee (hotel)

Friday 24th June

9.15 – 10.45	Welcome, Introduction, and Tour of Institute
10.45 – 11.00	Break
11.00 – 12.15	Shaikh Hamdan Bin Rashid Al-Maktoum's Vision: a New Agenda
	Professor Abd al-Fattah El-Awaisi, Principal and Vice-Chancellor, Al-Maktoum Institute
	Professor Malory Nye, Depute Principal for Academic Affairs
	Students: Sarah Hassan, Ramona Ibrahim, and Rosalind Anderson
12.15 – 2.15	Lunch at Institute
2.15 – 3.30	Shaikh Hamdan Bin Rashid Al-Maktoum's Vision.
	Practical models for global cross cultural understanding and cooperation: UAE and Scotland
3.30 – 5.00	Visit to Dundee city centre
7.00	Welcoming Dinner at Swallow Hotel

Saturday 25th June

Day out to Edinburgh including Castle and Royal Museum of Scotland

Sunday 26th June

Day with group at the hotel
Evening: 5.20pm, Coach to cinema, Odeon Dundee Kingdom of Heaven (starts 5.45)

Monday 27th June

9.15 – 10.45	English Language and Cultural Vocabulary in Scotland
	David Catterick, Centre for Applied Language Studies, University of Dundee

10.45 – 11.00	Break
11.00 – 12.00	English Language and Cultural Vocabulary in Scotland (cont)
12.15	Leave on coach for Edinburgh
2.15	Visit to the Scottish Parliament and Scottish Executive, Edinburgh: Talk on the Parliament and Democracy in Scotland, Robert Dunn Tour of new Parliament building at Holyrood Meet with: Mrs Margaret Curran, Minister for Parliamentary Business, Scottish Executive Mr Tom McCabe, Minister of Finance, Scottish Executive
6.00	Leave Edinburgh and return to hotel

Tuesday 28th June

9.15 – 10.45	Introduction to the history and culture of Scotland and Dundee Ian Flett, Dundee City Council
10.45 – 11.00	Break
11.00 – 12.30	History and culture of Scotland and Dundee (cont)
12.30	City of Dundee Chambers Lunch reception by Dundee City Council Formal welcome by Lord Provost, John Letford and Head of Administration, Jill Shimi Introduction to Dundee
3.30 – 4.30	Visit to Dundee Contemporary Arts
4.30 – 5.30	UAE and Qatar higher education and Al-Maktoum Institute for Arabic and Islamic Studies: links with UAE and other universities in the Gulf Professor Abd al-Fattah El-Awaisi and Professor Malory Nye, Al-Maktoum Institute

Wednesday 29th June

9.15 – 10.45	The new field of inquiry: Islamicjerusalem Studies Professor Abd al-Fattah El-Awaisi, Al-Maktoum Institute
10.45 – 11.00	Break
11.00 – 12.15	The new field of inquiry: Islamicjerusalem Studies (cont)
12.15 – 1.30	Lunch at Institute
1.30 – 2.30	Business leadership: Alliance Trust, working with the UAE Alan Harden, Chief Executive of Alliance Trust
3.00 – 4.00	Divide into 2 groups: • Tour of Alliance Trust, Meadow House, Dundee • Visit Verdant Works Heritage Centre, Dundee
4.00 – 5.00	Reverse group visits from 3pm

Thursday 30th June	
9.15 – 10.45	Historical issues in Islamicjerusalem Studies Dr Maher Abu-Munshar and Aminurraasyid Yatiban, Al-Maktoum Institute
10.45 – 11.00	Break
11.00 – 12.00	Historical issues in Islamicjerusalem Studies (cont)
12.00 – 1.00	Lunch at Institute
1.00	Visit to Ice Hockey arena
3.45	Return by coach to Al-Maktoum Institute for:
4.15 – 5.30	Talk with HSH Prince Philipp of Liechtenstein
	followed in evening by
7.00	Evening Reception and Dinner for HSH Prince Philipp of Liechtenstein with Tom McCabe MSP, Minister of Finance, Scottish Executive and invited guests at Apex Hotel, Dundee

Friday 1st July	
9.00	Depart on coach from hotel
10.30 – 12.30	Visit to Grampian TV studios, Aberdeen
1.30	Picnic Lunch, followed by tour of Balmoral Castle, Deeside
5.00	Back at hotel
6.45	Leave hotel at 6.45pm for visit to Byre Theatre, St Andrews to see 'Golf: the Musical' (starts 8pm)

Saturday 2nd July
Day out to Falkirk Wheel, Wallace Monument, and Blair Drummond Safari Park

Sunday 3rd July
Transfer to Altamount Hotel and Visit to Monikie Park (10.30 – 3.00)

Monday 4th July	
9.30 – 10.45	The challenges of multiculturalism Professor Malory Nye, Dr Julia Droeber, and Alhagi Manta Drammeh Al-Maktoum Institute
10.45 – 11.00	Break
11.00 – 12.00	The challenges of multiculturalism (cont)
12.00 – 1.15	Lunch

1.15 – 3.15	Media and leadership: Print and TV media in Scotland David Whitton Sandy McGregor, Chief Reporter of the *Courier*, Dundee
3.15 – 3.30	Break
3.30 – 5.15	Multiculturalism in Scotland and the UK: Islam, Muslims and British society Professor Malory Nye, Dr Julia Droeber, and Alhagi Manta Drammeh

Tuesday 5th July

8.15	Depart on coach from hotel
	Visit to Glasgow
10.00	Arrive for tour of St Mungo's Museum of Religion
11.00	Tour of McLelland Galleries
12.00	Tour of Burrell Collection, followed by
	Lunch meeting with Lord Provost, Liz Cameron, and Bridget McConnell, Director of Cultural and Leisure Services, Glasgow City Council, and city officials at Burrell Collection
2.30 – 3.30	Shopping in Glasgow
4.00 – 5.30	Visit to BBC studios, Queen Margaret Drive, Glasgow
5.30	Women as Global Leaders Wendy Alexander MSP, former Minister of State, Scottish Executive
6.30	Return on coach to Dundee

Wednesday 6th July

9.30 – 10.30	Islam and the West: globalisation, multiculturalism, and Muslims (short discussion)
10.30–10.45	Break
10.45–12.15	The British Council and Education UK Scotland: British educational initiatives in the Gulf Liz Neil, Education UK Scotland, British Council Scotland
12.15 – 2.00	Lunch at Institute
2.15 – 4.00	The future development of the study of Islam and Muslims: the Dundee Declaration
4.15 – 5.30	Scottish Country Musical Traditions, Laurie Mills

Thursday 7th July

9.30 – 11.00	Islam and the West: globalisation, multiculturalism, and Muslims Discussions and debates, with Al-Maktoum Institute academic staff
11.00 – 11.15	Break

11.15 – 1.00	Islam and the West: globalisation, multiculturalism, and Muslims
1.00 – 2.30	Lunch at Institute
2.30 – 4.00	UK and Scotland – 'Engaging with the Islamic World' Frances Guy, Foreign and Commonwealth Office
4.00 – 4.15	Break
4.15 – 5.15	Dr Pia Beckmann, Mayor of Wurzburg, Germany Video presentation on women as global leaders

Friday 8th July

9.30 – 11.45	Discovery Point, Dundee Talk on 'Leadership and the Heroic Age of Polar exploration', Professor Stewart Brymer and 'Marketing of Tourist Attractions in Dundee', Mark Munsie Tour of Discovery Museum
12.00 – 2.15	Lunch at Institute
2.30 – 3.30	Opening of Al-Maktoum Multicultural Garden, Park Place Primary School, Dundee
3.30 – 4.00	Return to Institute
4.00 – 5.30	Women as Global Leaders: Meeting and discussion with Lorna Ferry, Education Officer, Dundee City Council

Saturday 9th July

Day out to Deep Sea World and Hopetoun House, Edinburgh

Sunday 10th July

Day with group at the hotel

Monday 11th July

9.30 – 10.15	Review of programme themes: multiculturalism and leadership Final discussion of coursework project
10.15– 10.30	Break
10.30 – 5.00	Work on Project, including breaks at:
12.30 – 2.00	Lunch
3.30 – 3.45	Break
5.00	Submission of Project

Tuesday 12th July	
9.30 – 10.30	Postgraduate studies in Scotland and Dundee: Representatives from local universities
10.30–10.50	Break
10.50 – 11.30	Evaluation session
2.00 – 4.00	Concluding ceremony with Lord Elder, Chancellor of the Al-Maktoum Institute, Professor Abd al-Fattah El-Awaisi, Principal and Vice Chancellor, and senior guests and dignitaries
4.00	Return to Hotel
7.00	Farewell Dinner at Altamount Hotel

Wednesday 13th July
Travel by coach from hotel to Glasgow: Departure from Glasgow Airport to Dubai

APPENDIX XIX

AL-MAKTOUM INSTITUTE SUMMER SCHOOL FOR UAE STUDENTS
(including students from Qatar University)

Training Programme in Multiculturalism and Leadership
27th June – 18th July, 2006

Tuesday 27th June	
Arrival: Welcome at Glasgow Airport and travel by coach to Dundee (hotel)	
Wednesday 28th June	
9.00 – 10.15	Welcome and Opening Remarks Professor Abd al-Fattah El-Awaisi, Principal and Vice-Chancellor, Al-Maktoum Institute
10.15 – 10.30	Break
10.30 – 12.00	Li ta'arafu (get to know one another) and introduction to the programme Professor Malory Nye, Depute Principal for Academic Affairs
12.00 – 12.00	Lunch
12.30	Coach leaves for Visit to Edinburgh: Scottish Parliament
2.30	Tour of Scottish Parliament building at Holyrood
4.00	Welcome at Scottish Parliament by • Mr Tom McCabe MSP, Scottish Executive Minister for Finance and Public Service Reform and • Mrs Margaret Curran MSP, Scottish Executive Minister for Parliamentary Business followed by Public Launch at Scottish Parliament of • HH Shaikh Hamdan Bin Rashid Al-Maktoum's Vision: A New Agenda
5.30	Return on coach to Dundee
Thursday 29th June	
9.15 – 10.45	English Language and Cultural Vocabulary in Scotland David Catterick, School of Applied Linguistic and Language Studies, University of Dundee

10.45 – 11.00	Break
11.00 – 12.15	English Language and Cultural Vocabulary in Scotland (cont)
12.15 – 1.30	Lunch
1.30 – 3.30	Shaikh Hamdan Bin Rashid Al-Maktoum's Vision Practical models for global cross cultural understanding and cooperation: UAE and Scotland continued…
3.30 – 3.45	Break
3.45 – 5.00	Al-Maktoum Institute 2006 Summer School Training Programme: Multiculturalism and Leadership Introduction to Summer School Assessed Project
5.00 – 5.30	Project work
5.30	Depart for hotel

Friday 30th June

9.15 – 10.45	UAE and Qatar higher education and Al-Maktoum Institute for Arabic and Islamic Studies: links with UAE and other universities in the Gulf Professor Abd al-Fattah El-Awaisi and Professor Malory Nye, Al-Maktoum Institute
10.45 – 11.00	Break
11.00 – 12.15	New Agenda for the Study of Islam and Muslims
12.15 – 1.15	Lunch
1.15 – 2.55	New agenda: Introducing Islamicjerusalem Studies
3.00 – 3.30	Launch of Al-Maktoum Institute DVD
3.45 – 4.45	New agenda: Introducing Multiculturalism
4.45 – 5.30	Project work
5.30	Depart for hotel

Saturday 1st July

| | Day out to Falkirk Wheel, Blair Drummond Safari Park, and Wallace Monument Stirling |

Sunday 2nd July

morning	at the hotel
12.00	coach to Taza restaurant for lunch
1.30 – 4.30	shopping opportunities in Dundee city centre

Monday 3rd July	
9.15 – 10.15	Islam and the West: globalisation, multiculturalism, and Muslims (short discussion)
10.15 – 10.30	Break
10.30 – 12.30	Women and Leadership: Business leadership • Dr Lesley Sawers, Chief Executive, Glasgow Chamber of Commerce • Alison McIntosh, Marketing Manager, Glasgow Chamber of Commerce • Jane Wood, Head of Corporate Affairs, The Boots Group (Board Member of Glasgow Chamber of Commerce) • Claire Dunning – Managing Director, Dunning Design Ltd (Deputy President of Glasgow Chamber of Commerce)
12.30 – 2.00	Lunch
2.00 – 3.15	New Agenda: The Challenges of Multiculturalism
3.15 – 3.30	Break
3.30 – 4.45	New Agenda: The Challenges of Multiculturalism (cont)
4.45 – 5.30	Project work
5.30	Depart for hotel

Tuesday 4th July	
9.15 – 10.30	Islamicjerusalem Studies: geographical issues
10.30 – 10.45	Break
10.45 – 12.00	Islamicjerusalem Studies: historical issues
12.00 – 12.40	Lunch
12.40 – 3.05	Film Showing: Kingdom of Heaven (145 minutes)
3.05 – 3.20	Break
3.15 – 4.45	Debate on Islamicjerusalem Studies
4.45 – 5.30	Project work
5.30	Depart for hotel

Wednesday 5th July	
9.15 – 10.45	New Agenda for the Study of Islam and Muslims
10.45 – 11.00	Break
11.00 – 12.15	Multiculturalism and Globalisation

12.15 – 1.30	Lunch
1.30 – 3.00	Meeting with Edward Oakden, UK Ambassador designate to UAE
3.00 – 3.15	Break
3.15 – 4.45	Open discussion with UK Ambassador designate to UAE
4.45 – 5.30	Project work
5.30	Depart for hotel

Thursday 6th July

9.15 – 10.15	Dundee City Council Leisure and Communities Department organised by Stewart Murdoch, Director of Communities and Leisure Presentation on Leisure and Communities Department by Stewart Murdoch
10.15 – 10.30	Break
10.30 – 11.30	Workshop presentations and discussion (in Shaikh Rashid Conference Hall and Michael Adams Seminar Room): • Equalities and Diversity: Olive Smiles, Unit Leader-Social Inclusion • Adult Learning: Marie Dailly, Adult Learning Manager Group discussion and dialogue
11.30 – 12.00	Signing of Memorandum of Understanding between Dundee City Council Leisure and Communities Department and Al-Maktoum Institute
12.00 – 12.50	Lunch
12.50	Depart on coach for visits to Leisure and Communities Department centres:
1.15 – 2.15	• Mitchell Street Adult Learning Centre
2.30 – 3.30	• Central Library – Tour and Multicultural Open Day
3.30 – 4.30	• Whitfield Activity Centre
4.45	Depart for hotel
5.15 – 6.00	Project work at hotel

Friday 7th July

9.15 – 10.45	Dr Pia Beckmann, Lord Mayor of Wurzburg, Germany How to become and to be a Lord Mayor as a woman
10.45 – 11.00	Break
11.00 – 11.30	Open discussion with the Lord Mayor of Wurzburg
11.30 – 12.15	Remembering the tragedy of 07/07/05

12.15 – 1.30	Lunch
1.30 – 3.00	Dr Pia Beckmann
	New ways of marketing, example: Wurzburg, Germany
3.00 – 4.00	Tartan Tea Party
4.00 – 4.45	Open discussion with the Lord Mayor of Wurzburg
4.45 – 5.30	Project work
5.30	Depart for hotel

Saturday 8th July

| | Day out to Edinburgh including Castle and Royal Museum of Scotland accompanied by the Lord Mayor of Wurzburg |

Sunday 9th July

10.30	Visit to Cathedral Church of St Paul, High Street, Dundee
12.00	coach to Taza restaurant for lunch
1.30 – 4.30	shopping opportunities in Dundee city centre

Monday 10th July

8.00	Depart on coach to Edinburgh
10.00	Visit to the Scottish Executive, Edinburgh:
	Talk on the Parliament and Democracy in Scotland, Robert Dunn
	Diversity and Equality, One Scotland Many Cultures
	Women and Leadership in Scottish Government
1.00	Return on coach to Dundee
3.00	Back at Institute: short refreshments
3.15 – 4.45	Briefing on Debate and Open Parliament
4.45 – 5.30	Project work
5.30	Depart for hotel

Tuesday 11th July

	Dundee City Council Social Work Department organised by Alan Baird, Director of Social Work
9.15 – 10.30	Presentation on
	'What is social work and why do we need it?'
	Alan Baird and Jenny Tocher
10.30 – 10.45	Break

10.45 – 11.35	Presentations by social work department:

Presentations by social work department:
- Promoting safer communities and protecting citizens
- Developing more personalised services and promoting greater self-determination of service users
- Promoting inclusion and reducing disadvantage and discrimination
- Developing partnership working

(divided into 4 separate groups)

11.35 – 12.00	Plenary Discussion and Dialogue in Shaikh Rashid Conference Hall
12.00 – 12.50	Lunch
12.50	Depart on coach
1.15 – 4.30	Visits to Social Work Centres in Dundee, one of following:

1.15 – 2.45	Group 1	Group 2	Group 3	Group 4
	Oaklands day care centre for older people	Mackinnon Centre physical and learning disabilities	Advocacy Group for service issues, venue to be confirmed	Seymour Lodge Child protection service
2.45	Coach transfer	Coach transfer	Coach transfer	Coach transfer
3.00 – 4.30	Bruce Street Family support centre	Eastport House Criminal justice and domestic abuse	Menzieshill Residential care for older people	Criminal justice service
4.30	Depart for hotel	Depart for hotel	Depart for hotel	Depart for hotel

6.00	Evening Reception, Lecture and Dinner at Hilton Hotel
6.30	Public Lecture:

Dr Fatima Al-Sayegh, United Arab Emirates University
'The Leading Role of UAE Women in the Twenty-First Century'

7.30 – 10.30	Dinner with invited guests, including programme of entertainment

Wednesday 12th July

9.30 – 10.00	Final briefing on debate
10.00 – 10.45	Leadership in the twenty-first century

Jill Shimi, Leader of Dundee City Council
Alan Harden, Chief Executive of Alliance Trust

10.45 – 11.00	Break
11.00 – 12.00	Leadership in the twenty-first century (cont)
12.00 – 1.30	Lunch

1.30 – 3.30	Women and Academic Leadership Professor Angela Black, Director of Graduate School, College of Arts and Social Sciences, University of Aberdeen
3.30 – 3.45	Break
3.45 – 4.45	Multiculturalism in Scotland and the UK: Islam, Muslims, and British society continued…
4.45 – 5.30	Project work
5.30	Depart for hotel

Thursday 13th July

9.30 – 10.30	Becoming a Great Leader: Historical Perspectives
10.30 – 10.45	Break
10.45 – 12.00	Becoming a Great Leader: Historical Perspectives (cont)
12.00 – 1.00	Lunch
1.00 – 3.30	Debate: Islam and the West: globalisation, multiculturalism and Muslims
3.30 – 3.45	Break
3.45 – 5.00	Open Parliament: Discussion on themes of: Multiculturalism, Leadership, the Study of Islam and Muslims, and Islamicjerusalem Studies
5.00 – 5.30	Project work
5.30	Depart for hotel
7.00	Dinner at hotel
8.00 – 10.00	Scottish Country Musical Traditions, Laurie Mills at Hilton Hotel

Friday 14th July

9.30 – 10.00	Review of programme themes: multiculturalism and leadership Final discussion of coursework project
10.00 – 11.00	Postgraduate studies in Scotland and Dundee: Representatives from local universities: Al-Maktoum Institute, University of Aberdeen, and Dundee University
11.00 – 11.15	Break
11.15 – 5.00	Work on Project, including breaks at: 12.30 – 2.00 Lunch 3.30 – 3.45 Break

5.00	Submission of Project
5.30	Depart for hotel

Saturday 15th July

	Day out to Deep Sea World and Hopetoun House, Edinburgh

Sunday 16th July

morning	at the hotel
12.00	coach to Taza restaurant for lunch
1.30 – 4.30	shopping opportunities in Dundee city centre

Monday 17th July

9.15 – 10.00	Evaluation session
10.00 – 10.15	Break
10.15 – 12.00	Preparation for ceremony
12.00 – 12.45	Lunch
2.00 – 4.00	Concluding Ceremony under the Patronage of HH Shaikh Hamdan Bin Rashid Al-Maktoum
4.00	Official Opening of Shaikh Maktoum Garden, Al-Maktoum Institute Lord Elder, HE Mirza al-Sayegh, and Professor Abd al-Fattah El-Awaisi Reception for Students and Guests
5.00	Return to Hotel
7.00	Farewell Dinner at Hilton Hotel, Dundee

Tuesday 18th July

Travel by coach from hotel to Glasgow: Departure from Glasgow Airport to Dubai